The Eagles

AN AMERICAN BAND

The Eagles

AN AMERICAN BAND

Andrew Vaughan

STERLING

New York / London

www.sterlingpublishing.com

STERLING and the distinctive Sterling logo are registered
trademarks of Sterling Publishing Co., Inc.

10 9 8 7 6 5 4 3 2 1

Published by Sterling Publishing Co., Inc.
387 Park Avenue South, New York, NY 10016

Distributed in Canada by Sterling Publishing
c/o Canadian Manda Group, 165 Dufferin Street
Toronto, Ontario, Canada M6K 3H6
Distributed in the United Kingdom by GMC Distribution Services
Castle Place, 166 High Street, Lewes, East Sussex, England BN7 1XU
Distributed in Australia by Capricorn Link (Australia) Pty. Ltd.
P.O. Box 704, Windsor, NSW 2756, Australia

Produced for Sterling Publishing by Essential Works
www.essentialworks.co.uk

Publishing Director: Mal Peachey
Managing Director: John Conway
Editors: Fiona Screen and Dipli Saikia
Designer: Michael Gray

Printed in China
All rights reserved

Sterling ISBN 978-1-4027-7712-7

For information about custom editions, special sales, premium and
corporate purchases, please contact Sterling Special Sales Department
at 800-805-5489 or specialsales@sterlingpublishing.com

CONTENTS

Introduction

IF THE BEATLES gave us the soundtrack of the '60s then the Eagles, America's most popular group ever, provided the sound of the '70s. The Eagles are, quite simply, the most popular rock band in American pop music history. While selling in excess of 100 million in records worldwide, they pioneered the incredibly popular Southern California country rock sound, which became world famous in the 1970s. Songs like "Hotel California," "Life in the Fast Lane," "Take It Easy," and "Desperado" have been in constant rotation on FM radio across America and the world ever since the tracks were first released. *Eagles: Their Greatest Hits 1971–1975* was the first album ever certified platinum and is currently tied with Michael Jackson's *Thriller* for the best-selling album of all time in the U.S. at twenty-nine million copies. The Eagles' chief songwriters, Don Henley and Glenn Frey, have proved peerless in their ability to observe the highs and lows of 1970s America.

The Eagles—Glenn Frey, Bernie Leadon, Don Henley, and Randy Meisner—originally formed in 1971. Each had at one time been in Linda Ronstadt's touring band and played sessions for her album. Finding each other with the help of Ronstadt's manager John Boylan, they decided to form a band. With musical virtuosity provided by multi-instrumentalist Bernie Leadon and bass player and singer Randy Meisner, the songwriting talent of Don Henley and Glenn Frey flowered and brought the band to the attention of some of the music industry's most dynamic executives. With music business whizz kid David Geffen fully behind them, it didn't take long for the Eagles to achieve success: their debut, self-titled album went Top 30 and gave the band three Top 40 singles,

the first of which, "Take It Easy," went to number 12. The Eagles went on to have fifteen hit singles (five number 1s) and release eight albums (four of them number 1s) before they split up in 1980. Throughout their eventful career, the Eagles also included among their ranks the legendary and flamboyant guitarist Joe Walsh, former Poco bassist Timothy B. Schmit, and guitar virtuoso and songwriter Don Felder (the man behind the music of "Hotel California").

Don Henley and Glenn Frey's songs of the 1970s reflect and express the underlying cynicism of the Nixon, Watergate, and late-Vietnam era. The fact that the Eagles grew out of the peace and love community of late 1960s Hollywood only gave their increasingly socially concerned and critical lyrics more poignancy and conviction as the decade progressed.

It was fitting for a band that so perfectly provided the soundtrack for America in the 1970s that it should all end by the beginning of the new decade—though the world wondered whether it was to prove a hiatus rather than a final end to Eagles proceedings.

As it turned out, the Eagles weren't disbanded forever. Following a few false starts, Don Henley and Glenn Frey managed to patch up their differences and resumed making music as Eagles again after what they called a "fourteen-year vacation." Their return in 1994, prompted by a country music tribute album, was a phenomenal success, and they continued to be in the top ten of any list of top grossing concert acts well into the twenty-first century. In 2008 they listed at number three behind Madonna and Celine Dion in concert ticket sales, grossing over seventy million dollars in the U.S. alone. Their seventh studio album, *Long Road Out of Eden*, which was sold exclusively through Wal-Mart, beat Britney Spears to the number one spot when it was released in late 2007.

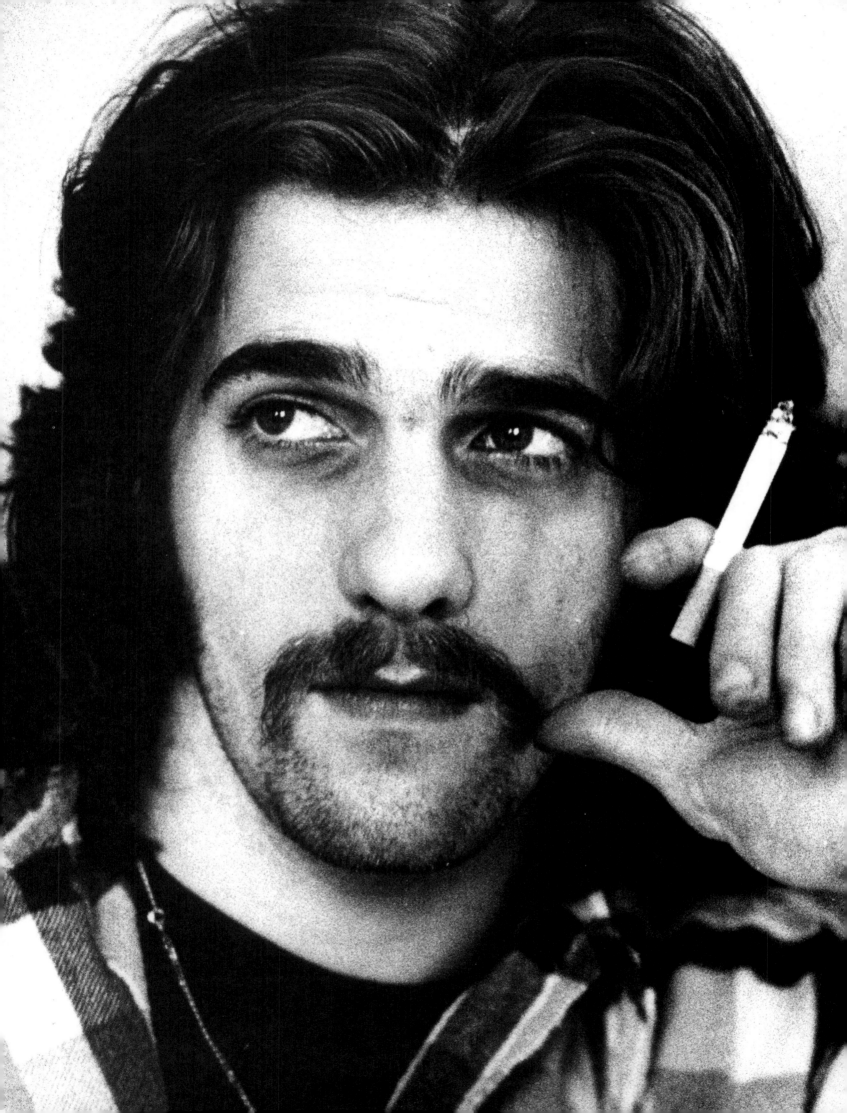

America had been searching for its own Beatles since 1964 and with John, Paul, George, and Ringo calling it quits in 1970, the new decade started with a rock and roll vacuum that the Eagles were more than capable of filling. They mixed folk with country, pop with rock, and created an immediately identifiable sound that ruled the airwaves for a decade and was clearly, definably American. Late 1960s California was alive with new sounds. The Byrds mixed folk and rock music, The Dillards made bluegrass exciting and cool, and Rick Nelson went from being a teeny bop star to country rock innovator with his iconic Stone Canyon Band. Gram Parsons burned brightly and pioneered the marriage of country and rock music, while Michael Nesmith left the madness of the

Monkees to follow his own country-meets-rock path with the First National Band. The musical environment of Los Angeles, centered on the Troubadour nightclub, was ready for a new band or artist to capitalize on the musical journeys of all those artists. If someone could take country rock to a mass audience, then the music would be legitimized and the artists in question would most likely become stars. The four original Eagles brought very different talents and skills to the band. However, once they came together, they were united in a determination to do what it took to make it to the big time.

Glenn Frey grew up on a diet of rock and roll and R&B, but also loved the purity of country music. Don Henley

came from Texas where country music was the only show in town. Bernie Leadon was an experienced musician, and Randy Meisner had an impressive track record as a working musician. Surrounded by talented friends and songwriters like Jackson Browne and J. D. Souther, the Eagles realized that by 1970 the music of rock and roll was still growing, changing, and developing as an art form while the business of rock and roll was growing ever larger and more corporate. At the beginning of the decade, the music business was worth many millions of dollars and it had a multinational reach. The Eagles knew they had to capitalize on this in their quest to take their music out of LA and into the world. They turned for help and representation to music empire-builder David Geffen, who ensured that their musical talents and vision would at least have a fair chance in the market-place. Throw in a manager, Irving Azoff, who was relentless in protecting his band and finding them the best deals imaginable and Henley and Frey's ability to reflect the times in their songs, and it is hardly surprising that the Eagles managed what bands such as Poco, the Burrito Brothers, and The Dillards had failed to do.

The most dedicated and organized of all the country rock bands that epitomized Californian music in the '70s, the Eagles went on to lead the way in breaking soft rock, album rock, and the new FM radio format. Their harmony-driven, well-crafted songs with country style vocals and tough rock guitar provided some of the most memorable songs of the time. Hits like "Take It Easy" and "Peaceful Easy Feeling" perfectly encapsulated the idealistic, easy-going lifestyle of affluent California. They released seven hit albums in that decade, with their best known, *Hotel California*, becoming a timeless seller that still evokes memories of the excess and decadence of the rock stars of that time.

However, while the image may have been post-hippy and laid back, these were competitive young rock stars

urged on by the ambitions of Geffen, on whose fledgling Asylum Records they first surfaced. Equally, the creative process for the Eagles' songs was often far from laid back. Glenn Frey, who exhibited all the swagger of a rock and roll punk from Detroit, found the perfect writing partner in the more pensive and intellectual Don Henley, but at times their personalities would clash. Yet their "creative tension," as Henley called it, would help them to write some of the most magical music of the decade. They were ambitious, talented, and determined to learn from the mistakes—as they saw them—that their other musician friends made.

America wasn't big enough for the Eagles and Geffen, however; their world tours became legendary, and not only for their length and global reach. The Eagles singlehandedly exported country, and country rock music, to the world, laying the groundwork for Nashville's bursting onto the global scene in the 1990s with Garth Brooks and Shania Twain—though none could really match the sheer force and popularity of the originals from LA. Even at the height of their fame, some of the U.S. rock press refused to see the depth and complexities in the Eagles' music, preferring to champion similar artists like Jackson Browne and Bruce Springsteen instead. But that critical oversight would change with time, and the band's 1998 induction into the Rock and Roll Hall of Fame was a clear signal that they had proven themselves to even their harshest critics.

Early press resistance to the band came in part because the Eagles' songs were definitively post-Woodstock, and they steered clear of overtly political lyrical content. As parts of the music business turned to punk and a new wave of harder, faster sounds in the mid-1970s, the Eagles' reliance and insistence on keeping with their trademark peaceful and easy style would fly in the face of fashion. Millions of new fans didn't seem to mind, though.

As with most rock bands of the time, fame brought its own problems. Excess, decadence, and hedonism became synonymous with mid-to-late '70s Eagles, especially on their world tours where their rock-star antics made the Who and Led Zeppelin look like choir boys. Money and drugs fueled the already inherent personality clashes, and when lawyers and accountants became more important than producers and musicians, it was inevitable that the band would implode. When songwriter and co-founder Bernie Leadon departed, fellow co-founders Glenn Frey and Don Henley gained power and control over the Eagles. Relationships were so strained within the band by the end of the 1970s that the individual members stayed in separate hotels when on tour.

Following an acrimonious break-up in 1980, each of the Eagles went on to solo careers and that seemed to be that for the most successful American rock band in history. Until, that was, 1993, when Irving Azoff's Giant Records, recognizing the huge impact of the Eagles

in modern country music, recorded the tribute album *Common Thread: The Songs of the Eagles*. Possibly a little flattered, the Eagles reunited to shoot a video for Travis Tritt's version of "Take It Easy." Don Henley had said that hell would freeze over before the Eagles would get back together, so naturally the reunion album was called *Hell Freezes Over*. It was released in 1994. In just a few months, the album was number 1 and had sold more than ten million copies worldwide.

When the Eagles were inducted into the Rock and Roll Hall of Fame, all seven musicians who had previously been members of the band performed together for the first time at the ceremony. There were more intermittent reunions, including a sell-out mini-tour in 1999 and a four-CD retrospective set, *Eagles 1972–1999: Selected Works*, in 2000. As was often the case with the band, though, frictions were never too far from the surface, and in February 2001 the Eagles fired guitarist Don Felder. He responded by suing the band for over $200 million. As the acrimonious court cases proceeded, in 2003 *The Very Best of the Eagles* was released along with a brand new single entitled "Hole in the World." Finally the legal disputes were settled out of court in May 2007, just as the Eagles completed their first new album proper in twenty-eight years. *Long Road Out of Eden* debuted at number 1 on the *Billboard* chart in October and it seemed that, once again, there was just no stopping them. The Eagles continued to play to sell-out crowds internationally into the second decade of the new century.

As they enter their fifth decade as a working band, the Eagles have come a very long way from those denim-clad hippies in the summer of 1971 who played backing for Linda Ronstadt at Disneyland. It has been a long and sometimes rocky road, but through all the line-up changes, the upsets and acrimony, the fights and the resentments, the Eagles have survived. Now in their sixties, whether playing live or in the studio, the Eagles

have never sounded better. Then again, with tunes like "Take It Easy," "Best of My Love," and "Hotel California," they have the material to sound better than most. Credit is deserved for surviving the decades, but the Eagles are far more than a band who simply weathered the storms.

The Eagles should be recognized as the creators of some of the most magical and significant music of the past forty years.

Andrew Vaughan, Nashville, 2010

Introduction

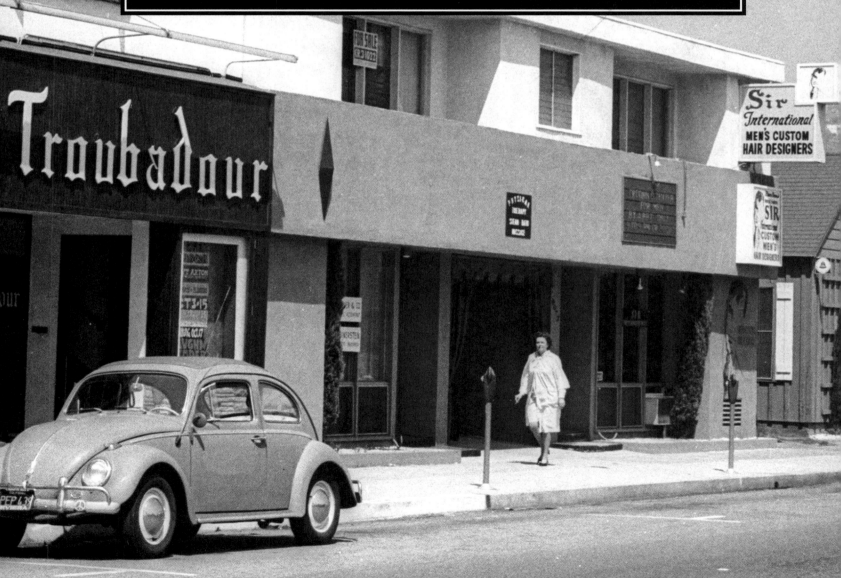

1

Los Angeles & Country Rock

I T WAS JUNE 1970 when a curly-haired drummer by
the name of Don Henley arrived in Los Angeles with his
band Shiloh. The band had traveled from Linden, Texas,
on the orders of their record producer Kenny Rogers, who
oversaw the making of Shiloh's one and only album at
Quantum Studios in Orange County. The album contained three
songs written by Henley, the first of which, "I'm Gone," sounds like an
early Eagles song, showing heavy influences of the Allman Brothers
with twin guitars, and the Flying Burrito Brothers in its falsetto
harmonies. It's a driving country rock song with more emphasis on the
rock. His other two songs—"Same Old Story" and "God Is Where You
Find Him"—are more country than rock. The album as a whole is very
self-consciously "American," from the band's name carved in wood on
the front of the sleeve to the band photo displaying checkered- and
cowboy shirt-wearing, longhaired, mustachioed country guys sitting in
a wood. Clearly, here was a band trying hard to show that they were
neither British nor affected by the British Invasion that had so altered
the rock and pop music scene in the 1960s.

As the 1970s dawned, that all-pervasive British influence on American
music finally gave up the ghost when in April Paul McCartney
announced to a disbelieving world that he was leaving the Beatles.
The 1960s had ended with the greatest pop group in music history in
disarray. The band that had inspired so many artists and musicians in
America since that famed *Ed Sullivan* TV appearance in 1964 would
never make music together again. Don Henley's first band, formed with
a couple of other school pals named Richard Bowden and Jerry Surratt,
had been inspired by the Beatles' appearance that night. They called
themselves The Four Speeds and Henley sang as well as played the
drums (like Dave Clark). Henley and Bowden carried on making music
while together at Texas State University and were joined by Richard's
cousin Mike Bowden, as well as Jim Ed Norman. The Four Speeds
changed their name to Felicity and, after a chance meeting with Kenny
Rogers in a boutique in Dallas (he was buying bell-bottomed jeans,
apparently), persuaded him to watch them perform live.

Rogers watched the live show, liked it, and so Felicity made their
first trip to LA and recorded a single titled "Jennifer," with Rogers
producing. It flopped, and the band returned to Texas—but only briefly.

Opposite: A young Don Henley
arrived in Los Angeles in 1970
armed with focus, drive, and
an ambition to succeed.

Linden, Texas is a small town located near the Louisiana and Arkansas border. There is nothing remarkable about the town, although it had produced Scott Joplin and blues legend T. Bone Walker in earlier times. There was little going on culturally in the early 1960s. Being longhaired and hippy-oriented, Henley stood out like the proverbial sore thumb. As he told *Rolling Stone* writer Cameron Crowe:

"In a town that size all you can do is dream. I had this one English teacher who really turned my head around. He was way out of place in this little college. A bohemian, the first one I'd ever seen. He'd come to class in these outrageous clothes and sit cross-legged on his desk. One day he told me: 'Your parents are asking me what your future career plans are. I know there's a lot of pressure on you to decide.' Then he said something I never forgot. 'Frankly, if it takes you your whole fucking life to find out what it is you want to do, you should take it. It's the journey that counts, not the end of it.'"

Back in Texas, Felicity gained a pedal-steel player named Al Perkins, changed their name to Shiloh, and once again headed west. Al Perkins was a Texas guitar prodigy, well known to every band on the scene. He excelled on the pedal steel, playing country music exhibitions around the state.

As he remembers it, "I was pretty well known in Texas as a steel guitar player. I was a longhaired kid but played traditional country music. Shiloh had lost their steel player, who died in a road accident, and they asked me if I'd be interested in joining them. Shiloh were pretty good, they were into early country rock—you know, *Sweethearts of the Rodeo*, Linda Ronstadt. They invited me to come play with them a few times, and finally I said I'd try it out. We went to their rehearsal place in the woods outside of town. I liked what they were doing but I didn't think country rock had any chance at all—people were listening to heavy blues and psychedelic and hard rock. But still, I felt good about joining them. So I did. I was in the National Guard and had to get away from that and I finally caught up with them in Aspen, Colorado, and watched them play a setup there at the Estes Park Rock Inn, a building made out of stone. Sound-wise they were early Eagles really. Don Henley was very talented. Before I joined the band we had some jam

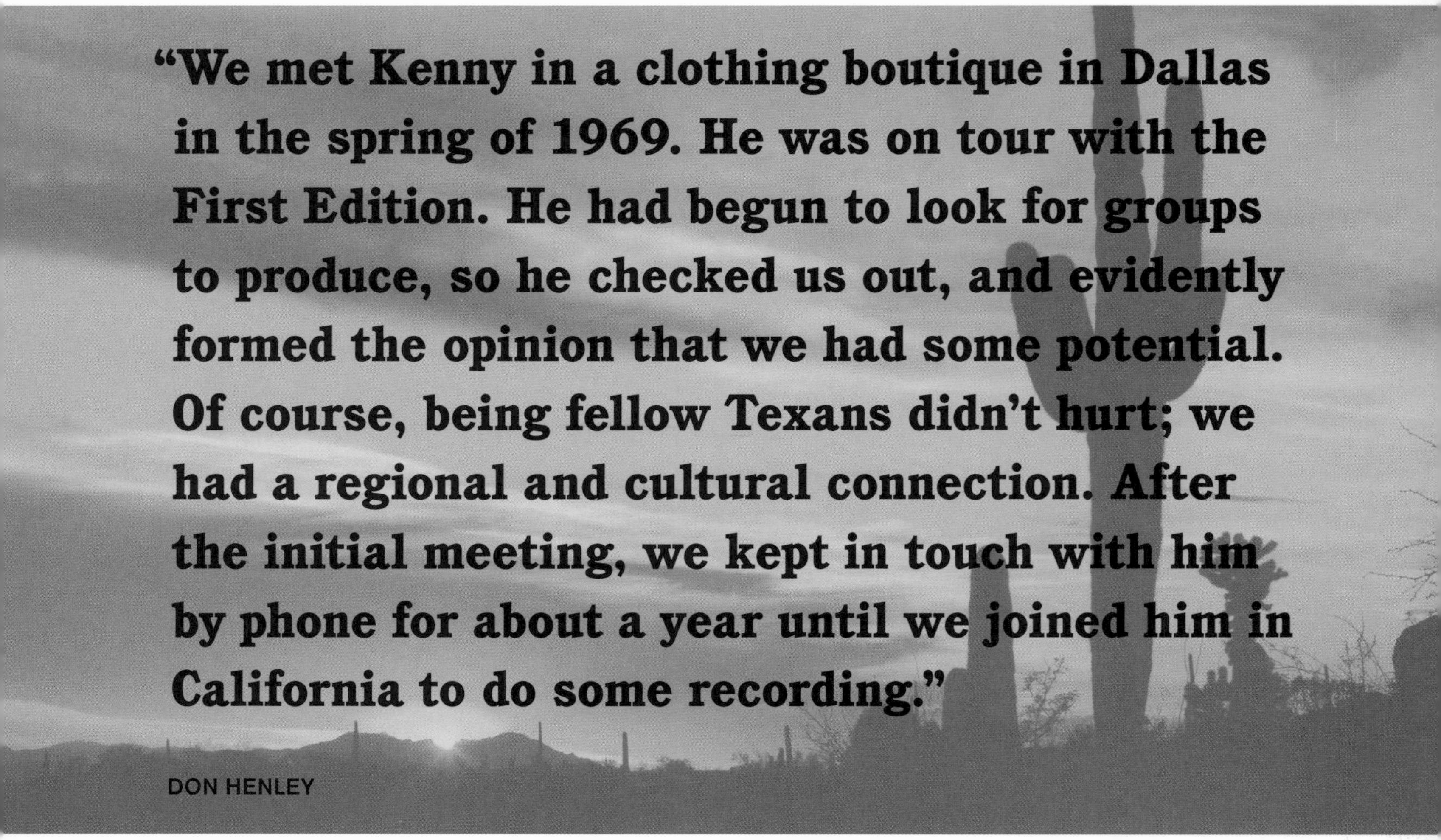

> **"We met Kenny in a clothing boutique in Dallas in the spring of 1969. He was on tour with the First Edition. He had begun to look for groups to produce, so he checked us out, and evidently formed the opinion that we had some potential. Of course, being fellow Texans didn't hurt; we had a regional and cultural connection. After the initial meeting, we kept in touch with him by phone for about a year until we joined him in California to do some recording."**
>
> **DON HENLEY**

sessions around town in Texas, so I knew Don from that and I told him he had a really good, distinctive voice. It was akin to early Rod Stewart in my opinion and Don was very serious about it. He had the drive and ambition to make it."

Felicity's single "Jennifer" had been through Amos Records, which had been set up by another Texan, Jimmy Bowen. When they signed up with Amos, Shiloh became label-mates with another country rock act named Longbranch Pennywhistle, comprising Glenn Frey and John David Souther, both originally from Michigan but long since settled in LA. Within a few short months the members of each band were well known to each other and were hanging out at the same bars in West Hollywood.

The self-titled *Longbranch Pennywhistle* debut album was released in 1969 by Amos, to little effect, despite featuring the musical talents of Elvis Presley's guitarist of choice James Burton, as well as Ry Cooder,

Name Mike Bowden
Born January 4, 1948
Place Dallas, Texas
Instrument Bass Guitar

Name Richard Bowden
Born September 30, 1945
Place Linden, Texas
Instrument Acoustic Electric Guitar

Name Don Henley
Born July 22, 1947
Place Linden, Texas
Instrument Drums

SHILOH

SIDE ONE
SIMPLE LITTLE DOWN HOME ROCK & ROLL LOVE SONG FOR ROSIE*
Michael McGinnis • 4 Star Music Co., Inc. BMI
I'M GONE*
Don Henley • The Jolly Rogers Pub. Co. ASCAP
LEFT MY GAL IN THE MOUNTAINS* (Traditional)
Adapted & Arranged by "Shiloh" • The Jolly Rogers Pub. Co. ASCAP
IT'S ABOUT TIME*
Richard Bowden • The Jolly Rogers Pub. Co. ASCAP
SWAMP RIVER COUNTRY*
Jim Norman • The Jolly Rogers Pub. Co. ASCAP
SIDE TWO
RAILROAD SONG*** (Traditional)
Arranged by Al Perkins • Summer Star Music BMI
SAME OLD STORY*
Don Henley • The Jolly Rogers Pub. Co. ASCAP
DU RAISON**
Jim Norman • The Jolly Rogers Pub. Co. ASCAP
DOWN ON THE FARM*
Richard Bowden • The Jolly Rogers Pub. Co. ASCAP
GOD IS WHERE YOU FIND HIM*
Don Henley • The Jolly Rogers Pub. Co. ASCAP

PRODUCED BY KENNY ROGERS FOR KEN-MAR PRODUCTIONS, INC.
Arranged by: Shiloh* — Jim Norman** — Al Perkins***
Engineered by Amos: Chuck Britz
Recorded at Quantum Studios
With Special Thanks To Don Sciarrotta
Strings through the courtesy of The Linden
Philharmonic Orchestra
Art Direction: Bruce Hinton
Cover Photography & Graphics: Ken Kim
Liner Photography: James Partain
Shiloh Wood Carving: David Fulks of "Smile"

AMOS RECORDS

STEREO
AAS7015

bell

Distributed by Bell Records, a Division of Columbia Pictures
Industries, Inc., 1776 Broadway, New York, New York 10019

Name Jim Norman
Born October 16, 1948
Place Fort Myers, Florida
Instrument Organ, Piano & Acoustic Guitar

Name Al Perkins
Born January 18, 1944
Place Bowie County, Texas
Instrument Steel & Electric Guitar

Above: The back cover of the first and last Shiloh long player.

Larry Knechtel, and Doug Kershaw. The album contained two original Frey compositions: "Run Boy, Run," a fast-paced country rocker with fuzz guitar, and "Rebecca," a Gram Parsons-like ballad. There were also six Souther originals, one by James Taylor and a number co-written by Frey and Souther entitled "Bring Back Funky Women" (which would have been perfectly in place on a Monkees album of the time).

Glenn Frey had begun making music around the same time as Henley and, like the Texan, had been inspired by the arrival in America of

"Only a few were making it out of Detroit. And in the late 1960s, Detroit was in a fake music boom. There were all these really terrible bands getting the attention—the MC5, the Scott Richard Case. As far as I was concerned, nobody except Bob Seger had a single ounce of talent. As soon as I got out of high school, I wanted to go to California."

GLENN FREY

the Fab Four to form his own band, The Disciples. After a while The Disciples became The Hideouts who became The Subterraneans, all of them covering British Invasion numbers. In 1966 Frey formed The Mushrooms, inspired by another British band, The Who. After some successful gigging around Detroit, a local musician and producer named Bob Seger got them onto a local label and produced a single for them, entitled "Such A Lovely Child." It was a big enough local hit to land Frey his first TV appearance, with The Mushrooms, on *Swingin' Time*. However, by 1968 The Mushrooms had ceased to exist, and Frey had supplied backing vocals and guitar to the title track of

Longbranch/Pennywhistle

AAS 7001

Amos Records Stereo

Above and previous page: The front and back covers of the Longbranch Pennywhistle album. Frey is the flying one.

debut album, *Ramblin' Gamblin' Man*. He also sang with a folk quartet (The Four of Us) at college in Detroit before forming The Heavy Metal Kids to play rock songs. However, the trip to LA with Seger to record *Ramblin' Gamblin' Man* at Capitol Records' studio had given him a taste of the sun, sights, and Strip, which proved to have a heavy pull. When a draft letter arrived at his house in Detroit he was no longer living there; he had moved to LA to share an address with an old girlfriend, whose sister just happened to be dating another former resident of Detroit, J. D. Souther.

It wasn't merely the threat of being drafted that drove Frey west, though. It was also the fact that he couldn't see any way of making it in music if he stayed in Detroit.

Frey and Souther hit it off from their first meeting, and were soon making music together. Their only album was an expensive production. The sleeve had a double fold-out design, and the musicians spent a day posing for a series of photos that showed them fooling around on a beach for the rear image, and sitting looking very mellow by candlelight for the front. The recording sessions took place at the TTG Studios on Sunset and Highland. In 1966, Frank Zappa had recorded *Freak Out!* there and, in 1968, Jimi Hendrix and The Doors would make use of the same two-inch, sixteen-track recording equipment. It was a hip, LA studio that, along with the Troubadour club on Santa Monica Boulevard, served as a meeting place for all the many different musicians thronging the scene as the 1960s became the 1970s.

Once he and Souther had found one another, and despite the failure of Longbranch Pennywhistle, there was no stopping Frey. One of their fellow strugglers was a young songwriter called Jackson Browne, with whom they lived in an Echo Park apartment complex.

"Jackson Browne, J. D. Souther, and I all lived at 1020 Laguna in Echo Park. J. D. and I shared a $60-a-month, one-room apartment—a couch and kind of a bed with a curtain in front of it. Right underneath us in an even smaller studio apartment was Jackson. He had his piano and guitars down there. I didn't really know how to sit down and work on a song until I heard him playing underneath us in the basement. He would work on 'Jamaica Say You Will,' and he had the first verse and chorus. Then he would sing the second verse—sing it five or six times—and then silence. Twenty seconds later, he would start again, and if he liked it, he'd sing it over and over again. I had never really witnessed that sort of focus—someone being that fastidious—and it gave me a different idea about how to write songs; that maybe it wasn't all just going to be a flood of inspiration. That's when I first heard 'Take It Easy.'"

JACKSON BROWNE ✳ FOR EVERYMAN

**Opposite: Jackson Browne feels
the vibe of early-1970s California.**

**Above: *For Everyman*, Browne's
second solo album, released in 1973.**

Timeless Flyte

Many musicians traveled to LA because, as Glenn Frey once put it, various magazine articles about "free love and free dope in California" made it sound like a hell of a place. Plus, there was the incredibly vibrant music scene too. Numerous successful rock acts from the mid-1960s onward had emerged from Los Angeles, San Francisco, and the Valleys. The Lovin' Spoonful, The Byrds, Poco, The Flying Burrito Brothers, Crosby, Stills and Nash, Buffalo Springfield, Neil Young, The Doors, Love, and later, of course, the Eagles all came into existence on the West Coast. Many formed as a direct result of the

Sunset Strip

The Sunset Strip refers to a mile and a half stretch of Sunset Boulevard that runs from Hollywood in the east to Beverly Hills in the west. It's the entertainment center of Los Angeles, famed for its nightlife, clubs, boutiques, restaurants, and towering billboards. The Sunset Strip's reign as the glamour center of Hollywood dates back to the golden days. Ciro's, on Sunset Boulevard, was perhaps the most swanky of several nightclubs on Sunset Strip back in the thirties and forties. Before Las Vegas became the gambling, glamour, and decadence capital of the world, Hollywood movers and shakers partied on the Strip. Laws were looser in West Hollywood than in neighboring Los Angeles, and cops turned a blind eye to celebrity bad behavior.

Ciro's was truly an A-list hangout. Marilyn Monroe, Errol Flynn, even John F. Kennedy had wined and dined there. Dean Martin was married there; it was where Martin and Jerry Lewis launched their double act and Sammy Davis, Jr. made his comeback after the car accident that took his right eye. Las Vegas, however, with its twenty-four-hour gambling and world-renowned entertainment, had ruined most of the Sunset Strip nightclubs by the end of the 1950s, and Ciro's under new ownership reopened as a rock and roll music club. One of the first bands booked was The Byrds, who debuted in March, 1965.

MONDAY

MARCH 1

Ciro's

★ **Night Club** ★

8433 Sunset Blvd. Los Angeles, CA.

On The " Sunset Strip "

INTRODUCING

The BYRDS

LIVE

MUSIC

★ **1965** ★

tremendous visual and musical impact that the Beatles had made in 1964, but by the end of the 1960s the bands who'd wanted to be British had discovered their American identities. Across the United States, as music, art, drugs, the hippie ethos, and a search for social change filtered into small towns and cities, teenagers joined local bands and, if they felt they were good enough, headed to Los Angeles. Southern California was, in the expression of the time, where it was at. Try as they might, no matter how good any of America's musical ripostes to the Beatles might have been—and some like The Byrds and The Doors came close—none could emulate or surpass the Liverpool originals. But in 1971, with John, Paul, George, and Ringo no longer dominating the airwaves, perhaps a new band could spring from the still-vibrant and creative LA scene and continue the work begun by The Byrds in 1965.

"We just wanted to be the Beatles— that was it, four guys in a band playing rock and roll and getting the girls."

DAVID CROSBY OF THE BYRDS AND CROSBY, STILLS AND NASH

In the mid-1960s, dressed in the thrift-store clothes of the street, The Byrds understood that image and cool counted for as much as songs and musicianship. Indeed, drummer Michael Clarke was recruited more because he looked like a Beatle than for his ability with cymbals and snare drums. One day he was just another kid in a club, the next he was the drummer for a groundbreaking rock band. The distance between audience and performer had closed. For the 1960s generation, artists and audience were much the same—same age, same mentality, and same spiritual vision. Hundreds of young kids joined and formed beat combos to emulate The Byrds, creating an LA sound that perfectly encapsulated Hollywood in flux circa 1965. Sunset Strip became a musical playground. Nightclubs sprung up everywhere and were packed to the rafters on weekends when it could take up to four hours to drive along the one and a half miles of the Strip. David

Above: David Crosby, Stephen
Stills, and Graham Nash
enjoying life in LA in 1969.

Crosby remembers, "This was the center of the music universe. There
were so many clubs that you could see incredible live music every night,
club after club—there were bands like The Byrds, Sonny and Cher,
Buffalo Springfield, The Turtles—it was pretty incredible."

So You Wanna Be a Rock 'n' Roll Star

David Crosby, a young singer-songwriter in Los Angeles in the early 1960s, seized his chance to emulate his Liverpool heroes with The Byrds, the most visible of a slew of young Los Angeles bands inspired by the Beatles, Bob Dylan, and the folk music boom to mix folk and rock music, pop blues and country. The Byrds hit big and West Hollywood, especially the magically named Sunset Strip, quickly

Above: The Byrds in 1965 (l–r): Chris Hillman, David Crosby, Mike Clark, Jim (Roger) McGuinn, and Gene Clark.

became as famous worldwide as Carnaby Street in London, or the Haight-Ashbury district of San Francisco. No band in the California scene would have as much impact on the Eagles' story as The Byrds.

On stage, The Byrds presented themselves as wannaBeatles. They wore suits and ties, let their hair fall over their collars, and delivered their rock-and-roll-meets-folk songs with Beatles-inspired harmonies that gave every song punch and impact. They were hip, cool, and from the streets. But it wasn't their look that appealed to Henley or Frey; it was their sound.

Such was the immediate impact of The Byrds on the scene that West Hollywood and indeed southern California would never be the

Below: Police seal off Sunset Strip after the teenage riots of December 1966. The sidewalk is jammed with people while the road is deserted.

same again. Where once young starry-eyed hopeful actors headed to the streets of Los Angeles, now long-haired hippies, armed with nothing more than a guitar, a backpack, and a bag of weed, came to join the party. Some wanted to join the New World, to partake of this burgeoning idealist community, while others saw their chance to bake their own musical pie and, like The Byrds, jump from being club musicians to rock stars overnight.

Pamela Des Barres remembers that there were "hundreds of kids on the street, half-naked girls, young boys, everybody was beautiful, everybody was wearing antiques and feathers. It was a revolution, I felt like I was part of a revolution."

For What It's Worth

As the 1970s began, LA was arguably already the center of America's pop music universe. When psychedelia, folk music, blues, and rock and roll were bursting out of the clubs on Sunset Strip—played by the likes of The Doors, Love, The Seeds, The Turtles, Moby Grape, and Janis Joplin—the full flowering of music power was accompanied by its share of troubles. Teenage riots on Sunset Strip in the fall of 1966 were hardly on the scale of Watts in 1965 or Chicago in 1968, but they were enough to alter the music environment of Hollywood. In response to the mid-1960s youth-dominated scene on the Strip, the police introduced curfew laws and would, according to activist Mike Davis, "humiliate curfew-violators with insults and obscene jokes, pull their long hair, brace them against squad cars, and even choke them with billy clubs, before hauling them down to the West Hollywood Sheriffs or Hollywood Police stations where they [would] be held until their angry parents [picked] them up."

In early December 1966, over two thousand protesters had assembled at Pandora's Box coffee shop to show their displeasure at the curfew laws and the police harassment. The heavy-handed police reaction led to Stephen Stills writing the powerful protest song "For What It's Worth," which his band, Buffalo Springfield, recorded. Clubs suffered financially, those arrested faced heavy fines, and several activists organized committees to plan a benefit concert featuring The Byrds, Buffalo Springfield, and The Doors to help them pay their fines. The concert would end up as the groundbreaking 1967 Monterey Pop

Festival, which in many ways provided the blueprint for Woodstock two years later.

Appalled by the police treatment of the crowds, club owner Doug Weston started booking rock bands at his Troubadour folk club situated a mile or so from the Strip and thereby exempt from the laws that applied to clubs on Sunset Strip. The Troubadour would be the creative home of the LA music scene for the next three years and provide the launch pad for the greatest country rock band of them all, the Eagles.

> "The year that we were all there, 1969, was a bumper crop year for songwriters. A lot of things came to fruition. Hanging out at the Troubadour was Laura Nyro, Joni Mitchell, James Taylor, Kris Kristofferson, Carole King— every major writer of the next twenty-five years was there and every one of them was serious about their music and doing it right."
>
> J. D. SOUTHER

If the Beatles had the Cavern then the Los Angeles country, folk, and singer-songwriter scene had the Troubadour. Named after London's Troubadour, it opened in 1957 and would become a Mecca for folkies and folk rockers through the early 1960s. In 1961, owner Doug Weston moved the club to larger premises with elegant mock Tudor walls at 9081 Santa Monica Boulevard. A short walk from the Strip in West Hollywood, the Troubadour became the hangout of choice for countless 1960s musicians, among them Neil Young, Buffalo Springfield, The Byrds, Jackson Browne, Linda Ronstadt, and Janis Joplin, and as the 1960s turned into the 1970s, those musicians who would soon become the Eagles.

Monday Monday

In 1968, New York record producer John Boylan traveled to LA to produce 1950s pop star Ricky Nelson's comeback album *Another Side of Rick* and discovered that the Troubadour scene was every bit as vibrant as the one in Greenwich Village. "The Troubadour was this incredibly influential place—it was like the New York folk scene had been part transported to California. Everyone would gather and play songs in the lobby—it was the most amazing and creative place. There was this circle of incredibly talented musicians; Jackson Browne, Linda Ronstadt, The Dillards, Poco, the Eagles. It was this huge talent pool."

Weston booked bands into his LA club for up to a week at a time but kept Monday as Hootenanny Night—or "open mic" night in modern parlance. Jackson Browne remembers those nights with misty affection.

> "There I was, this young kid sitting next to folk legends like Odetta. You'd see David Crosby cruising through with beautiful women on his arms. There'd be all these people, Steve Stills, Roger McGuinn, Linda Ronstadt, the Dillards. Monday night you'd show up early, like at 4 pm, and get in line to sing your three or four songs."

Monday nights saw agents, record company executives, managers, bookers, TV producers, and talent scouts crowding the Troubadour's bar. Says Browne, "It was the club you played at [in order] to get hired. Other clubs didn't hire you. But I played the Monday night at the Troub and ended up getting a job supporting Linda Ronstadt."

The early form of a new musical hybrid that would become country rock and be perfected by the Eagles was born in the Troubadour and in the hills of nearby Laurel Canyon. The musicians and artists played music at the Troubadour and then headed north into the hills where many had made themselves homes in an enclave of leafy canyon roads, small rustic cabins, and A-frame houses. It was back to the country, the hippie reaction to corporate America and a desire for community and a new way of living. This was the time of shared living arrangements, of passing joints around campfires, pulling out guitars, and sharing songs and poetry. The music being played was usually acoustic, and while some of the experimentation explored by musicians in the Canyon

was heading toward the strange sounds of jazz (as played by Frank
Zappa and Captain Beefheart), there were enough players at parties
carrying all manner of stringed instruments, from banjos to mandolins,
fiddles to Dobros, for the sound of American folk and country to fill
the mellow evening air. With the Beatles no longer around to set the
musical agenda, it was left to all-American musicians to show the way.

Bob Dylan, a cultural guru whether he liked it or not in the 1960s, had
been out of the public eye after a motorbike crash in 1966. When he
emerged in 1968 from the farm in upstate New York where he'd been

recuperating, he did so to promote a country music album, recorded in
Nashville and titled *Nashville Skyline*. The album's opening track was
a duet with Johnny Cash ("North Country Girl"), and the rest of the
record proceeded to mix pedal steel with acoustic guitars and rock bass
and drums. Even Dylan's voice sounded "country." When the album
made Number 3 on the *Billboard* Hot 100 in the summer of 1969, it set
thousands of American musicians on a journey to discover the roots of
country music and attempt to marry them with rock sensibilities.

Of The Canyon

Laurel Canyon runs from Sunset Boulevard in West Hollywood up into the winding tree-lined Hollywood Hills, across the majestic Mulholland Drive, and down into the San Fernando Valley.

The canyon had been a convenient getaway from the frenzy of Sunset Boulevard for LA's artistic community for many years. Now, with the influx of so many musically inspired youngsters, it became home to Hollywood's alternative music community. Musical groups rented cabins, and young and old artists of all kinds either found their own places there or slept on friends' floors and spent much of their time in artistic endeavors, convening at some house or other for social and spiritual discussions mixed with some poetry, marijuana, and music.

When Joni Mitchell wrote "Our House" about her domestic bliss with ex-Hollie and future Crosby, Stills, Nash and Young singer Graham Nash, she was living in a charming and simple A-frame cottage in Laurel Canyon. Graham Nash recalls that it was in Joni's house that he, David Crosby, and Stephen Stills first blended vocals. Frank Zappa moved into silent western movie star Tom Mix's rambling cabin, Laurel Tavern, which became the hub of all musical and artistic happenings in the local community. It was a peaceful and easygoing setup with its own country store where neighbors met up, arranged the next listening party, or talked about music. This being the late 1960s, not a lot of communal activities happened without copious quantities of marijuana and cocaine. Passing the guitar followed by a joint was the order of the day.

New York Times' journalist Susan Gordon Lydon visited Mitchell in her Laurel Canyon house in 1969 and gave a delightful description of Canyon life.

"Joni Mitchell lives in Laurel Canyon, in a small pine-paneled house lovingly cluttered with two cats, a stuffed elk's head, stained glass windows, a grandfather clock given her by Leonard Cohen, a king's head with a jeweled crown sticking out from the brick fireplace, votive candles, blooming azaleas, a turkey made of pine cones, dried flowers, old dolls, Victorian shadow boxes, colored glass, an ornamental plate from Saskatoon, Saskatchewan, where she grew up, an art nouveau lamp in the shape of a frog holding a lily pad, a collection of cloisonné boxes, bowls and ashtrays, patchwork quilts, Maxfield Parrish pictures, various musical instruments, and Joni Mitchell and Graham Nash."

Sweetheart of the Rodeo

Musically, the young singer-songwriters of the Canyon were inspired by first folk and then the Dylan-led rebirth of country music. The 1960s in California had already witnessed a bluegrass revival and now with The Byrds and Dylan leading the way, another musical revolution was about to take place, one that would flower spectacularly with the Eagles.

In 1967 The Byrds changed their lineup. Out went Crosby and in came Gram Parsons, a wayward rich kid from Kentucky who had star quality and a love of country music. With Crosby gone, Parsons and Chris Hillman pushed The Byrds toward a country music sound. In March 1968 they appeared on stage at Nashville's Grand Ole Opry, the mother church of country music. The "hippie" Byrds were not exactly accepted in straight-laced Nashville, despite cutting their hair especially for the performance. Undaunted, they recorded what is regarded as the first country rock album, the seminal *Sweethearts of the Rodeo*.

Below: Two of future Byrd Gram Parsons' earliest recordings.

Above: Gram Parsons and Bernie Leadon perform with The Flying Burrito Brothers. Leadon would, of course, soon take his country sound to the newly formed Eagles.

"We'd already known that a country influence could work in pop music—we'd heard the Beatles' song 'Act Naturally,' and I'd written 'Mr. Spaceman,' which was a 2/4 kind of country-ish sound. So we started going in that direction and decided to do an album in Nashville and hired some country guys to come and help us out."

Although Gram Parsons' voice was too often lost in the final mix of the *Sweethearts of the Rodeo* album, his influence and songs clearly shaped the direction of the group. He left The Byrds in 1968, refusing to tour South Africa, but continued to pioneer country rock with another ex-Byrd and bluegrass aficionado Chris Hillman. Their band, The Flying Burrito Brothers, would become legendary in country and rock circles. Their breakthrough album, *Gilded Palace of Sin* (1969), filled with a delicate mix of backwoods country and rock and roll beats, completed the cosmic cowboy vision with the LP cover showing a group of long-haired hippies wearing country and western Nudie suits embroidered with marijuana leaves. They, and the album, were everything that Don Henley's Shiloh aspired to be, but only came close to.

The Burritos would undergo several personnel changes over the next few years with a young multi-instrumentalist and future Eagle, Bernie Leadon, joining for a while. He worked with Parsons and the band on their second album, *Burrito Deluxe*, which featured the first recording of a new Jagger-Richards song, "Wild Horses." Parsons and Rolling Stone Keith Richards had become pals after first meeting in London in 1968, and Richards had invited the American to spend time at his mansion in France to which he had retreated in order to write songs. Other Stones' numbers to emerge from the era of their friendship include "Honky Tonk Women" (also recorded by Parsons), "Country Honk," "Dead Flowers," "Sweet Virginia," and "I Just Want to See His Face," all of which are country flavored.

The Flying Burrito Brothers effectively lost their creative spark when the drug-addicted Gram Parsons left them after the second Burritos album flopped commercially and critically. Parsons died three years later of a drug overdose, aged just 26, in a hotel room in Joshua Tree in the California desert.

Bernie Leadon stayed with the Burritos for the recording of their third, eponymous, album. Although born in Minneapolis, he received his musical education in the booming folk era of late 1950s and early 1960s California, hanging out at a musical instrument store, the Blue Guitar Shop, in Los Angeles. There he mixed with folk singers, bluegrass players, assorted bohemians, and would-be troubadours. One of them, Chris Hillman, then in bluegrass band The Scottsville Squirrel Barkers, drafted the young Bernie in on a few gigs in 1964. When Leadon's father got a job at a university in Florida, Bernie went with him, still playing music, honing his craft, and teaming up around town with a young Don Felder, who would join the Eagles some time later.

In 1967, the year of flower power, *Sergeant Pepper*, and the Summer of Love, Leadon trekked the 3,000 miles back to Los Angeles to find a thriving and exciting folk music scene in the clubs of Hollywood. Larry Murray, the Dobro player for Squirrel Barkers, asked Bernie to join

PICKERS
DOUG DILLARD – Vocals, Banjo, Guitar and Fiddle
DONNA WASHBURN – Vocals, Tambourine and Guitar
GENE CLARK – Vocals, Guitar and Harp
BYRON BERLINE – Fiddle
JON CORNEAL – Drums and Tambourine
DAVID JACKSON – Vocals, Bass, Piano and Cello
SPECIAL PICKERS
SNEAKY PETE – Steel Guitar
CHRIS HILLMAN – Mandolin
BERNIE LEADON – Guitar and Bass

Producer: LARRY MARKS
Engineer: DICK BOGERT and RAY GERHARDT
Art Director: TOM WILKES
Photography: JIM McCRARY
Manufactured under licence
from A&M Records Ltd.

ED CD 195

his Hearts and Flowers band, which was achieving minor success with the album *Now Is the Time for Hearts and Flowers*. Their sound would predate much of the soft rock, country, and rock brews that colored the South California landscape. Leadon worked with them on their second and final album, *Of Horses, Kids and Forgotten Women*.

When that musical ensemble dissipated, he started playing with his then-housemate Doug Dillard and ex-Byrd Gene Clark as they moved increasingly toward country music and contemporary bluegrass. The stunning and influential *Fantastic Expedition of Dillard and Clark* album came out in 1968 and included the first version of "Train Leaves Here this Morning," which would resurface on the Eagles' debut album.

Band associations were loose in the pre-corporate rock and roll of the 1960s, though, and Leadon left Dillard and Clark prior to completion of their second and final album, *Through the Morning, Through the Night* (1969), in order to play live shows on the east coast with Linda Ronstadt's backing band, The Corvettes. Before long, Leadon would join old pal Chris Hillman in The Flying Burrito Brothers, but an important link had been made during his time with The Corvettes, one that would eventually lead to the creation of the Eagles.

Above: Dillard and Clark's second album, *Through the Morning, Through the Night*. Bernie Leadon actually quit the band before the album was completed.

Pickin' up the Pieces

The band Poco appeared from the ashes of the Buffalo Springfield, with Richie Furay, Jim Messina, Rusty Young, and future Eagle Randy Meisner on bass, recording prototype country rock on their *Pickin' up the Pieces* debut album in 1969. Born to sharecroppers in Nebraska, a starry-eyed ten-year-old Meisner had seen the Beatles' breakthrough performance on *Ed Sullivan* and somehow got himself a guitar. A series of local bands followed and, on leaving school, already married, he played gigs across Nebraska to support his young family. Eventually one such band, Soul Survivors, found enough ambition and cash to make the journey west to Los Angeles and try their luck with the big boys.

They struggled, sleeping in Hollywood dives and making poorly paid gigs. Renaming the band The Poor didn't help, but they did get the attention of ex-Buffalo Springfield managers Charlie Green and Brian Stone. Nothing much transpired, but Meisner was asked to audition for Buffalo Springfield to replace Jim Messina. Although selected, Meisner quickly quit when the band's Richie Furay left to form Poco. Meisner stayed with Poco for a year before bailing out of that group as well, to be replaced by yet another future Eagle, Timothy B. Schmit. Unhappy at not being treated as an equal part of the Poco band, Meisner was quick to respond to producer John Boylan's call to play for Rick Nelson in The Stone Canyon band. A short tour of Europe and playing on the *Rick Nelson in Concert* album was all he achieved before Boylan suggested Meisner for another of his acts: Linda Ronstadt.

Meanwhile, Michael Nesmith, a veteran of the Troubadour Hootenanny Nights, had written the country-flavored hit "Different Drum" for Linda Ronstadt and the Stone Poneys in 1967 before finding television stardom with *The Monkees*, where he brought a Texas twang to the mix. Nesmith turned his back on celebrity in 1969, though, to establish another of country rock's most significant musical groups, The First National Band.

John Boylan was in LA looking for musicians to work with Rick Nelson, and working on an album for the Association. Next he was recruited by bluegrass band The Dillards, a move which would have a huge impact on Boylan and play no small part in his eventual role in bringing the Eagles together. "I realized that the most exciting music

The Albums

Linda Ronstadt

Producer: John Boylan

Recorded: United and Western, Hollywood; Muscle Shoals Sound, Alabama; live at the Troubadour, Hollywood 1971

Label: Capitol Records

Released: 1971

Chart positions: U.S.A. Billboard Pop Albums #163

TRACKS

Side One

1. Rock Me on the Water
2. Crazy Arms
3. I Won't be Hangin' Round
4. I Still Miss Someone
5. In My Reply

Side Two

1. I Fall to Pieces
2. Ramblin' Round
3. Birds
4. I Ain't Always Been Faithful
5. Rescue Me

for me was rooted in the American folk tradition," he remembers. "I began to think of ways that I could combine those roots with contemporary rock and roll." When Boylan was charged with finding musicians for Linda Ronstadt, he naturally turned to the Troubadour.

"I heard that Randy Meisner had left Poco so I quickly hired him to play for Rick Nelson's Stone Canyon Band, and when I needed to find a band for Linda Ronstadt's tour I thought of Randy straightaway. There was this kid who had given me a tape of his band Shiloh—looking to pitch songs to Linda—and he had talent. His name was Don Henley and at the time he was on a label formed by Kenny Rogers, and Kenny's wife Margo was booking their gigs. I asked Don if he wanted to play with Linda, but he said that he was playing at the Golden Bear and couldn't make it. Now I happened to know that those shows had been canceled so I pursued Don and eventually got him for the band. Next I approached Glenn Frey, who was in a duo with J. D. Souther, Longbranch Pennywhistle, and I offered him $250 a week. Then Henley called me and said he was in and we were on the road with Linda—first gig was at The Cellar Door in Washington D.C."

When Boylan later recruited Bernie Leadon for a Linda Ronstadt Los Angeles show he had effectively created the Eagles—Don Henley, Glenn Frey, Randy Meisner, and Bernie Leadon, four young men who had paid their country rock dues, and who would very quickly take the genre to unheard of heights of critical and commercial success. One of the finest female singers in Los Angeles during the late 1960s and early 1970s, Linda Ronstadt eventually became a pop superstar with numerous platinum albums, hit singles, and multiple Grammy awards to her name. She played a significant part in blending country and folk music and making it palatable and marketable to a mainstream audience in the early country rock days. While a student at Arizona State University, Ronstadt hooked up with guitarist Bob Kimmel and, fired by the folk rock boom in California, both moved to Los Angeles where they formed the Stone Poneys with guitarist/songwriter Kenny Edwards. Regulars on the folkie circuit and part of the vibrant Troubadour crowd, they scored a record deal and a Top 20 hit with "Different Drum," written by Mike Nesmith of Monkees fame.

Right: When news spread that
Randy Meisner had left Poco, the
Eagles seemed his natural home.

With Ronstadt's sultry Latin good looks bringing media attention
and the group's effortless fusion of folk and rock positioning them as
a cross between Sonny and Cher and The Byrds, it seemed stardom
was inevitable. It wasn't to be, however, and the Stone Poneys failed
to capitalize on that success. Ronstadt reemerged in the early 1970s
with a more country-influenced sound and played a significant role in
the development of the country rock genre. *Linda Ronstadt*, her third
album, was a pivotal record in her career. The album also featured all
four Eagles—Bernie Leadon, Don Henley, Glenn Frey, and Randy
Meisner—although the foursome never worked together during the
recording as Boylan recorded the album in different locations and used
musicians as and when they were available. The album only made it
to #163 on the *Billboard* chart but it highlighted the work of some of
the Troubadour scene's most talented young songwriters. Ronstadt also
brought traditional country music to the attention of her young rock
audience by recording country standards like "I Fall to Pieces" and "I
Still Miss Someone." The live tracks on the album, recorded at the
Troubadour, provide a perfect snapshot of the blossoming country rock
style that Ronstadt along with Frey, Henley, Leadon, and Meisner were
creating on Sunset Boulevard in 1971.

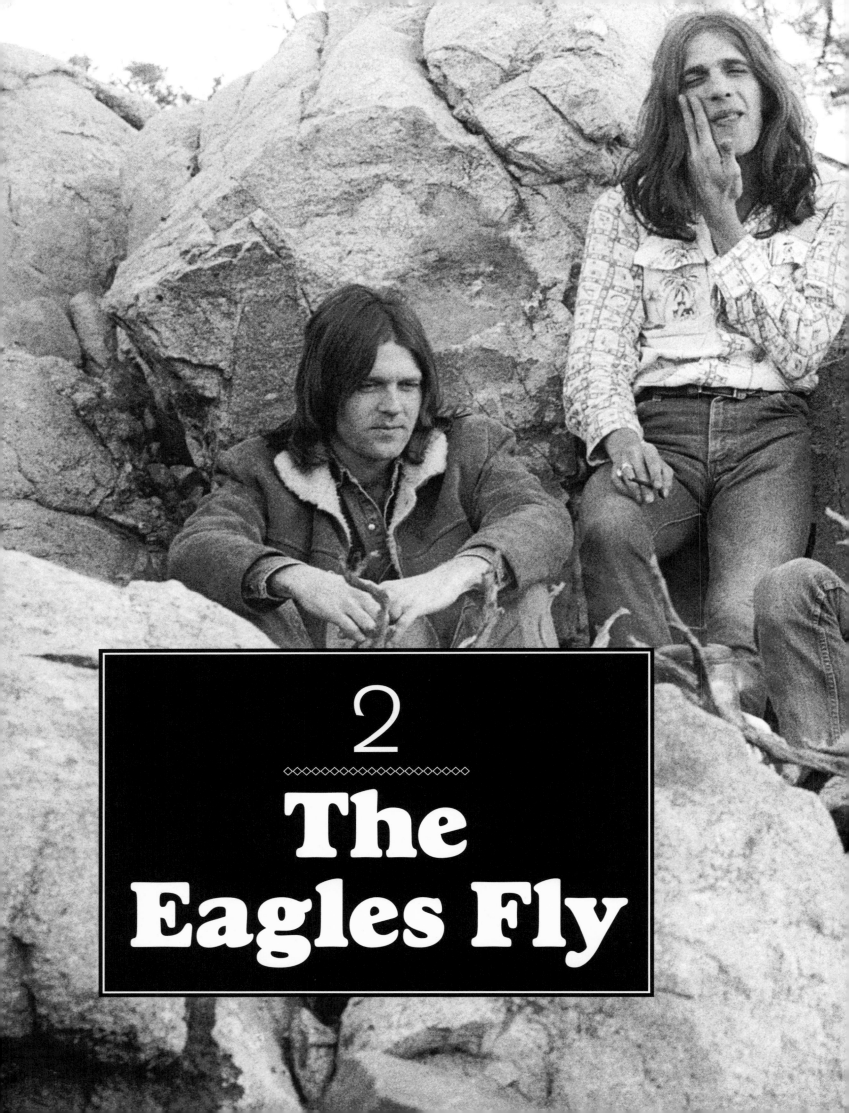

2
The Eagles Fly

DON HENLEY AND GLENN FREY saw one another at the Troubadour enough to be on nodding terms, but they didn't get to know each other well until they were brought together by producer John Boylan to help make up Linda Ronstadt's backing band. From the moment they started working together, it was clear that here was a formidable musical pairing. As Boylan noted, "It was Glenn and Don; they had a musical chemistry, and on top of that they had the talent and the drive to make something happen." That "something" began happening very quickly on the Linda Ronstadt tour. As Frey recalled, "the first night of our tour we decided to start a band."

J. D. Souther, who had become very much a part of the Henley and Frey inner circle from the off, was considered a fifth Eagle but despite conflicting reports as to why he was not part of the original band, Souther himself claims it was a musical decision. "I went to a rehearsal after they got together and played with them but they were so good as a unit that there was no need for me."

> **"Right from the start the Eagles were good. Don had this thing about working hard and rehearsing so that you had a solid foundation if anything went wrong on stage. He took that with him to the Eagles."**
>
> **AL PERKINS**

After sharing time on the road, it's unsurprising that, musically, the men who would become the Eagles were tight as a unit, but there was more to their unity than just the music. While Henley and Frey bonded on the road—and when back in LA, at late-night drinking sessions at the Troubadour—they also shared a powerful determination to do whatever it took to emerge from the LA scene as winners, but

to do so with professionalism. Similarly, Bernie Leadon and Randy Meisner had been through more than their fair share of highs, lows, and fragile band politics to also have the desire for something new and solid. All four agreed that they would make a concerted effort to make it big, work incredibly hard, and bring a rare professionalism to the proceedings.

"We had it all planned," said Don Henley, looking back. "We'd watched bands like Poco and the Burrito Brothers lose their initial momentum. We were determined not to make the same mistakes. This was gonna be our best shot. Everybody had to look good, sing good, play good, and write good. We wanted it all. Peer respect. AM and FM success. Number one singles and albums, great music and a lot of money." He

added, "Money was a much saner goal than adoration. They'll both drive you crazy but if I'm gonna blow my brains out for five years I want something to show for it."

That was a break from the previously ruling ethos of 1960s' hippies in LA and the Canyon, which was based on community, art, and music for music's sake. Maybe it was because they were from working cities which had seen their share of poverty and misery that the two lead Eagles felt they would need a different approach. When the band teamed up with a young and ambitious music business executive called David Geffen, they were ideally placed to bridge the gap between the idealism of the '60s and the more cynical new decade in which rock music was fast becoming Big Business.

It's no coincidence that the Eagles surfaced in 1971. Just as the Beatles had reacted to the changes and trends of the early 1960s and become the mouthpiece of that era, so the Eagles seemed intuitively to respond to a different set of social circumstances and, like the Fab Four before them, would come to write the soundtrack for their era. The Beatles succeeded at a time of mourning in America, a mere three months after the assassination of President John F. Kennedy. Their ebullient music and hard-edged sense of fun offered something of an antidote to the prevailing mood of fear and uncertainty among the young: the Cold War was raging, troops were being deployed in Vietnam, and the draft was coming.

Similarly, when the Eagles announced their arrival on the music scene, America was also living in fear and depression. The Cold War might not have been quite so threatening to national security, but the Vietnam War was still raging and America seemed to be losing. There was also an impending oil crisis and economic downturn on the horizon. Plus, the promise of a brave new world borne aloft on hippie ideals had proven to be a false prophecy. Two pivotal events in 1969 had changed the social and musical climate. They also proved to have definite bearings on paths and decisions made by the Eagles.

The first of these events occurred in August 1969. Laurel Canyon was shocked to its core when members of the so-called Manson Family went on a murderous rampage though the Hollywood hills.

Helter Skelter

Charles Manson—a self-styled cult leader who recruited wayward waifs and strays, usually young hippie women looking for a home amid the drug-fueled confusion of Hollywood—moved from commune to commune in the Los Angeles area. He looked and acted very much like all the other flower-power canyon hippies of the time, and his communes were strikingly similar to those dotted all over Hollywood. Manson also had links with the music fraternity, having befriended Beach Boy Dennis Wilson and Byrds' producer Terry Melcher. He had designs on being an artist and studied Beatles lyrics avidly, reading in them messages of hate and dark warnings of a blood race war to come, especially in the Lennon/McCartney song "Helter Skelter."

Terry Melcher (also the son of movie star Doris Day) had shown interest in producing some demos for Manson after having been introduced to him by Dennis Wilson (who had met Manson after picking up a couple of the "family" women while they were hitchhiking). The Beach Boys had been persuaded by Melcher to record a couple of Manson's songs while he was producing them. Intrigued by Manson's living arrangements and role as a cult leader, Melcher had, over several meetings with him at the house Melcher was renting at 10050 Cielo Drive in Benedict Canyon, suggested he make a movie about Manson's "family."

However, having got to know him, Melcher backed out of their putative arrangement after seeing Manson erupt into a violent rage and deciding that he couldn't possibly work with him. Melcher left the house on Cielo Drive soon after, which was subsequently rented out to new tenants, and got word to Manson that he couldn't make any recording sessions. A furious Manson returned to Cielo Drive and was turned away by the new tenants. It is presumed, however, that he believed Melcher to be still living there.

Not long after, Manson sent various "family" members on a bloody rampage in the area, lasting over two terrible nights in August 1969. Sharon Tate, the actress wife of movie director Roman Polanski who was almost nine months' pregnant, was killed at 10050 Cielo Drive. Four others perished in the attack and the word "Pig" was scrawled in human blood on the front door of the house.

The following night, Manson and some of his family members drove to the LA suburb of Los Feliz. At a house on Waverley Drive, next door to a residence at which Manson had previously attended a party, husband and wife Leno and Rosemary LaBianca were tied up by Manson who then left, after ordering his followers to murder once again. The LaBiancas were killed and a misspelled "Healter Skelter" was written on the door of the refrigerator in blood. The murderers then showered and sat in the yard of the house feasting on milk and cheese taken from the fridge before hitchhiking back to their canyon commune.

Above: A poster for the Stones'
infamous Altamont concert, which
would end in violence and the
tragic death of a young fan.

Opposite: Jefferson Airplane,
another band to witness
the Altamont violence.

Following double page: The
crowd at Altamont, 1969.

Gimme Shelter

The violence and magnitude of the murders committed by the Manson
Family, especially of the pregnant Sharon Tate, sent waves of fear
and paranoia through the hippy communities of Los Angeles. The
counterculture was diametrically opposed to and wary of the "straights"
and the "suits," as they labeled corporate and federal America. In the
face of such violence perpetrated by murderers who looked just like
them, the scions of the underground felt under attack and had no
real form of protection from it. They needed the "straight" world to
save them from monsters; the "Peace Not War" dream faded. Never
again would the Canyon community know the innocence, trust, and
communal spirit that was their bedrock.

As if that wasn't enough, the hopes and ideals of the flower-power
generation would be challenged again a few months later at a music
festival set up as the West Coast's answer to Woodstock. It was
supposed to be another showcase of the power of peace and love, but it
erupted in violence and ended in death.

In December 1969, over 300,000 music fans gathered at the Altamont
Speedway arena in northern California to see the Rolling Stones,
Crosby, Stills, Nash and Young, Santana, and the Jefferson Airplane
perform for free. The Stones, further courting their reputation as "bad
boys" of rock, decided to call on the local chapter of the Hell's Angels
to provide security following the almost successful precedent of their
use at a free concert in London in July. The notorious and often
criminal Hell's Angels biker chapters were perceived by the flower
children as fellow members of U.S. counterculture in a shared struggle
to change corporate America. The Angels had provided security for
the Grateful Dead on several occasions without any real incident.
But Altamont was different. On the second day scuffles broke out in
the crowd and the Hell's Angels, who were being paid in beer, were
intoxicated and in no mood to be jostled and harassed by concert-goers.
When a motorcycle was knocked over, tempers flared. A nervous Marty
Balin was assaulted and knocked unconscious during the Jefferson
Airplane show. Shaken and perturbed, the Grateful Dead refused to
go on stage at all and left the venue in a hurry. The headlining Rolling
Stones stepped on stage several hours late to an extremely rowdy
reception. When a young audience member rushed the stage waving

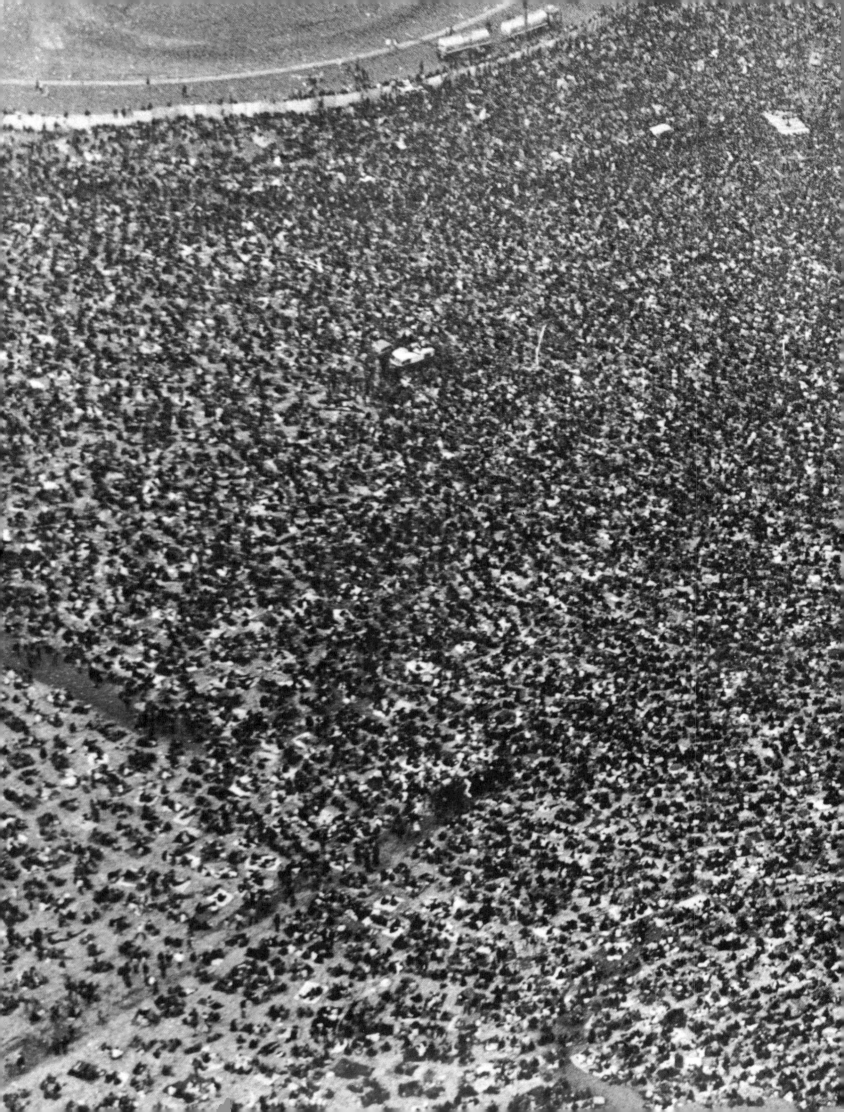

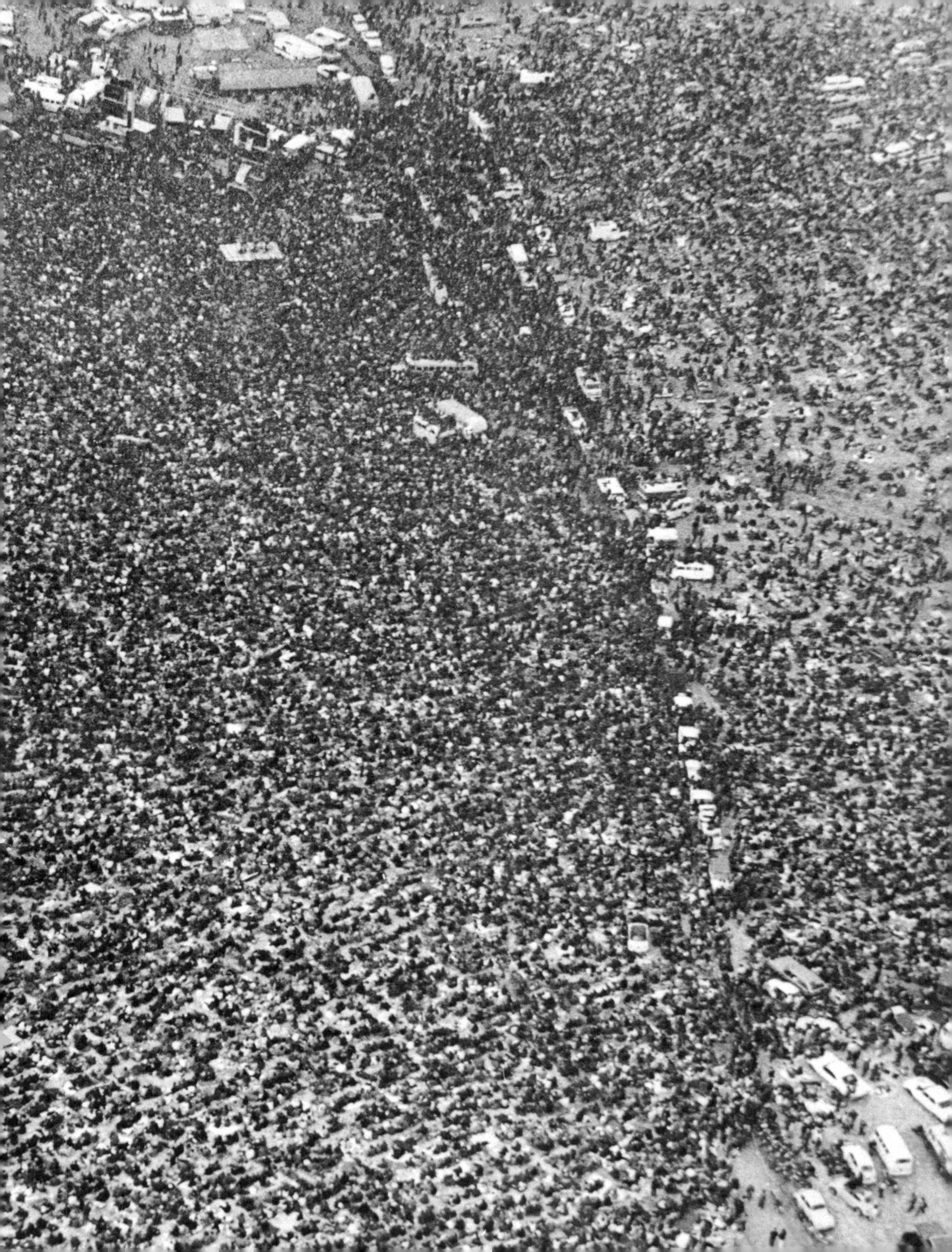

a gun, the Hell's Angels wasted no time in taking him down. The eighteen-year-old Meredith Hunter was beaten and stabbed to death.

As with the violence surrounding the Sharon Tate murders, the horrors at Altamont shattered the idealism and optimism of the counter culture, undermining the new generation's beliefs and faith in the possibility of change. Throw in the cynicism engendered from the assassinations of Robert F. Kennedy and Martin Luther King just a year before in 1968 and the drink- and drugs-related deaths of Janis Joplin, Jimi Hendrix, and Jim Morrison, and it was no wonder that the rock and roll class of 1971 would approach things in a different way to that of their more idealistic predecessors. Musical and financial success in the record business would quickly replace loftier notions of peace, love, and social change through music.

Asylum

The mega-successful Eagles would later be criticized by some sections of the still largely idealistic rock press in the mid-1970s for putting materialism and professionalism above art and expression in their career. But those critics always missed the very essence of the Eagles. What made this band different was their united desire to be successful as a band, to instill a disciplined work ethic, and to take on the music business—not as poor artistic victims but as smart, business-savvy equals. Each of the Eagles had witnessed the harshness of the music business, the dangers of drugs and alcohol, and the need to be strong in the face of record company machinations and politics. And while Henley and Frey embraced the '60s lifestyle in Hollywood, neither were ever idealistic flower children. Meisner was a veteran of several band implosions as was Leadon, who was ready to devote his talent and energy to a musical project that would have direction and follow-through. They were still, of course, primarily musicians and naturally somewhat naïve about much of the business side of the music industry, but shrewdly, and unlike many of their musical peers, they recognized that weakness and hitched their horses to someone who could be trusted to deal with the corporate executives on their behalf.

It may have been the smartest decision they ever made. The band's relationship with David Geffen, already managing Crosby, Stills, Nash and Young and Joni Mitchell when they approached him, would be

Above: The Eagles' first manager, David Geffen, seen here with one of his charges, singer-songwriter Laura Nyro.

Following double page: Geffen with another of his stars, Joni Mitchell.

pivotal on many levels. That relationship, like so many, started in the Troubadour where Geffen was a regular.

Glenn Frey, along with J. D. Souther, might not have gone far with their duo project Longbranch Pennywhistle, but their album did get circulated around the song-hungry music community of Hollywood. One of the non-musicians who frequented the Troubadour, enamored by the scene and determined to make his mark in the record business, was a young talent agent by the name of David Geffen. He would go on to become one of the most successful and colorful media moguls in America and to launch the Eagles to unimaginable heights around the world. Younger than most music business executives at the time, he started by hanging out on the Hollywood music scene as ostensibly just another longhaired, denim-clad kid eager to make a name for himself. Geffen, originally from New York, famously worked his way

Opposite: Jackson Browne, who co-wrote "Take It Easy" for the Eagles. The track would encapsulate the sound and feel of California in the early 1970s.

up in the entertainment business from the mailroom at the William Morris Agency, where his street smarts and overt ambition quickly won him promotion to artist agent. From there he first managed young singer-songwriter Laura Nyro, who became a huge sensation with "Stoney End," before representing Crosby, Stills, Nash and Young and Joni Mitchell from a hip, musician-friendly office on Sunset Boulevard. Geffen and his partner Elliot Roberts were young enough to relate to the musicians they represented but sufficiently business-minded and tough to deal, on their behalf, with the record industry.

"At the beginning he was an executive, but he was also one of us. He was into the music and you have to remember that back then the record company guys were a different generation to us. David Geffen seemed like he was on our side and would represent us and our music better than anyone."

JACKSON BROWNE

David Geffen straddled both camps perfectly, and in the early days at least had the complete trust of his artists. He was aware of Longbranch Pennywhistle and the songwriting potential of J. D. Souther, and he told Glenn Frey that he was suited to being part of a band rather than a solo act. But it would be the influence of another of Frey and Henley's artist cohorts who would open the doors for the Eagles to sign with Geffen and eventually make records for his new Asylum Records company. Don Henley told Cameron Crowe, "A lot of credit has to go to Jackson who convinced David we were good."

Jackson Browne, who would provide the Eagles with their first hit with his Echo Park-penned song, "Take It Easy," had already allied himself with Geffen.

In one of those wonderful Hollywood stories, Jackson Browne, at David Crosby's suggestion, sent a demo of his songs and an 8 × 10 photograph to Geffen's office. Even in the beginning of his executive career, Geffen was not in the habit of accepting unsolicited material and tossed the package. The picture of a strikingly handsome young Browne, however, was rescued by Geffen's secretary who, taken by the image, listened to a few songs and then recommended that her boss give the kid a chance. The strength of the prodigious Browne's songs did the rest.

Browne had been on the LA scene since the mid-60s, and had even joined the Nitty Gritty Dirt band for a while in 1967. While still only seventeen he signed a deal with Elektra, worked the Greenwich Village scene in 1968, and then returned to the Troubadour and LA in 1969, where he became part of the circle that would launch the Eagles.

Geffen, tired of the politics and squabbling of Crosby, Stills, Nash and Young at the time, made Browne his new priority and determined to get the young songwriter a record deal. When legendary executive Ahmet Ertegun turned him down, he offered instead the possibility for Geffen to run his own record label via a distribution deal with Atlantic. So, in 1971, David Geffen and Elliot Roberts launched Asylum Records, signed Jackson Browne, and determined to tap into the country rock and singer-songwriter veins of LA that he deeply believed were the future of rock and roll in America.

Mountain Boys Trial

With the Leadon, Meisner, Henley, and Frey lineup firm, committed, and rehearsed, Glenn Frey was able to approach Geffen, as part of a band rather than a solo artist, just as Geffen had recommended he do. Jackson Browne had been championing his friends for some time, so that when Frey and co., led by their spokesman (at that time) Bernie Leadon, visited Geffen in his sumptuously hip offices, they didn't even take a demo tape of them playing together.

Bernie Leadon strode up to Geffen and asked quite simply, "Ok. Here we are. Do you want us or not?"

Impressed at their confidence, track record, and buoyed by Jackson Browne's testimonial, Geffen wasted no time in agreeing to manage the

Above: Bernie Leadon. His "Witchy Woman," co-written with Don Henley, would be one of the standout tracks on the Eagles' first LP.

band and then signing them to his new Asylum label. He sent them to Aspen, Colorado to formulate their sound, play four sets a night every night, and write material. Given how fast things would move for the Eagles once their first album was released, these weeks away from the spotlight were essential in giving them the opportunity to become a tight and proficient musical unit and would prove to be valuable in the following months. They also needed a name. Don Henley recalls that "at the time everything was Strawberry this and Electric that, you know, so we wanted something simple and we wanted something American and we wanted something that was easy to remember and something with a little spiritual value. Somebody—I think Glenn—was reading some book about Hopi mythology. Also it sounded very American, football teams and street gangs."

The Eagles worked perfectly from Day One. They all instinctively understood where the fusion of country and rock had failed so far and recognized that a stronger rhythm section was necessary to cross over into the mainstream. Frey's rock and roll attitude was perfectly suited to a more conventional rock-band formula but with the inspired

Glyn Johns

Glyn Johns, rock and roll royalty in London by 1972, had begun his music career as an artist, releasing a handful of soon-forgotten singles in the early 1960s. Realizing that stardom was not in his astrology chart, Johns found work as an apprentice under legendary producer Shel Talmy of the Kinks and the Who fame. By the mid-1960s, he was engineer on tracks by the Rolling Stones and Led Zeppelin. He then produced Steve Miller, the Who, and the Faces. He was even brought in by the Beatles to save the doomed "Get Back" sessions.

Glyn Johns was a disciplined taskmaster who liked to use a particular studio in West London, the hi-tech Olympic Studios—in its day rivaled only by

Abbey Road as the recording facilities of choice. But rather than just sending the Eagles to London, Geffen shrewdly first flew Glyn Johns to Colorado to see the fledgling band in action and get a feel for the group of musicians he might be working with. However, Johns was initially unimpressed with the live shows he witnessed and swiftly returned to England. He had to be cajoled back to the U.S.A. by Geffen to reconsider. Given time with the band in a rehearsal studio, he was able to better witness the natural blend of voices and the harmonious balance between Leadon's country bent and Frey's natural rock and roll instincts.

songwriting from the band and their circle of trusted friends—topped off with the adoption of CSN&Y-style harmonies—they knew immediately that they were on to something. Not that their producer Glyn Johns was so instantly impressed. In fact his initial take on the Eagles was that they weren't really his cup of tea.

Yet it made sense for Geffen to select Glyn Johns as producer for his new band. Johns was English, which carried considerable credibility with the American music business at the time—and indeed the Eagles themselves. Bernie Leadon told the *NME*, "We all wanted to record in London ever since we heard those early Beatles and Stones records—the mystique of British rock!"

Tryin'

Once Johns had satisfied himself that here was a band that he could do something with, he agreed to a deal with Geffen to record the Eagles—in England. What was to become the quintessential sound of West Coast America, the record that would put the sun up in the sky over America's troubled horizon, mixing country, rock, and laid-back sounds, was recorded in a gray, cold, and wet England. It would be overseen by an Englishman who, right from the start, Glenn Frey felt, had too quickly pigeonholed the band as a country outfit. Frey envisioned a tougher, more rock and roll sound; the differences between Johns and Frey would produce friction right through to the recording of the Eagles' third album. However, for the early recording sessions tensions were forgotten as the band, excited to be in London, were enthused by working with a producer with a track record like Glyn Johns.

The Eagles arrived in London in February 1972. Fresh from the relative luxury of LA, they were thrust into an economically depressed capital city and a dismal British winter. California seemed a million miles away.

Cold, gloomy London wasn't exactly what the California boys were used to, but it was what the producer ordered, Henley told BBC Radio in 1977. "He pretty much insisted that we use the studio over here because of the equipment." In February 1972, London was even colder and more miserable than usual; a miners' strike was in full swing, the first such since 1926, and the country was at a standstill. Miners picketed power stations across the country and then moved on to steelworks and coal depots. From February 9th a state of emergency was declared by the Conservative government who introduced a three-day working week in order to save power. The Eagles' recording sessions were interrupted when Olympic Studios had to bring in generators to keep things running. The social life for the band, in a country where pubs closed by 11pm and TV had only three channels to watch, was a major culture shock. "We were driven to the studio and driven back to the apartment every day. We'd just sit in the apartment and drink tequila and wait for the next day," said Henley. On top of that, the disciplined Glyn Johns stood for no nonsense in the studio and was never afraid to criticize.

"We thought 'we'll get to see London and get away from Los Angeles and all its distractions, with the phone ringing and people coming in to the studio and bothering us and stuff.' And we were left alone because we didn't know anybody and it was miserable."

DON HENLEY

Henley remembers that Johns' approach was his way or the highway. "Glyn had a very particular style. He was not about to change anything for anybody. He was a star, good at what he did, and respected within the industry. We were sort of new and green so he did it in his way. And he was very strict about how many takes we could do. I'd sing a song maybe three or four times and just be getting in to it and he'd say 'OK there you go, that's fine, the best you can do.' It got a bit frustrating after a while. He was great to work with in a way because we needed a psychologist and a band sorter-outer so to speak. He was good for that and we learned a lot from working with him. But he was very strict and had definite ideas of what we could do and what we couldn't do."

Below: The grimy streets of strike-hit London in early 1972, where the Eagles recorded their first album.

Besides differences over musical styles and overall direction of the band sound, Glyn Johns irked the California freewheelers with some heavy-duty rules of behavior. He greatly frowned on Frey and Meisner disappearing at regular intervals to partake of some light recreational drugs. Perhaps because Johns was a no-nonsense producer or maybe because the band were eager to get out of strike-hit London, the album was recorded in just over two weeks. A ridiculously short time considering the months the band would take to complete just one track a few years later, but first albums typically flow quickly. Songs have piled up and the chance to work on that long-dreamed-of debut project is enough to fire up and inspire any group, however awkward the circumstances. Whatever the reason, *Eagles* was done, dusted, and ready to be shipped, all within four months.

The Albums

Eagles

Producer: Glyn Johns

Recorded: Olympic Studios, London, February 1972

Label: Asylum Records

Released: June 1972

Chart position: U.S.A. Billboard pop albums #22

TRACKS

Side One

1. Take It Easy
2. Witchy Woman
3. Chug All Night
4. Most of Us Are Sad
5. Nightingale

Side Two

1. Train Leaves Here
   This Morning
2. Take the Devil
3. Earlybird
4. Peaceful Easy Feeling
5. Tryin'

Some critics still claim that the Eagles' debut album is their finest work. Undoubtedly it is crammed full of great songs and their trademark free-flowing country-rock style is already evident, effortless, and beautifully melodic. There's a strong band feel of four independent voices pulling together as one, an element that would slowly diminish as Frey and Henley became more powerful within the group. The record was well received by the then-hugely influential *Rolling Stone* magazine, which described the opening track and first single "Take It Easy" as "simply the best sounding rock single to come out so far this year."

The song, a co-write between Jackson Browne and Glenn Frey, had started life in Browne's tiny Echo Park apartment. He had never finished it, but with Frey's urging and help the song was completed. Frey always saw it as the stand-out track on the album. The song starts simply with Frey's chiming acoustic and Leadon's Byrds-like guitar playing before launching into a mid-tempo country rock song. The delicate harmonies finish off the song perfectly. Until "Hotel California" came along, "Take It Easy" would serve as the band's trademark number.

"Witchy Woman," co-written by Leadon and Henley, is a different thing altogether. It is darker, the arrangement less breezy and more musically complex. Then Glenn Frey chips in with his "Chug All Night," a much heavier rock piece predating the tougher sound the band would go on to perfect in later years. Leadon's crystal-clear high tenor vocals work delightfully on "Train Leaves Here This Morning," which he co-wrote with ex-Byrd Gene Clark and which sounds like something from The Flying Burrito Brothers. It's an outside song, "Peaceful Easy Feeling" written by Jack Tempchin, which brings the band back to the country rock sound with which they would dominate the airwaves.

The Eagles' use of imagery and their extolling of a freewheeling lifestyle would play a major role in their popularity all over America and then the world. Not since the Beach Boys' somewhat twee early 1960s odes to surf, sea, sand, and girls had a group found a way to capture the essence of the West Coast lifestyle. Where the Beach Boys had focused on sand and surf, the Eagles delved deeper into California's high desert mythology and folklore. For the debut album photo shoot, the band and photographer Henry Diltz headed to the California desert, took plenty of the Native American drug peyote, and posed in various locations in the mountain locale. The cover is sparse, dominated by a gorgeous blue sky, a cactus in silhouette, and an eagle at the top incorporating the band's name into an impressive logo. Inside the gatefold the Eagles are pictured sitting around a campfire, lit only by the light of the flames and looking very much like outlaws on the run from a posse in some 1970s alternative western movie.

The music and the image had been planned, orchestrated. It was well received by the press, and was now available to the public. It was time for the verdict.

3
Outlaws

ITH THE EAGLES' debut album
scheduled for a June 1972 release, David
Geffen arranged for the band to spend
the summer on the road opening shows
for some well-known acts: Jethro Tull, the
J. Geils Band, and Yes. Whether intended by Geffen or not, playing
before the colorful, sometimes outrageous, and always progressive-rock
oriented Tull and Yes was no easy feat for the more restrained Eagles,
but the challenges of the situation served to unite the new outfit.
Occasionally the pressure of playing for an openly hostile audience
led to moments of regrettable outspokenness from the sometimes
prickly Glenn Frey, who attacked the New York music scene and the
New York Dolls in particular during one less-than-satisfactory show in
the Big Apple. It marked the start of what was to become a negative
relationship between the band and the city, one that would continue
right through the 1970s.

Fortunately perhaps, Frey's band were by no means household names
at the time, which meant the outburst wasn't reported outside New
York. "Take It Easy" proved a modest hit and received decent FM and
AM radio play across the country, but the slow build toward national
fame meant that the Eagles were able to learn their trade as a musical
unit with a degree of anonymity. They soon realized that their best
approach was to keep things laid back, just play the songs and, as
a support act, not get too involved with the audience. At a time of
eccentric onstage performances from bands in the progressive rock
and fledgling glam rock scenes, the Eagles came across as sober, almost
conservative musicians, simply pleased to be given the chance to sing a
few songs. It proved to be a masterstroke of presentation that not only
suited the different personalities in the band but also helped to set
them apart from the crowd. Their album's follow-up singles, "Witchy
Woman" and "Peaceful Easy Feeling," also caught radio play and by the
end of 1972, the Eagles were beginning to see their first rewards. When
the album went gold (500,000 units) it was an understated but clear
message to the music business that a new band had arrived.

David Geffen recruited a record promotions specialist named Paul
Ahern, who had made his reputation at Atlantic Records, to work
for the Eagles and concentrate on getting them radio play. He spent

**Above: The cover of the Eagles'
eponymous debut was the
first in a long line of spare,
minimalist album sleeves.**

**Opposite: Glenn Frey pictured in
the early 1970s, leaning on his
Chevy. The car would go on to be
the star of the track "Ol' 55" from
1974's *On the Border* album.**

his time essentially schmoozing and calling key radio station heads and programmers, persuading them to add the Eagles to their playlists. Ahern was hugely successful and went on to work on several more Eagles projects before discovering and managing the melodic metal act Boston (whom he helped to sell millions of copies of their debut album). Geffen was constantly adding layers of professionalism to his company, and he also called in favors and used his industry influence

Above: Meisner, Leadon, Henley, and Frey photographed in Topanga Canyon, California.

to give leverage to the promotion team's efforts. The strategy did not go unnoticed by the increasingly business-aware Glenn Frey who realized that the key to their early success was that "we had David Geffen behind us. (He) was a big difference. He was a star on radio because he was the manager of Crosby, Stills, Nash & Young and Joni Mitchell. We benefited by having him become a star along with Asylum Records. Because of him we got our initial notoriety."

"It's sad when you learn what the rock and roll business is all about. That's basically what the Desperado album deals with. With growing up and learning what the real world is about and learning that there are certain compromises and sacrifices you have to make. In other words you have to do what everyone else wants you to do for a while. And during that time you have to maintain your identity, remember who you are and what you want to do. And then after you've achieved your position of power then you can say screw you to all those people and do what you want to do."

GLENN FREY

While touring as an opening act was not ideal, with a successful album behind them the band was at least able to enjoy the first flush of rock star fame, wealth, and life on the road. Tellingly, none of the Eagles allowed the influx of groupies, illicit drugs, and cash turn them from their avowed intent to make it really big as a group. More intelligent perhaps than some of their counterparts, and certainly less naïve, the Eagles exhibited an unusual degree of self-awareness during this period of blossoming fame and success. They used their experience of playing together and living life on the road as outsiders among the Prog Rock fraternity to create what may be their finest ever album, *Desperado.*

While the Eagles were playing support to apparently mismatched headliners, the rest of the music business—and the world in general, it seemed—was getting weirder, more diverse, and harder to predict. The industry was proving to be a big business. In 1969 a previously unknown band from England called Led Zeppelin had, without releasing singles, become such a success that by 1971 they were being booked into massive venues, selling out Madison Square Garden and two nights at the Inglewood Forum, CA. On their next U.S. tour they were booked into even larger venues, including the Long Beach Arena. Zeppelin's fourth album in as many years, released in 1971, had become the biggest selling rock record ever, and their eighteen-date (in twenty-two days) tour of America in June 1972 had sold out within days of tickets going on sale. At the same time, Grand Funk Railroad had also emerged onto the live scene, becoming the self-proclaimed loudest band in the business and also selling out massive venues.

Meanwhile the pop charts were being filled with singles by acts who were more used to topping the specialist charts, such as the country and soul charts. New musical and fashion trends were coming out of every American city, it seemed.

Horses, Snakes & Spiders at 4AM

In February 1972, former Beatle Paul McCartney launched his new musical project into the world when Wings took flight at a small university gig in England. An old Beatles' favorite, Harry Nilsson, was number 1 in the U.S. and England with "Without You," written by a band who signed to Apple Records, Badfinger. Not everything in music was connected to the Beatles, though. In March a three-piece band called America scored their first and greatest number 1 hit single with "A Horse with No Name." The single and subsequent self-titled album were recorded in London, where each band member had been born and raised—although they all had American servicemen fathers who had settled there. The sound and subject of the album and single came out of the band members' desire to see and experience the land of their fathers. The country-tinged rock song could easily have been an Eagles number with its laid-back beat, bluesy harmonies, and nostalgia-tinted subject matter. The album featured a photograph of the band sitting in front of a large image of three Native Americans, and the Wild West imagery complimented perfectly that of the Eagles' *Desperado*.

At the end of the 1960s, Detroit's Alice Cooper (born Vincent Furnier) had said that his band was "the last nail in the coffin of hippy." Like many other bands, Furnier and Alice Cooper—which was the whole band's name at first—traveled to LA to "make it." However, their confrontational and theatrical style, with Furnier dressed as a futuristic witch, turned so many people off that they famously took only ten minutes to clear the Cheetah Club in Venice, CA, of all customers. Frank Zappa, the arch contrarian, loved the band and signed them to his label Straight. After putting out two albums, in 1971 they enjoyed a Top 30 hit single with "I'm Eighteen" and Top 40 album with *Love It to Death* in February that year.

By the end of 1971 Alice was signed to Warner's and the album *Killer*, featuring a photograph of Yvonne, Cooper's pet boa constrictor, on the cover was released. In June 1972 the band hit the big time with the release of the single "School's Out," which made the Top 10 charts in several countries around the world, including America. Here was a very different America to the one idealized in "A Horse with No Name"—one full of screaming, wild school kids hysterical about finishing school and being led in their celebrations by a cross-gendered witchy-woman wrapped in a snake.

Opposite: The cover of Alice Cooper's 1971 *Killer* album was a far cry from what the laid-back Eagles were doing in the early 1970s.

Below: The cover of T. Rex's 1972 *Slider* album, showing Marc Bolan in typical pose. This album was the band's most successful in the U.S.

alice cooper

killer

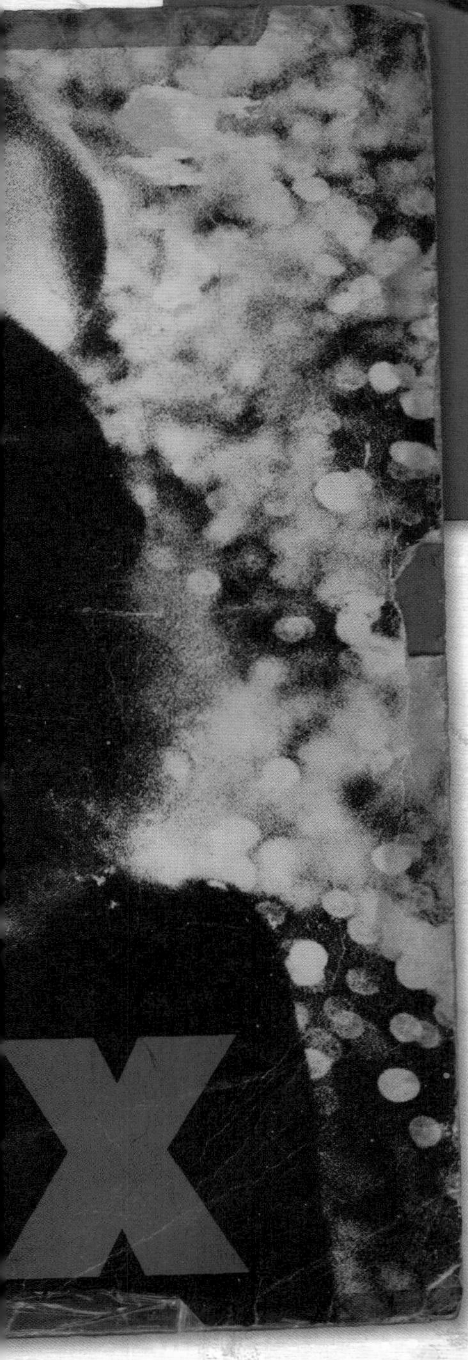

With fashion entering a unisex phase, perhaps it was no surprise that the coolest thing to emerge in music in 1972 came from the UK and was androgynous—and alien, apparently. David Bowie's Ziggy Stardust persona and his band The Spiders from Mars looked otherworldly, with their dyed hair cut into feminine styles, cakings of mascara and rouge, skin-tight leotards and high-heeled shoes. Bowie, a former Mod and failed pop star of the 1960s, had embraced the look of another British former Mod, Marc Bolan, but went one better by adding the alien concept to his identity. Where Bolan and T. Rex relied on three-chord boogie and songs with catchy, repetitive, and nonsense lyrics—and had earned a reputation in the UK as "the new Beatles" due to being followed everywhere by hordes of screaming girls—Bowie's first hit had been an acoustic song about the Moon landing in 1969. Unable to capitalize on it as a long-haired hippy, he radically remade himself in the image of alien Ziggy and became a star in the UK. Six previous single releases failed to chart before "Starman" made number 10, and the album it was taken from reached number 5. In 1972, as he was preparing to "kill off" Ziggy in a live performance in London, the album *Ziggy Stardust* crept to number 75 on the *Billboard* album chart. In September 1972, Bowie as Ziggy began his first U.S. tour in Cleveland.

"The Eagles proved to everyone watching that country music was a valid format for mainstream music fans."

DWIGHT YOAKAM

As a suitable end to such a diverse and bizarre year, a forty-year-old country singer whose last number 1 hit had been in 1961 made the top of the pop charts around the world with a pure country song entitled "It's Four in the Morning." Faron Young had made his name in 1954 with "Live Fast, Love Hard, Die Young," his first country chart number 1. Young's first crossover hit came in '61 with "Hello Walls" (a U.S. pop number 12). Despite "It's Four in the Morning" only making number 92 on the U.S. pop charts, by January 1973 it had sold over 750,000 copies in America—and had only been released in November 1972. The single also sold over 500,000 copies in the UK. A standard, medium-paced country song, the success of "It's Four in the Morning" gave heart to all music acts who believed in the power of country music to sell everywhere in the world, not just the Midwest. In 1973 former Sun Records pianist and recording artist Charlie Rich would score an international smash hit single with the similarly country-style song "Behind Closed Doors," and a few weeks later "The Most Beautiful Girl in the World" made number 1 in the U.S. pop and country charts. Records by Tammy Wynette and Marie Osmond were huge crossover hits not long after. The world seemed to be enjoying the sound of American country music. Record executives and various Eagles in LA took note.

Way Out West

Not many young groups offer a record company what they refer to as a concept album as only their second release. The Eagles proposed one with an Old West gunfighter and outlaw theme that would draw parallels between life as an outlaw and life as a musician. In retrospect, talk of *Desperado* being a concept album may have been stretching the definition. It's certainly no rock opera; more a collection of songs connected by a theme and an image. Henley and Frey were, at the time, sincere in their belief that the album's themes of outsiders and outlaws reflected their own position in the music business but only industry execs could really appreciate those connections. For the public and critics, however, it was more a collection of songs connected by mood, feel, theme, and time. The cowboy metaphor reflected in the artwork certainly gave the project the look of a concept album, and Geffen, who prided himself on being in touch with the artistic community, supported the venture when many executives would have quite reasonably passed on the idea. Bands like the Who, the Beatles,

"We didn't use any fake blood, but they sure looked plenty dead. J. D. had this book about the old west with real pictures of dead outlaws and we modelled the shoot on that. The band were so into it. They were like a bunch of kids playing at cowboys."

HENRY DILTZ ON THE DESPERADO SHOOT

Above: Few bands can have had as much fun as the Eagles did on the famous *Desperado* photo shoot.

and the Rolling Stones were all mainstream stars who could afford a risky venture. The Eagles were less in a position to push rock and roll's boundaries. But Geffen, as was his wont, supported the band's ideas, recognizing that his talents lay in selling not creating music.

So to capitalize on the promising and largely successful debut album Frey, Leadon, Meisner, and Henley decided to finally complete an idea for a music project that assorted members and friends of the band had been kicking around since 1970.

Opposite: J. D. Souther and Bernie
Leadon examine their accessories
on the *Desperado* shoot.

Below: The Eagles still found time for
side projects during this period, with
Bernie Leadon contributing guitar
to four tracks on Rita Coolidge's
1972 *The Lady's Not for Sale* album.

The story of the *Desperado* album goes back to a few years earlier when Troubadour buddy (and solo act in his own right) Ned Doheny gave Glenn Frey a book about outlaws of the Old West. Frey was struck by stories of the Dalton and Doolin bank robbing gang, which focused on that fine line between good and evil where lawmen and robbers were often indistinguishable in the anarchy of America's Wild West. Referring to the book, Frey noted that "it contained the story of Bill Dalton and Bill Doolin. Dalton had two brothers who were bank robbers and their whole gang except one was killed while they were trying to rob two banks at the same time. Bill Dalton was working in the California State legislature when he heard of his brothers' deaths. He quit his job, went to Kansas and teamed up with the only surviving member of his brothers' gang to carry on their work." Frey tossed the idea around with J. D. Souther and Jackson Browne and even took it so far as to book some studio time to work on song ideas.

"Doolin-Dalton" was written by Frey, Browne, and Souther—with Henley contributing at the finish. Frey and Henley had already worked together on the song "Desperado," which Henley had started writing back in Texas in the Shiloh days. It seemed clear that the band had the beginnings of an album.

Hold Your Horses

Geffen, however, held the eager Eagles back from following their debut release too quickly. After all, sales were good and the album was maintaining a healthy chart position. So, to fill in the time between live shows, the individual Eagles played on friends' projects and worked on songs and ideas for the next set of studio recordings. Bernie Leadon showed up on Rita Coolidge's *The Lady's Not for Sale* album and Glenn Frey contributed plenty of guitar to J. D. Souther's debut album.

The Eagles also got to play dress up for the album artwork, which saw the band dressed as western outlaws. Photographer Henry Diltz and art director Gary Burden took the band and a posse of buddies including Jackson Browne, J. D. Souther, and Brit producer Glyn Johns to Western Costumes, a Hollywood movie rental store, and outfitted the band in authentic Wild West attire. They then drove out to an old Paramount western movie set in Malibu Canyon armed with 1,500 rounds of blank ammunition and guns. The photo sessions provided

some remarkable images, especially on the back cover, where they are pictured, in full western garb, lying on the ground along with buddies Souther and Browne, towered over by producer Glyn Johns and assorted Eagle friends.

That was December 1972; the debut album was still doing nicely and Geffen was ready to arrange the recording sessions for *Desperado*. The band flew to London in January 1973, with no strikes or power outages hopefully, for the recording sessions. This time around the band were at Island studios with Glyn Johns, better equipped to deal with the culture shock of 1970s London and determined to focus on the business in hand. Henley and Frey had bonded since the first album and their perfectionist work habits started to cause minor issues with the rest of the band. "The only two people who tend to think alike in this group are Glenn and me," said Henley, "and we've always wanted every song to be the best it can be. We didn't want any filler. No stinkers. When somebody hears a bad song they're not gonna say 'so and so wrote a bad song,' they're gonna say 'that's a shitty song on an Eagles album.'"

"The Eagles took things to another level, mostly I think because Glenn and Don were talented and dedicated."

JACKSON BROWNE

Desperado was supposed to be a culmination of those glory years at the Troubadour when friends and community were as much a part of the Eagles' lives as limousines and security guards would later become. Songs were worked on in advance with buddies like Browne and J. D. Souther before the foursome sat down in London with Johns to record the ambitious album. The finished article would receive mixed critical acclaim at the time but become a classic in retrospect. *Desperado* more significantly established Henley and Frey as a credible songwriting partnership and gave Henley a stronger performing platform than on the debut album, where his input was more limited to the drums.

The Albums

Desperado

Producer: Glyn Johns

Recorded: Olympic Studios, London, January 1973

Label: Asylum Records

Released: April 1973

Chart position: U.S.A. Billboard pop albums #41

TRACKS

Side One

1. Doolin-Dalton
2. Twenty-One
3. Out of Control
4. Tequila Sunrise
5. Desperado

Side Two

1. Certain Kind of Fool
2. Doolin-Dalton (instrumental)
3. Outlaw Man
4. Saturday Night
5. Bitter Creek
6. Doolin-Dalton/
Desperado (reprise)

EAGLES
DESPERADO

Doolin-Dalton, Twenty-One, Out of Control, Tequila Sunrise, Desperado
Certain Kind of Fool, Outlaw Man, Saturday Night, Bitter Creek, Doolin-Dalton (reprise) Desperado (reprise)

Produced by Glyn Johns. Recorded at Island Studios, London. Engineer: Glyn Johns. Assistant: Howard Kilgour. Mastered at: The Mastering Lab, Hollywood
String Arrangements: Jim Ed Norman. Art Direction & Design: Gary Burden for R. Twerk. Photography & Lettering: Henry Diltz. Direction: The Geffen Roberts Co
Our Thanks to: Leslie Morris, John Hartmann, Rico & the Mudsharks and Charles Blocker. Front cover left to right: Don Henley, Glenn Frey, Randy Meisner & Bernie Leadon

K53008
(SD 5068)

ASYLUM RECORDS

℗ & © 1973 Elektra/Asylum Records. Distributed by WEA Records Ltd. ⓦ A Warner Communications Company. Sleeve printed and made in England by Gothic Print Finishers Ltd., London SE9 2EQ

Henley kicks off the album with a raspy, world-weary vocal on the haunting "Doolin-Dalton" ballad. Henley would also perform magnificently on the title track, a song that has since become an Eagles standard, though which oddly was never released as a single. It was Linda Ronstadt's version that ruled the airwaves in the early 1970s. Lyrically the song best expresses the idea of rock band and outlaw that Frey and Henley were pursuing in the concept behind the album. A young twenty-one-year-old kid, determined to make a name for himself in the Old West, buys a gun, practices til he's a master, and embarks

Above: The back cover of *Desperado*. The Eagles (plus Souther and Browne) have been captured and tied up by producer Glyn Johns (center) and assorted Eagles extras.

Below: Henry Diltz said of the *Desperado* shoot: "The gear they got really could have been worn by John Wayne because it came from the same rental place that supplied all the big movies. The band loved those clothes so much, they refused to return some of them, which must have cost David Geffen . . ."

upon a life of crime and excess. Expanding on the allusion, Frey explained, "When a kid sees a guitar in a shop window today he sees it in the same way the kid in the old west saw the gun. It's the mark of a new kind of man. A way he can make a fortune and a name for himself while thumbing his nose at the things society wants him to be."

Bernie Leadon brings his bluegrass background into play in the jaunty "Twenty-One," a song that doesn't quite fit the outlaw motif but which works in the overall "rock-star-as-outlaw" conceit as a joyous ode to the innocence of starting out as a musician. Musically it's fresh and frothy, more "Sweethearts of the Rodeo" by The Byrds than "Take It Easy," and is one of Leadon's Eagle highlights.

The tough, rock-oriented "Out of Control" from the budding new writing team of Henley and Frey is the nearest thing on the album to the dirty rock and roll sound that Frey always wanted and producer Glyn Johns avoided. Lyrically it neatly reflects the first flushes of success-induced hedonism that the Eagles had recently experienced, with its tales of gambling (the Eagles were habitual poker players), boozing, and carousing. The song segues into one of the first two

songs that Henley and Frey wrote together, "Tequila Sunrise"—about a young guy who's dealt with so much rejection, disappointment, and his girl "out runnin' 'round" on him that he's got to get into a heavy drinking session even to be able to talk to a girl. Showing an ability as writers to tap into the consciousness of the day with their songs, Frey and Henley throw in the "Tequila Sunrise" reference. A Tequila Sunrise drink, containing tequila, orange juice, and grenadine, was one of the drinks of choice of the rock community in Hollywood in the '70s, probably not readily available to outlaws in the Old West who were not best known for their consumption of orange juice.

"Desperado," a brooding and slow ballad, is sweetened by subtle string arrangements courtesy of Jim Ed Norman (see opposite), a colleague of Henley's from the Shiloh days. It is significant mostly in the way it highlights Don Henley's awakening vocal talent within the Eagles. Never again would he be anonymous at the back, playing drums and contributing a few telling harmonies. Henley had the voice of a star.

Henley and Frey asked Randy Meisner to come up with a song that would fit the outlaw theme, and "Certain Kind of Fool" is performed in typically accomplished fashion by Meisner, but it's "Bitter Creek," another Leadon tune, that gives the album a serious edge. The sound is early '70s country rock and the themes are pure desert mysticism, Carlos Castaneda, peyote, and mescal—elements that played an intrinsic role in early Eagles music.

Shot Down

Everyone—from band members to Glyn Johns to Geffen—expected the album to continue where the debut had left off. Yet sales and reactions to *Desperado* were disappointing. It peaked at number 41 on the *Billboard* album chart and its strongest single, "Tequila Sunrise," pushed its way to only number 64 on the singles chart.

However, despite failing commercially and critically in 1973, *Desperado* would come to be regarded as a great 1970s album and among the band's strongest work. In 1973, *Desperado* was significant in less obvious ways. The album served as a catalyst for the events that would change the band's direction and its relationship with management and record company. Henley started talking about the creative tensions within

Above: Legendary photographer Henry Diltz, who masterminded the *Desperado* shoot. Of the Eagles he said, "They were restless young men and rock and roll kept them out of trouble."

Jim Ed Norman

A key figure in the west coast music scene of the late 1960s and early 1970s, Jim Ed Norman started out playing keyboards for Don Henley's Shiloh. He then worked as an arranger and keyboard player on numerous Eagles albums before becoming one of the most respected producers in Nashville. Jim Ed worked with numerous music heavyweights including New Riders of the Purple Sage, Anne Murray, Kenny Rogers, Linda Ronstadt, Faith Hill, Dwight Yoakam, Randy Travis, and Hank Williams, Jr. Before retiring to Hawaii in 2004, Jim Ed Norman was president of Warner's Nashville.

"I met Don at college in Texas and we became friends. We shared the same musical interests and the two of us would pack up and head off on trips. I remember traveling to Fort Worth to see The Dillards, who we loved. Don had been in a band for years in Texas, which became Shiloh, and their keyboard player was killed in a motorcycle accident. So they needed a keyboard player and I went to the little town in Texas where Don was from and had an audition which was probably more of a social audition than it was a musical audition.

"I hadn't listened to the Shiloh album in at least twenty years but I was recently transferring it to my iPod and it's an interesting record. Generally it is a mish-mash of different kinds of material and there's a lack of consistency which would make it difficult on a marketing level. But I was also reminded about the songwriting talent of Don. I was an instrumentalist; I grew up with classical music, so it took me a while to understand the role of the lyrics in music. Don was the one who understood. He got the importance of lyrics. We never really talked about it but it was obvious that Don, with his English major background, understood the value of the lyric.

"I started working with the Eagles on *Desperado* in London with Glyn Johns. I did all those arrangements. I did all the orchestral arranging that happened through *Hotel California* and I also played piano on a lot of sessions, whenever I was asked to come in and play. 'Lyin' Eyes' I remember, and 'Outlaw Man' on the *Desperado* record. A lot of people over the years would say to me 'So, you were in the Eagles right?' I say no, but I was honored to be involved. I liked working with them because Don and Glenn were great guys.

The energy came from both of them. It would have never worked if it wasn't both of them; just look at their solo work—it's not the same. But together they had something magical. Don was a hard worker. I remember working on *Desperado* and Don would be outside the studio with a legal pad in his hand at the eleventh hour still writing. He would not give up til it was right—an incredible work ethic. And I loved him for that. And I also loved that Glenn had this R&B thing and he was a little more fun-loving. It was a good match.

"I talk to kids about music these days and now they have all the technical equipment and computers that we didn't have, but I always tell them that without a good song you don't have anything. I've wanted to use Eagles songs on projects but it's hard when the original is just so good. That's what made the Eagles so great. They had some of the best songs ever written."

the band, and the album would be the last complete recording to be produced by country-music enthusiast and Bernie Leadon–champion Glyn Johns. Don Henley had arrived as a singer, and Frey and Henley were clearly the chief song architects. This meant that Frey's constant battle to move into a rock sound was closer to becoming a reality. Leadon and Meisner were becoming isolated from the decision-making and were feeling less valued as members of what had started out as a very democratic band. Initially they had shared all publishing royalty money, but after *Desperado* it was decided to split the publishing by songwriter—clearly a move that would benefit Henley and Frey, who were implicitly in charge of song selection from this point onwards.

Tensions of another kind had surfaced over at Asylum Records and with the Geffen-Roberts management. At the end of 1972 Steve Ross, head honcho at record company giant Warner, offered David Geffen $7 million for Asylum Records, with the added bonus that he could stay on as president and have a prestigious place on the board. Moreover, the new move saw Elektra merged with Asylum. Warner Elektra Asylum, or WEA, would operate under Warner Communications, with Geffen in the driving seat. More importantly for the Eagles, Geffen felt it appropriate to relinquish all involvement in his management company for fear of being accused of conflict of interest. Elliot Roberts renamed the company Lookout Management and included on his roster Jackson Browne, Poco, the Eagles, Joni Mitchell, and Crosby, Stills, Nash and Young, among others.

There were no immediate effects on the individual Eagles from the Asylum sale, but it may have helped them realize that they were no more special to Geffen than any of his other acts, and that Geffen was set on his own path to success. When the *Desperado* album stumbled at the starting gate, Frey and Henley, both of whom had begun taking a greater interest in the business side of things, wondered if their second album had received less marketing and promotion attention than their debut because of the diversions of the record company sale and merger. That Geffen reportedly did not tell the band of his decision to sell did not sit well with the Eagles. However, Lookout appointed a young Geffen wannabe named Irving Azoff to take care of the Eagles' affairs and the band got to know him well. It was the beginning of a relationship that would have tremendous repercussions for them all.

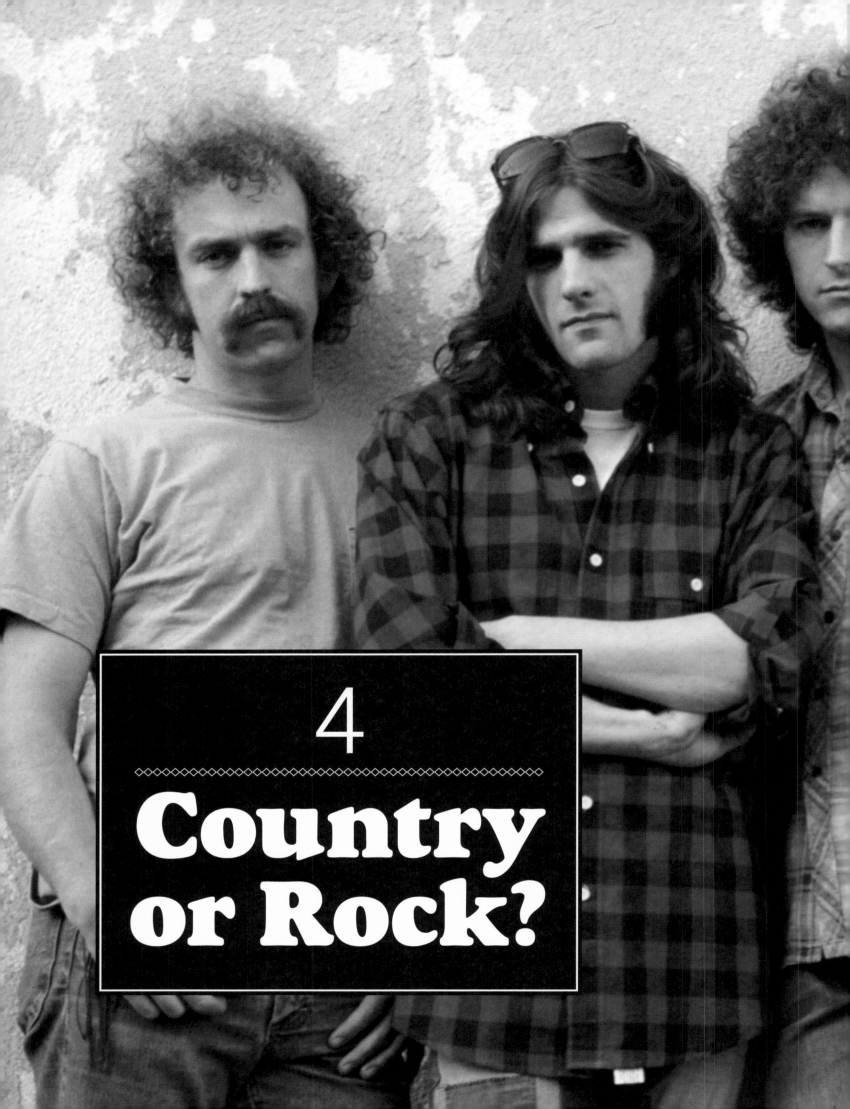

4

Country
or Rock?

THE RELATIVELY POOR critical reception of *Desperado* brought home to Henley and Frey the inherent danger of playing both country music and rock and roll within a rock band format— they could too easily fall between the two worlds of country music and rock music. Rather than attracting fans and pleasing critics from both camps, the Eagles alienated many from both. Nashville would embrace the Eagles in the 1990s, but back in 1972, Music City still hadn't got over the longhaired Byrds appearing on the *Grand Ole Opry*.

Mainstream America really wasn't ready for a fusion of country and rock and roll, no matter how passionate, as in Gram Parsons' case, or how skillfully executed, as with the Eagles. There was a market for country rock but not enough to launch a band to superstardom. Bernie Leadon was not a purist in hardcore bluegrass terms, but his musical affinity was with country and folk music, not pop or rock. Henley and Frey, however, shared a deep love of R&B and rock music and sensed, correctly, that to find mass appeal they needed to approach their music with a tougher, louder rock sound.

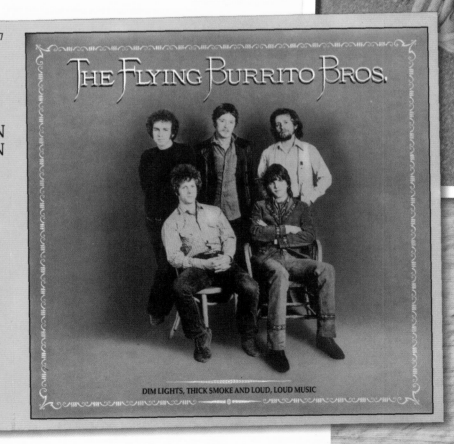

ED CD 197

THE TRAIN SONG*
CLOSE UP THE HONKY TONKS**
SING ME BACK HOME**
TONIGHT THE BOTTLE LET ME DOWN
YOUR ANGEL STEPS OUT OF HEAVEN
CRAZY ARMS
TOGETHER AGAIN
HONKY TONK WOMEN
GREEN, GREEN, GRASS OF HOME
DIM LIGHTS
BONY MORONIE**
TO LOVE SOMEBODY**
BREAK MY MIND**

PRODUCED BY JIM DICKSON FOR TICKNER/DICKSON PRODUCTIONS EXCEPT * PRODUCED BY LARRY WILLIAMS, AND ** PRODUCED BY THE BURRITO BROTHERS.

COVER PHOTO BY JIM McCRARY
ALBUM DESIGN BY PHIL SMEE AT WALDO'S

MANUFACTURED UNDER LICENSE FROM A&M RECORDS LTD.
℗ 1976 A&M RECORDS INC., EXCEPT *℗ 1969 A&M RECORDS INC.,
AND **℗ 1974 A&M RECORDS INC.

A DIVISION OF DEMON RECORDS LTD.,
BRENTFORD, MIDDLESEX.

THE FLYING BURRITO BROS.

DIM LIGHTS, THICK SMOKE AND LOUD, LOUD MUSIC

Above: The Eagles ready for take-off in early 1973.

Desperado proved to be country rock's last hurrah. The country rock movement in many ways died with the poor reception of that album. Gram Parsons, the catalyst for so much pioneering country and rock collaborations, had already removed himself from the picture. Dismayed by his lack of commercial success and the relatively poor reception of his first album, he fell into a slump and a drug-fueled depression from which he'd never recover. Even on their more country outings, Parsons let it be known that he felt that the Eagles had sold

Gram Parsons *and the* Fallen Angels -
featuring Emmylou Harris

Opposite: This Gram Parsons album was recorded as a live radio broadcast in March 1973, just six months before the singer was found dead. It was not released, however, until 1982.

out on the ideals of country rock. Then again, it was easy for Parsons to be a purist; money was not an issue. "He came from a very wealthy southern family and had a sizeable trust fund," explains fiddle player and one time Burrito Brother, Byron Berline. "The thing about Gram was that he died young, so he has this mystique and people remember his influence differently. He wasn't regarded as the creator of country rock back then; he was too difficult to work with for us to really see beyond that. Definitely his own worst enemy."

> "It was difficult for artists like Gram Parsons and the Eagles and the Byrds back then because they would not be wanted by either group. The country folk thought they were too rock and the rock fans thought it was way too country."

EMMYLOU HARRIS

Grievous Angels

After leaving the Flying Burrito Brothers Gram Parsons spent a short time with Keith Richards in his château in France, but Parsons was banished from the Richards' château by Anita Pallenberg for being in a constantly incapacitated state through drug use and quarreling endlessly with his girlfriend, Gretchen Burrell. Sent to London, he had taken an apartment for a while in 1972 and undergone treatment for heroin addiction. It apparently worked, and he returned to America to form a partnership with Alabama-born singer-songwriter Emmylou Harris. Their professional relationship revived Parsons' music career, and their work together on two fabulous albums, *GP* and *Grievous Angel* (released posthumously), show how much he had moved musically toward a purer country music sound and away from country rock. After a successful tour of America with a band he named The Fallen Angels, and with enough recordings completed for two albums,

Parsons spent the summer of 1973 living in Topanga Canyon until a fire left him homeless (and with only a guitar rescued from the flames). He subsequently moved in with his road manager, Phil Kaufman, and in September traveled to the Joshua Tree National Park where on the 19th of September he died from a lethal combination of drugs and alcohol. While Parsons' body was waiting to be flown back to Florida for burial, Kaufman and an accomplice stole the coffin with his body in it, drove to the Joshua Tree Park and attempted to cremate the remains of the singer, which, according to Kaufman, was what Parsons had requested.

There was nothing so dramatic to mark the end of The Byrds; their death as a viable country rock outfit was slow and pitiful. The 1971 album *Byrdmaniax* was a musical disaster thanks to overblown string arrangements contributed by Terry Melcher, their longtime producer who never really recovered mentally from his brush with near-death at the hands of Charles Manson's "family." Various Byrds lineups continued to tour in the early 1970s, but with little success, and in 1972 an original Byrd's reunion was discussed but failed to come to any kind of fruition.

Former Monkee Michael Nesmith, who had done so much for country rock with his First National Band albums, had started a country label to showcase Los Angeles' country and country rock talent. However, when David Geffen took over Elektra, Nesmith's Countryside imprint was closed. Poco moved slowly from country rock to a mellow California soft rock that would maintain them through the 1970s, while two impressive country rock–fueled "supergroups," Stephen Stills' Manassas and the Souther Hillman Furay Band, started brightly but faded quickly, and both failed to set the charts or concert halls alight. Linda Ronstadt crept towards a pop and rock audience and while Emmylou Harris continued the work of Gram Parsons after his death, hers was a more Nashville-dominated country rock than anything brewed in California.

It wasn't that the Eagles necessarily perceived themselves as a country rock band—most musicians resist labels of any kind and leave it to their record companies and the media to categorize and judge—rather, it was clear to Henley and Frey that the country music-influenced

Above: The Souther Hillman Furay band. Left to right: Chris Hillman, J. D. Souther, and Richie Furay.

sound they had created, and that Glyn Johns still envisioned for them, was just not going to work. At least, it was not going to work on the level they both desired. It was not the right sound for the time, and it wasn't the right sound for Henley and Frey, both of whom now had more influence over the band than Bernie Leadon, who was the group's real purist when it came to country music.

Gram Parsons
The Fallen Angel

Gram Parsons' lamentably short life was full of tragedy, mistakes, regrets, and broken relationships. Born Cecil Ingram Connor to a wealthy Florida family in 1946, his father "Coon Dog" Connor committed suicide on Christmas Day 1959. His mother remarried a local businessman named Robert Parsons and Gram took his stepfather's name. His mother died of causes arising from her chronic alcoholism on the day that Gram graduated from high school. All of these could either provoke psychological depression in a sensitive young man or set him on the path to a career as a country singer perhaps. Parsons was a gifted musician and began playing in a local band at twelve years of age. He played with several local acts in Florida before enrolling at Harvard to study Theology—which ended when he joined the International Submarine Band in 1965. Their folksy country music did well in certain circles and resulted in a meeting between Parsons and Roger McGuinn, then of The Byrds. Impressed with Parsons' passion for the music, the head Byrd offered him an invitation to join the band. He brought a strong country influence to bear on The Byrds, notably on what is now considered to be a classic album, 1968's *Sweethearts of the Rodeo*. But the relationship was short lived. Byrds fans did not take to the country music experiment while country fans were definitely not yet ready for longhaired hippy music on their stages or radio stations, and so Parsons left for pastures new.

DISCOGRAPHY

1968 ★ Safe at Home, with The International Submarine Band; LHI Records. Did not chart.

1968 ★ Sweethearts of the Rodeo, with The Byrds; Columbia Records. Reached #77 on Billboard hot 200 LP chart, September 1968.

1969 ★ The Gilded Palace of Sin, with The Flying Burrito Brothers; A&M Records. Reached #164 on Billboard hot 200 LP chart, March 1969.

1970 ★ Burrito Deluxe, with The Flying Burrito Brothers; A&M Records. Did not chart.

1973 ★ GP, Gram Parsons; Reprise Records. Did not chart.

1974 ★ Grievous Angel, Gram Parsons; Reprise Records. Reached #195 on Billboard hot 200 LP chart, January 1974.

1976 ★ Sleepless Nights, Gram Parsons and The Flying Burrito Brothers; A&M Records. Reached #185 on Billboard hot 200 LP chart, April 1976.

1979 ★ Gram Parsons' The Early Years, with The Shilohs; Sierra Records. Did not chart.

1982 ★ Live 1973, Gram Parsons and the Fallen Angels; Sierra Records. Did not chart.

2000 ★ Another Side of This Life: The Lost Recordings, Gram Parsons; Sundazed Records. Did not chart.

2006 ★ The Complete Reprise Recordings, Gram Parsons; Reprise Records. Did not chart.

2007 ★ Gram Parsons Archives Vol. 1: Live At the Avalon Ballroom 1969, Gram Parsons and The Flying Burrito Brothers; Amoeba. Reached #45 on the Billboard country LP chart, November 2007.

Enter Irving

With *Desperado* failing to sell, despite a huge concerted band effort to produce a legitimate country rock album, it seemed the Eagles were going to have to change something. Irving Azoff had taken to the road with the Eagles as they toured in support of *Desperado* and it proved a paradoxically good time for an ambitious manager with designs on launching his own management company. He was able to witness firsthand the psychology of a band in distress and was there to help create a plan that would solve both their problems and establish himself in the music business.

Azoff had started booking bands in college and hooked up with a couple of young acts, Dan Fogelberg and Joe Walsh, before becoming part of Eliot Roberts' Lookout Management. Not that he was overconfident about joining Lookout, as he remarked in an interview in 1978: "I was a nervous wreck," he told Cameron Crowe. That didn't last for long, though.

Henley and Frey were not happy with the direction in which they were being taken by their management and record company, and sensed that the young, overtly ambitious and aggressive Azoff could be a great help in changing that for them.

As Glenn Frey recalls, "The first night we met Irving, Henley and I got him in a room. There was something about it. We started telling him about our problems with the band, our producer, how we wanted our records not to be so clean and glassy and how were getting the royal fuckin' screw job. . . . We determined that night that Irving would manage us."

As it transpired, Azoff would not take over management of the Eagles for some time, but he slowly built a solid working relationship with them, especially with Henley and Frey. He always ensured that they felt looked after and important, which wasn't the case with everyone at Lookout or Asylum. Talking of their period under Geffen and Roberts' management, Henley later declared that they were "always the young guys down there. Nobody paid much attention to us. We found out our management company had signed Poco and America by reading *Melody Maker*."

PENTHOU
Approx. 1200 sq.ft.
unobstructed hill view.
inside partition to suit.
Available May. 1970
call 527-7728-4

Azoff's management tactics were simple. He created a siege mentality for his artists, completely protecting them from the outside world. He'd get the best deals possible, buffer them from the media, and defend his artists to the death. Intuitively he understood what artists wanted and needed in a manager. Money was important, musical fulfillment too, but what really mattered was being made to feel significant and important. With an album failing, concerts not selling, and Geffen apparently moving on to bigger and better things, the Eagles needed a skilled man manager like Azoff to bring them out of their slump. After all, they had a new record to make.

Over the Border

Despite their frustrations with Glyn Johns and still disappointed about *Desperado*, the group pulled together again early in 1973 to record their next album, *On the Border*. They began the process in London again and had to deal with more overbearing and country-heavy production from Johns, at least that's how Henley and Frey saw it. For six weeks they tried things out, fought, argued, despaired, and, at times, played wonderful music. But the creative tensions that Henley had talked about as being good for inspiration had grown like cancers and something was about to give. They were given a break from the studio to support Neil Young for a series of UK shows on his *Tonight's the Night* tour, but, despite this, change was inevitable. Either the Eagles would fire a member, break up completely, or change producers. Finally, Frey and Henley decided to remove Johns from the equation and they returned to California for a new start. They had finished only two songs: "You Never Cry Like a Lover" and "Best of My Love."

Irving was firmly in their camp and was representing the young Joe Walsh who had just released the fiery *The Smoker You Drink, the Player You Get* album. For their new producer, the Eagles naturally gravitated towards the man who had produced Walsh, Bill Szymczyk.

"They had already had a couple of hits from that first record—'Take It Easy' and 'Peaceful Easy Feeling,' but the second record didn't sell as well as the first. They started the third record with Glyn in London and had completed most of it when they decided to work with me," recalled Szymczyk. "They were willing to start all over. I agreed, but on one condition: that I check with Glyn and that he was OK with it. He

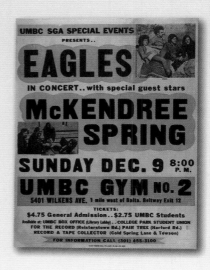

Above: Poster for an Eagles gig at UMBC (University of Maryland, Baltimore County) from December 1973, here supported by McKendree Spring who would achieve critical acclaim but, in contrast to the headliners, little commercial success.

was one of the producers I had looked up to for a long time. I called him in London and I guess the feeling was mutual, because he said 'Better you than me, mate!'"

There were many reasons why the Eagles-Johns collaboration had failed. Some personal, others musical. Henley had never been happy with the way Johns had produced his drum sound. "Don Henley asked me how many microphones I used on drums," Szymczyk said of their first sessions. "I said I used about eight or so. He was stunned; Glyn used two or three at the most. Don wanted to be a rock drummer, and he heard the sounds they were getting on rock records. That's what he wanted and he was convinced that was how you got those sounds."

Freed from Johns' direction, the band could form a different relationship with their new producer. This time around they were going to have their say and get things right. As Henley put it, "Glenn and I assumed this bulldozer attitude of 'We ain't gonna put up with any weaknesses. Every song's gonna be great.' There was a lot of fighting. Don Felder who we just added to the band in the middle of the album was so scared he'd joined a band that was breaking up."

Another Don

Supremely skilled guitarist Don Felder was well known on the rock and roll circuit and had been close friends with Bernie Leadon for years. He had recently made quite a name for himself touring with David Crosby and Graham Nash. As he tells the story, Felder recalled that he'd known the Eagles for a while when they asked him to join them.

"When I was living in New York, I'd go jam with them when they came through town. I'd built a relationship with them in the days when they were still kind of a small band playing 2,000 to 2,500 seat halls. It wasn't like sitting in with the Rolling Stones. So when they were doing *On the Border*, Glenn recalled that I played a little slide and they asked me to come play on 'Good Day in Hell.' The next day they called and asked me to join the band. And I said, 'Well, I don't know. . . . 'Cause every time I talked to Bernie, it sounded like the band had just broken up. And I didn't want to join a band that was going to break up every day. I mean I was very excited about their offer. But it felt like I was joining a band that was crumbling apart."

So Felder was well aware of the infighting within the Eagles, and he'd been close to Bernie Leadon for long enough to understand the group personality dynamics. Plus, he was currently earning good money in David Crosby and Graham Nash's touring band. He decided to talk to Nash about the situation—and Nash advised him to join the Eagles.

Below: With the arrival of Don Felder, the Eagles became a five-piece for the first time. It wouldn't be the last . . .

With a new guitarist Henley and Frey finally had the musical muscle to move away from the gentle acoustic sound so beloved by Johns. And with a new, more malleable producer, they could push more toward rock than country. As Frey saw it, "The biggest problem that we had was that we couldn't do double guitar solos and still have a rhythm instrument as a foursome. We thought five pieces would work to some advantage."

Don Felder had attended the same high school as Bernie Leadon in Gainesville, Florida, and joined his first band, the Continentals, when he was fifteen years old, along with a teenage Stephen Stills. When

Stills left, Felder recruited his high school buddy Leadon for the group. As a sideline he gave guitar lessons at a local music shop, where eager pupils included a very young Tom Petty. Eventually the Continentals broke up and Felder headed to New York to play with a jazz fusion band, Flow. He didn't take to life in New York, however, and felt that an unsatisfactory life in bar bands was looming. Asking around, Felder found himself a job in a recording studio in Boston. It would change his career. By day he worked on engineering, writing charts, producing vocals, and playing guitar on sessions. At night he had a residency at the Harvard Square Holiday Inn, playing standards in the restaurant.

"Glenn called me up and said 'I think we better get this guy in the band,' and I said 'I think you're right.'"

DON HENLEY

Felder kept in touch with Leadon while the Eagles started their journey and he met the rest of the band through Leadon while they were on their first U.S. tour. A couple of years later he and his wife packed up their Volvo and drove to LA, initially staying on the floor of Leadon's house in Topanga Canyon. So when Felder was finally invited into the Eagles circle for real he was well aware of their story. While Felder may have thought he was joining a band on the verge of breaking up, the Eagles themselves, despite some internal conflicts, were much happier as a recording unit than they had been before. Recording in LA at the famed Record Plant appealed more to their California sensibilities, and Bill Szymczyk was younger and more on their cultural and social wavelength; he'd even join them for a drink after recording sessions.

The Record Plant was a huge modern recording studio complete with lounges, recreation areas designed for musicians to take their time, relax, and partake of their favored narcotics—and record when the fancy took them. It was a far cry from the more austere London experience and the Eagles at least were able to argue and fight in luxury surroundings.

The Albums

On The Border

Producers: Glyn Johns and Bill Szymczyk

Recorded: Olympic Studios, London, January 1974
and Record Plant, Los Angeles, February 1974

Label: Asylum Records

Released: March 1974

Chart position: U.S.A. Billboard pop albums #17

TRACKS

Side One	Side Two
1. Already Gone	1. James Dean
2. You Never Cry Like a Lover	2. Ol' 55
3. Midnight Flyer	3. Is It True?
4. My Man	4. Good Day in Hell
5. On the Border	5. Best of My Love

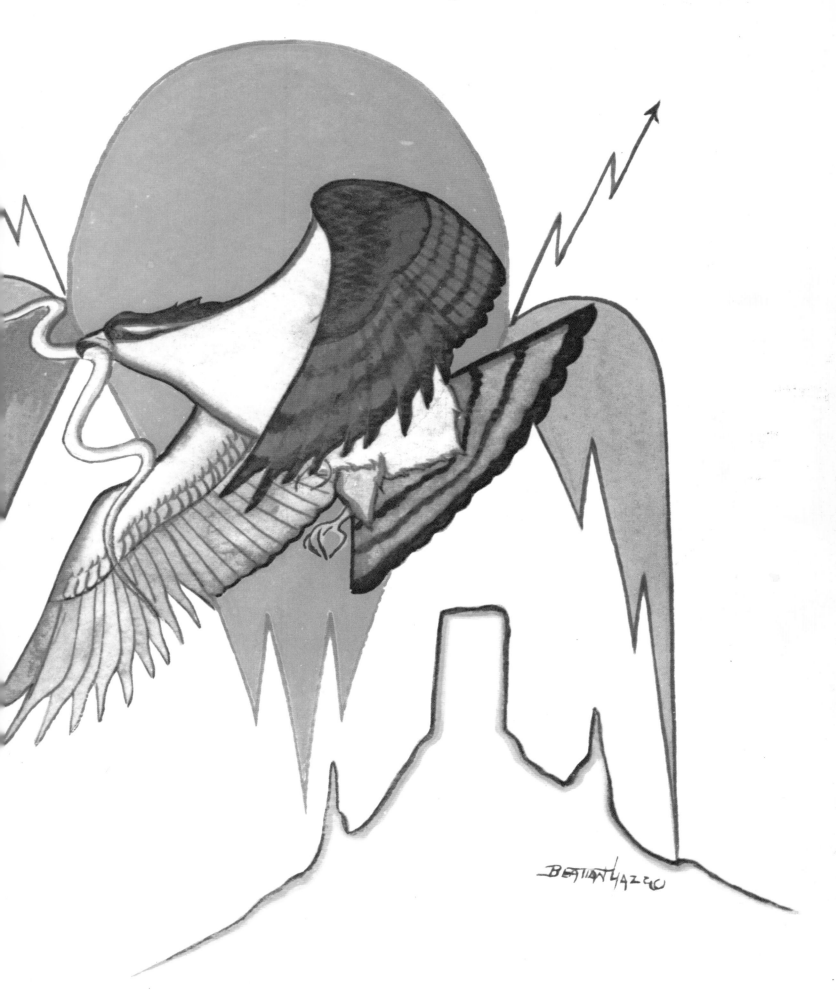

EAGLES ON THE BORDER

...LES ARE: GLENN FREY: VOCALS, GUITARS, PIANO – DON HENLEY: VOCALS, DRUMS – BERNIE LEADO...
...BANJO, STEEL GUITAR – RANDY MEISNER: VOCALS, BASS – LATE ARRIVAL: DON FELDER: ELECT...

SIDE ONE —

...READY GONE : LEAD VOCALS; GLENN, SOLO GUITARS; GLENN & DON FELDER,
WRITTEN BY; JACK TEMPCHIN & ROBB STRANDLIN

NEVER CRY LIKE A LOVER : LEAD VOCALS; DON HENLEY,
WRITTEN BY; DON HENLEY & JOHN DAVID SOUT...

MIDNIGHT FLYER : LEAD VOCALS; RANDY, SLIDE; GLENN,
WRITTEN BY; PAUL CRAFT

...Y MAN : LEAD VOCAL; BERNIE, PEDAL STEEL GUITAR; BERNIE, WRITTEN BY: BER...

ON THE BORDER : LEAD VOCAL; DON HENLEY, T.N.T.S; COACH, CLAPS: THE CLA...
WRITTEN BY; DON HENLEY, BERNIE LEADON, GLENN F...

SIDE TWO —

JAMES DEAN : LEAD VOCAL; GLENN, SOLO GUITARS; BERNIE,
WRITTEN BY; JACKSON BROWNE, GLENN FREY, DON HENLEY,...

OL '55 : LEAD VOCALS; GLENN & DON HENLEY, PEDAL STEEL GUITAR; A...
WRITTEN BY; TOM WAITS

IS IT TRUE : LEAD VOCALS; RANDY, SLIDE GUITAR; GLENN
WRITTEN BY; RANDY MEISNER

...OOD DAY IN HELL : LEAD VOCALS; GLENN & DON HENLEY, SLIDE; DON F...
WRITTEN BY; GLENN FREY & DON HENLEY

THE BEST OF MY LOVE : LEAD VOCAL; DON HENLEY, PEDAL ST...
BERNIE, THANKS TO GUIDO FOR T...
WRITTEN BY; DON HENLEY, JOHN DAVID SOU...

PRODUCED & ENGINEERED BY BILL SZYMCZYK FOR PANDORA PRODUCTIONS LTD. RECORDED AT THE RECORD PLANT, LOS ANGELE...
...STED BY ALLAN BLAZEK & GARY LADINSKY. "THE BEST OF MY LOVE" PRODUCED & ENGI...
..."...ER CRY LIKE A LOVER" & ... RECORDED AT OLYMPIC STUDIOS, LOND... ...GARY BURDEN FO...

Don Felder introduced himself to Eagle fans on the opening cut, the feisty and tough "Already Gone." This was Bob Seger-style rock and roll, a sound Frey had been pushing for since the early days and a million miles from "Take It Easy." Not that the band wanted to leave their musical roots and country and folk influences behind completely; it was more that they wanted some extra sonic weapons, especially when playing concerts in stadiums and arenas where they had at times felt lightweight ahead of a loud rocking headliner.

"Good Day in Hell," the track Felder was initially recruited for, mostly for his slide guitar expertise, is similarly explosive. The song, written as a tribute to Gram Parsons by Henley and Frey, is as good as anything they had written up to that point. Ironically, the album's other stand-out song is Bernie Leadon's "My Man," another tribute to Parsons, although it had started as a song about Duane Allman, the Allman Brother guitarist who died in 1971 in a motorcycle accident.

> ## "'My Man' was written by Bernie about Duane Allman because he and Duane used to be friends and every time Duane would see him he'd say, 'Hey, My Man.'"
>
> DON HENLEY

"James Dean" is an outtake from the *Desperado* sessions, and the band's version of "Ol' 55" from another young writer on the LA scene, Tom Waits, is a group harmony complete with inspired pedal steel work from Henley's old Shiloh buddy Al Perkins. Don Henley had promised much with his vocals on *Desperado* and, after his astounding vocal on *On the Border*'s title track, would never again be relegated to singer number two. The voice alone would have made anyone a star, but add in the emotion and the songwriting talent, and it was a sign that Henley had the potential to overshadow Glenn Frey as the unofficial face of the group.

Al Perkins

Perkins was the pedal steel genius from Texas who played with Don Henley's early band, Shiloh. He was a quick learner when it came to musical instruments. "I loved the steel guitar and when I was still a kid, you know, maybe eleven, I was already playing pedal steel and steel for numerous local bands. And then I'd go around the state doing demonstrations for steel guitar manufacturers. I grew up listening to country music—Buck Owens, George Jones, traditional country. Most of us in Texas liked rock and roll and country music; that's where Don Henley was from and he had the same influences. And I played a lot of traditional country music. Shiloh might have made it at that point if we had been with a bigger record company. Kenny Rogers wasn't a huge star then. He'd been on the charts with First Edition by then but it was before he went out on his own.

"The Troubadour was this cool music club in Los Angeles that everybody would gravitate toward. Being married at the time, I didn't hang out as much at the Troubadour as the single guys. The actor, Cesar Romero, once asked me what the instrument was that I was playing. He was referring to the Fender 1000 pedal steel and I don't believe he'd ever seen one before.

"I was a Christian and I kind of kept myself to myself. I'd take a tennis racket on the road and try and find a game. Keep healthy. There were some things which I didn't like about the business and sometimes I'd say something but mostly I just did my job and avoided all the excesses. A lot of people from back then have had bad health problems, and died even, so I'm always grateful to God for leading me in a good direction.

"That California country rock period was a pretty cool time. I got to play with some great musicians and artists—I was with Stephen Stills and Manassas, the Burritos, and I even got to play for Don Henley again with the Eagles. I did an overdub for the *On the Border* sessions. They kept both tracks of steel in the final mixes of 'Ol' 55.' Unusual, but it worked effectively. I think country rock could have existed without pedal steel, though. Rick Nelson's early country records with James Burton would be a good example of early country rock without the steel. It wasn't until later that Rick added Tom Brumley on steel with the Stone Canyon Band. And of course Don Felder would play steel parts with the Eagles later on. The Eagles took country rock to a different level mostly I think because of the songs. There were lots of great artists doing country rock, you know. But they had the songs. Gram Parsons wasn't as big a deal back then as he became later. As with so many public figures, they become more popular in death, especially if they die young amidst the climb toward fame and success."

Almost Famous

The first two singles from *On the Border*, "James Dean" and then "Already Gone," did little better than anything from *Desperado*. Ironically it was the Glyn Johns–produced "Best of My Love," the final single from the album, that gave them their first number 1. Frey and Henley may have had their way about creating a rockier sound and in the long run that change did result in world superstardom, but there was no small irony in the realization that it was a heavily country-

Above: The Eagles performing in 1974 against a faux Old-West backdrop.

tinged song from the London sessions that would provide the band with their breakthrough to the next level.

Those four months between the album's release in April 1974 and their first number 1 in November were spent touring the United States. The Eagles world that Felder entered in 1974 was as dramatic as any Hollywood movie. The sex, drugs, and rock and roll of the *On the Border* tour would surface later as inspiration for the movie *Almost*

Famous, in which a naïve teenage music journalist on assignment from *Rolling Stone* magazine goes on the road with fictional rock band Stillwater. The writer and director of the movie, Cameron Crowe, had started his writing life as a teenage *Rolling Stone* reporter on the road with the Eagles during that very tour. The tour was a frantic and often chaotic blur of hotel rooms, concert halls, limousines, and airplanes.

Determined that the third Eagles' LP shouldn't suffer the same fate as their second, Irving Azoff wasted no time in getting the band noticed while they were touring. If a radio station was playing the Eagles heavily, they'd get a visit from the members of the band. The Eagles did press and promotional visits whenever they could. Azoff had the band working all day every day if he felt it was necessary.

What with the traveling, performing, and PR duties, the Eagles needed some playtime to balance all that hard work. Thanks to Henley and

Above: A scene from the Cameron Crowe movie *Almost Famous*, loosely based on the director's experiences as a music reporter on the road with the Eagles, among other bands.

Frey's sensitive and sometimes vulnerable lyrics, the Eagles attracted more female fans than most of their contemporary rock bands. They were approached by hundreds of women in every town they played, some of whom gratefully received backstage passes and with them the chance of a sexual liaison with their favorite rock stars. On the tour the Eagles had a policy of performing just two encores, both consisting of two songs at the end of every show. However, under direction, roadies and crew would distribute buttons bearing the sign 3E, which was shorthand for "third encore." After the show the forty or so 3E pass holders, along with the band, management, radio promoters, and anyone else the organization wanted to impress, would meet and greet backstage for an adult party, fueled with champagne and cocaine.

There was nothing unusual about the Eagles' drug use in the early 1970s. It was considered recreational and normal practice in California, if not across America. The charming hippy habits of sharing weed and indulging in the occasional LSD tab had been slowly replaced by greater cocaine usage among the rock music fraternity. With the Eagles' hectic work schedule, the drugs on offer were often as much practical as they were pleasurable. Cocaine kept them moving and alert, marijuana and Budweiser kept them chilled and mellow. But having seen what heroin had done to their friend Gram Parsons, none of the Eagles allowed drugs to become anything more than a tool, a means to an end. For Henley and Frey, the pursuit of women easily surpassed any need for narcotics. However, nothing matched the search for musical perfection, especially for the increasingly persnickety Don Henley.

Miami Vices

All the hard work that went into promoting *On the Border* did its job. The album went gold quickly, eventually yielded a number 1 single in "Best of My Love," and launched the band to a new audience. A performance on nationally syndicated TV's *Don Kirshner's Rock Concert* saw the new five-piece run through several early songs before providing back-up to Linda Ronstadt. They were now genuine pop stars.

Irving Azoff, with his aggressive promotion, was proving priceless in his daily dealing with the Eagles—so naturally the Eagles followed him to his new management company, Frontline Management. Azoff wasted no time in getting things organized and set up Eagles Ltd., with each of the now five members being named as equal partners in their own company. But the commercial success, the new musical power of a five piece, the debauchery of the road, and the seemingly never ending supply of great songs couldn't hide the personal animosities between band members for long. The strong-willed Leadon was increasingly clashing with Frey and was disturbed by the way in which Henley and Frey often operated behind closed doors and clearly felt empowered to make decisions by themselves. Yet the band still came first for Leadon and he settled down to work on the next album, *One of These Nights.*

Henley still felt that conflict aided creativity. Partner in rhyme Glenn Frey agreed. "We fight with our manager, we fight with each other. Don and Bernie nearly had a fistfight the other day. We fight about everything." At least the fighting was taking place in warm climes— Miami, to be precise.

Recording in new American surroundings gave the Eagles, especially Henley and Frey, a perspective on California and LA that had been lacking on the first three albums. Already the band's chief songwriters had begun to explore the culture that had launched them, and in which they were enjoying such incredible success. Only 300 miles to the north, Henley and Frey had moved into an exclusive house high in the Hollywood Hills with an astounding 360-degree view of Hollywood.

The two men were beginning to move away from earlier themes to write about the world they inhabited and would find their greatest glory with the immortal "Hotel California," a song that said as much about LA in the mid-1970s as any PBS documentary ever could. Criticized by some at the time for not writing personal material à la Jackson Browne and Joni Mitchell, Henley and Frey were in fact providing a journalistic eye on life from the epicenter of Californian self-indulgence, self-absorption, and luxury living. The songs that emerged from this perspective would be seen as either aspirational or mere reportage.

The album kicks off with a brand new sound for the Eagles and yet more evidence of Henley as a star in waiting as he finds a pre-Bee Gee falsetto for the R&B surprise of "One of These Nights." As Frey recalls, it was an intentional experiment to start a new style with the Eagles.

Below: Poster for the *One of These Nights* world tour.

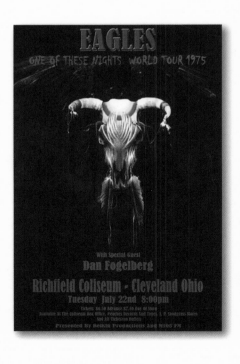

Right: Don Henley playing drums at an Eagles concert in Anaheim, California, October 1975.

"We wrote that when we were just getting into our R&B period. With his gravelly voice, Don was the ideal candidate to sing anything that was in an R&B or hard rock vein. So we wrote it with his voice in mind. I can picture me at the piano playing chords and Don sitting next to me making stuff up. Those kinds of songs came easily, beautifully. The best Eagles songs sounded natural."

Just to remind everyone that he remained a top vocalist himself, Randy Meisner provided a gifted vocal on "Take It to the Limit," a song that would go on to become a band staple and Eagle fan favorite over the next thirty or so years. "Lyin' Eyes" would win the band their first Grammy and see Glenn Frey in mellow country rock vein once again. Similar in tone to "Lyin' Eyes" but more observational and lyrically accomplished, is the somewhat ambiguous "Hollywood Waltz." The

The Albums

One Of These Nights

Producer: Bill Szymczyk

Recorded: Criteria Studios, Miami, and Record Plant, Los Angeles, 1974

Label: Asylum Records

Released: June 1975

Chart position: U.S.A. Billboard pop albums #1

TRACKS

Side One

1. One of These Nights
2. Too Many Hands
3. Hollywood Waltz
4. Journey of the Sorcerer

Side Two

1. Lyin' Eyes
2. Take It to the Limit
3. Visions
4. After the Thrill Is Gone
5. I Wish You Peace

song is in many ways an early take on the themes that would come to the fore in "Hotel California," a thoughtful look at the good, the bad, and the ugly of the City of Angels.

Just to prove that the band could rock with the best of them, Henley and Felder's "Visions" is given full throttle and sounds unlike anything the band were doing just a few years earlier. Meanwhile, Bernie Leadon creates the instrumental "Journey of the Sorcerer," which certainly marked a departure for the band. Perhaps the track was inspired by those long nights supporting Jethro Tull. Leadon also contributed the soon to be prophetic "I Wish You Peace," co-written by the love of his life at the time, Patti Davis. It's a beautiful song about letting go of acrimony and parting peacefully. Leaving was presumably on his mind.

Go Your Own Way

If *On the Border* had given the group a commercial rebirth after the disappointment of *Desperado,* then *One of These Nights* made them international stars. The first single, the title track, quickly went top 10 in America and the band embarked on a huge world tour of major stadiums, culminating in a vast arena show in Anaheim, California. *Rolling Stone* gave them their first cover, and *Time* magazine nominated the Eagles as the top band in America in 1975. Joining the Eagles for that Anaheim concert (which marked the twentieth anniversary of James Dean's death) were Jackson Browne and Linda Ronstadt. The Troubadour class of '69 had done what they set out to do.

By the end of 1975, the Eagles had the world at their feet. Backstage shenanigans on the road were as well organized and carefully orchestrated as their painstaking recording techniques and the highly structured choreography of their live shows. Henley was sending for beautiful women in Learjets and embarked on several celebrity romances, starting with an affair with Stevie Nicks from Fleetwood Mac, soon to be the Eagles' only real rivals in the new California soft rock sound.

However, one Eagle had had enough of the still-constant infighting among band members. Leadon had found contentment in a new romantic relationship, albeit one that courted a fair bit of controversy. Patti Davis was the free-spirited and liberal-minded daughter of

Top: The back cover of the *One of These Nights* album.

Above: The distinctive artwork of the *One of These Nights* album, shown here in the black and white inner sleeve.

California governor Ronald Reagan, and when she and Leadon became involved, the romance made the gossip papers across the country. Perhaps feeling isolated from the group, Leadon started bringing Davis to Eagles' recording sessions, much to the chagrin of Henley.

The lifestyle was taking its toll on Leadon. A rock and roll veteran by this time, he decided he'd had enough. He quit the band while they were on the road in December 1975 for the peace and quiet of Hawaii. Reflecting on the decision to quit from almost twenty years distant, Leadon said, "Mainly, I was burnt out. I wanted to go to the beach and get healthy. I started working professionally so young, I sort of missed the going-to-the-beach stuff, I'd been smoking from the time I was 13 til the time I left the Eagles, which was when I quit cigarettes. It was sort of a minor thing but a big thing to me at the time. It was sort of emblematic that I wanted a change of lifestyle and to get healthy. I think I made a good choice."

Once again, the Eagles were four; could they now become as one?

5

Welcome to the Hotel California

W HEN LEADON QUIT the Eagles close to Christmas 1975, Irving Azoff stepped in immediately and issued a press statement that Bernie Leadon had left the band. Barely a month earlier, the third single to be taken from the number 1 album *One of These Nights*, "Take It to the Limit," had made number 4 on the pop single charts. The previous single, "Lyin' Eyes," had made number 2 in September and the album

Edited: Derek Johnson

Leadon quits line-up, and ... JOE WALSH JOINS EAGLES

BERNIE LEADON, long-standing member of the Eagles, has left the band. And he has been replaced in the line-up by renowned rock guitarist Joe Walsh, who makes his live debut with the Eagles when they tour Australia, New Zealand and Japan from January 15 to February 10. Walsh, who left the James Gang three years ago to pursue a solo career, will add depth to the Eagles' sound with his heavy-metal guitar — although he will also be featured on keyboards.

Leadon's departure from the band is described as "amicable", cables Lisa Robinson from New York. It comes about because he does not relish the prospect of continued extensive touring and was rumoured by NME as long ago as June. Walsh has played with the Eagles in the past, and shares the same manager as the band, Irv Azoff.

Future recording plans for the Eagles are still uncertain. Much depends on whether Walsh remains with them on a permanent basis; if he does, he will be playing on their next album in the spring. Otherwise, Leadon may return briefly for the sessions.

It has been common knowledge for some time that Leadon has not been keen about gigging.

BERNIE LEADON

However, strong rumours in Los Angeles that he may join the Flying Burrito Brothers have been emphatically denied, as have suggestions that he is planning to record a solo album.

Hammond-Hammond leaves Jethro Tull

JETHRO TULL have parted company with their bass player of nearly five years' standing, Jeffrey Hammond-Hammond. He has reportedly left the band to return to painting, which has always been his principal interest. Our correspondent in Switzerland, where Jethro are at present recording, says that he has been replaced in the line-up by a young American musician named John Glasscock.

Tull are in the process of recording 18 new Ian Anderson songs, from which the best 10 or 12 will be selected for inclusion on a new album, planned for May release. Anderson said in Montreux that the songs are all about people from different walks of life — an ageing rock star, a housewife, an artist, and so on. Some

IAN GILLAN'S BAND FOR MARCH DEBUT

IAN GILLAN, the former Deep Purple vocalist, this week announced the line-up of his own band. It comprises Johnny Gustafson (bass), Mark Nauseef (percussion), Mike Moran (keyboards) and Ray Fenwick (lead guitar). Gustafson, who recently had a spell as guest bassist with Roxy Music, will also be featured on some vocals. The band are already in the process of cutting their debut album, and will spend the whole of January and February rehearsing a stage act. Gillan, who left Purple last year to be replaced by David Coverdale, plans to go out on the road toward the end of March — coinciding with the release of their album.

Heep cancel date

URIAH HEEP were forced to

ncerts
s who
during

by two
23 and
he gigs
ge tour.

t to the
charts.
a Silver
h their

Above: Irving Azoff, manager of Steely Dan, REO Speedwagon, and, of course, the Eagles. His style was in marked contrast to that of the band's previous manager, David Geffen, and this was welcomed by pretty much all concerned.

was still selling well. The Eagles were big news. Naturally wary of the press, Azoff refused all requests for interviews following Leadon's departure; he was well aware that the matter would take far more time to deal with than had the simple addition of Don Felder. Anyway, a replacement wasn't far away, and it would make a better story than the defection. Azoff asked one of his other management clients, the mercurial guitar hero Joe Walsh, if he'd like to join the band. And he said, "Yes."

As 1976 loomed, the Eagles' manager was making himself very busy indeed. He had filed a lawsuit against Warner for the return of copyrights in Eagles material. Realizing that they were in a delicate situation with their biggest-selling act of the moment, Warner stalled negotiations and released a greatest hits album while they did so, *Their Greatest Hits 1971–1975*. David Geffen wanted to capitalize on the Eagles while they were riding high in the charts, but the massive success of the compilation, which also helped to reinvigorate sales of the first three albums, soon had the band selling up to a million albums a week.

The huge success of a greatest hits package, culled from just three studio albums, was some achievement. The next album would have to be something pretty good, especially once the world knew that they were about to add a rock and roll guitar hero to the line-up. Of course, the band did not complain about it. The success of the greatest hits package gave them more time to deliver their next studio album.

And they'd need that time, especially given that both Henley and Frey intended the next studio album to be something "special" and different from the previous ones. It might only have been four years since their debut album, but the band were a million miles away from their starting point, both personally and professionally. While they mostly enjoyed their life as rock and roll royalty—the fast cars, multiple houses, helicopters and Learjets, designer drugs, groupies, and celebrity romances—there was a downside to it. Henley and Frey were feeling stressed by the pressure to compete with themselves. "We were scared," recalled Frey a couple of years later. "We had to go out and prove we were still happening." They also had to introduce the new guy to the Eagles' way of doing things, both live and on record.

Their Greatest Hits 1971–1975

Producers: Glyn Johns and Bill Szymczyk

Recorded: 1971–1975

Label: Asylum Records

Released: February 1976

Chart position: U.S.A. Billboard pop albums #1

TRACKS

Side One

1. Take It Easy
2. Witchy Woman
3. Lyin' Eyes
4. Already Gone
5. Desperado

Side Two

1. One of These Nights
2. Tequila Sunrise
3. Take It to the Limit
4. Peaceful Easy Feeling
5. Best of My Love

The Player You Get

Joe Walsh was already legendary in rock and roll circles. With his trademark "Flying V" guitar slung low like a gunfighter, Walsh played with a fierce aggression but combined it with a natural affinity for melody. He was the nearest thing America had to Led Zeppelin's Jimmy Page. Walsh was from the school of hard rock in Cleveland, and generally speaking, the Midwest was more into the kind of rock played by Cream than that of The Byrds. Walsh would naturally bring a rougher and tougher element to the Eagles sound, clearly marking their move away from their mellow beginnings.

Joe Walsh was originally from Wichita, Kansas, but grew up in Columbus, Ohio, before moving east to New York City and New Jersey. Like everyone else in the 1960s it was John, Paul, George, and Ringo who got him started in music.

"I was tremendously influenced by the Beatles, really that's what did it. I saw them on *Ed Sullivan* and I said 'Hey, those guys are cool.'"

Walsh attended Ohio's Kent State University, where he became the best-known guitarist in the area. He played with several local bands, although initially he played bass with them. Recalling his college days, Walsh said:

"I majored in English, minored in music, and took a lot of electronics courses. I didn't go to class very much though. I got in a band at a bar downtown and never really went home after that. My parents were kind of upset that I wasn't doing well in school but I was playing four sets a night, four nights a week, doing the Top 20. In those days if you knew Beatles and Rolling Stones songs you could play anywhere. I played lead and tried to copy what George Harrison had played pretty much note for note. Eventually I was studying Clapton, Page, and Beck, learning their songs note for note. That's really the way to learn guitar."

It was not surprising that Joe Walsh's parents were wary of their son opting for rock and roll; his mother was a trained musician, a pianist with the New York City Ballet. Surrounded by classical music as a kid, Walsh enjoyed a broader musical education than most of his rock counterparts, and was more adventurous than many in his choice of

The soap doesn't change.
& the room smell's the same.
Bottled & shipped to hypnotize
travelling salesmen.
& what the hell am I selling
so far from home?
I miss home.
Mine.
Yours.
Anybody's.

material. While playing with the James Gang between 1968 and 1971, he persuaded them to record a rocking version of Ravel's "Bolero," for instance. (Walsh also recorded Ravel's "Pavane" on his debut solo album of 1974, *So What*.)

The James Gang were the biggest band in the region in 1968, as Walsh confirmed. "[They] were a good, five-piece band, one of the top bands in Cleveland." When the band's lead guitarist Glen Schwartz left for California, Walsh got the call. Internal disagreements soon reduced

Above: The tedium and loneliness of life on the road as captured in a 1976 tour program.

Following double page: And then there were two . . . Don Felder gets a guitar mate, and the Eagles get a fuller sound.

"**Around that time, I was just fed up with a solo career—I didn't have the energy to do it, and it didn't really look like it was going anywhere. Irving met the Eagles, who were kind of disillusioned with their management and the way they were being represented, and they also had some internal friction—it was kind of being in the right place at the right time, but what ended up was that the Eagles asked Irving to represent them and formed kind of a little family. I got to know the guys [when] they helped me a little bit with 'So What.'**"

JOE WALSH

the Gang to a three piece and they released their debut, *Yer' Album*, in 1969. "It was good training for me," Walsh told a radio station in 1982. "I was the only melodic instrument in the band of guitar, bass, and drums. I learned to enjoy playing lead and rhythm at the same time, and also had to sing because I was better than the other two guys."

Walsh so impressed Pete Townshend, who saw an early James Gang/ Walsh gig, that he had the band open several Who shows in America during 1969. The guitarist stayed with the trio for two more studio albums, *James Gang Rides Again* and *Thirds*, both, like their first, produced by Bill Szymczyk (there was also a live recording, *James Gang Live in Concert*, released in December 1971). For those three years Walsh had to consistently balance his love of melody with the hard rock format, and in doing so proved himself a very adaptable,

flexible singer and writer—as well as one of the best guitarists around. Eventually tiring of the James Gang, and looking for a more varied musical landscape, Walsh relocated to Colorado in 1971 to work with his rock and roll mentor—and future Eagles producer—Bill Szymczyk.

As he explained the move, Walsh said, "So I went to Colorado, took an amount of time off, and began forming Barnstorm, which was an arrangement of players conceived in a way to express what I was hearing and what I thought a band should be. They were strange times and it was hard, but it took me back to basic survival, which is always very positive in terms of creative energy—when you have to get yourself together and you're talking in terms of basic survival, you play differently from when you're rich."

Barnstorm released a self-titled album in September 1972, which Walsh co-produced with Szymczyk, and it featured the pedal steel playing of ex-Shiloh member Al Perkins. When it failed to make Walsh a solo star, stalling at number 73 on the *Billboard* album chart, he recorded more songs with pretty much the same musical team in the studio, but released it in June of 1973 as a solo artist. This was *The Smoker You Drink, the Player You Get.* The opening track was released as a single and became an enormous hit. "Rocky Mountain Way" helped lift the album into the Top 10 of the album chart. Walsh's next solo album, *So What,* recorded between December 1973 and March 1974, saw Walsh, now managed by Irving Azoff, receiving some help in the studio from Don Henley and Glenn Frey.

They also helped with a live recording in March 1976, playing on "Help Me Thru the Night" for *You Can't Argue with a Sick Mind.* By the time the album was released in October 1976, Walsh had officially joined the band. Not that the move was made without some trepidation on everyone's part. Sure, they had a manager in common and had worked with each other before, but Walsh was a well-known artist in his own right, unlike Felder who was very much a sideman when he joined the Eagles. Walsh, moreover, had a reputation as an eccentric, colorful, and sometimes outrageous character. He was seen as quite a party animal and hell raiser, so much so that in his Eagles days he was inclined to carry a chainsaw on tour with him in case the furniture was not up, or rather down, to his size requirements. However,

the feeling was that perhaps his addition would provide the bite and street credibility that the Eagles were missing. Frey was nervous, though. "I personally thought that adding Joe Wash was a dangerous move. 90% of the people who heard about it couldn't figure out how it was ever going to work."

ROAD CREW (left to right)
Tom Nixon, Dave (Snake) Reynolds,
Richard Fernandez, Tony Taibi & Jage Jackson.

Straight Outta LA

For some time the Eagles had been opening concerts with Frey simply announcing, "Hello, we are the Eagles from Los Angeles." The more the East Coast press mocked them for not having the same social relevance of new kid in town Bruce Springsteen, the more they would turn toward their adoptive state for inspiration. The next album would take a year and a half to make, become one of the best-known albums in pop history, and make pertinent social comment like nothing they had attempted before. The album would be called *Hotel California*.

Henley and Frey, now firmly established as the songwriting hub of the band, had begun to exploit Hollywood and the California lifestyle for *One of These Nights*, especially with the song "Hollywood Waltz."

They had all migrated to California in search of their own musical version of the American Dream. Frey in particular began talking about Hollywood, Los Angeles, and California in press interviews, and was clearly dismayed and fascinated by the highs and lows that LA offered, with its immense wealth on one side and bloody riots

on another. California in the 1970s had become home to hippies, surfers, and free-thinking liberals, and there was "fun, fun, fun" to be had in the sun for anyone wealthy enough to be able to afford the copious amounts of readily available weed and cocaine. "Intellectual" Californians read Carlos Castaneda, headed into the desert for retreats, and uttered "far out" as they explored their universe. Meanwhile, a few miles away, economically depressed South Central LA filled up with poor, unemployed immigrants. California had beautiful weather, a strong economy, and some of the richest people in the world in Beverly Hills. But as those with a social conscience began to look closer at LA, they could see the downside; in the crime-ridden area of Compton, the previously hidden economic issues surfaced in the mini-recession of 1974. It was obvious to anyone with eyes to see that there were serious problems brewing among the underprivileged in east LA, not least with the growth of drug-related gangs. The rich and famous started to become aware of the vacuous nature of their materialism and wealth.

As songwriters, Henley and Frey were smart enough to see that living the California lifestyle of excess and abandon was not necessarily desirable, and knew that experiencing the downside of excess was a dark and scary affair. The new album, they decided, would be a concept album, but one much darker and more unsettling than *Desperado*. The album would prove universally popular with its catchy tunes and lush production but, like California and indeed America in the 1970s, its sweetness was masking something very sour indeed.

"We're not exactly going to win friends with this album," Henley told *Hit Parader* magazine, "but that's what it's about. We're just saying, 'Look what's happening.' I don't feel totally that way about California. I love it and I hate it at the same time."

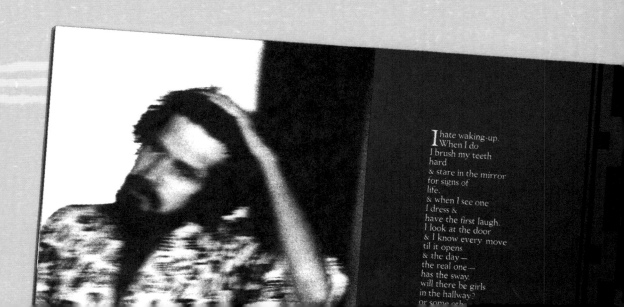

What You Make It

Before settling into a recording groove with the new member, Azoff and the Eagles undertook a tour of Japan and Australia in order to ease Walsh into the band structure. They were away from the prying eyes of the U.S. media, of course, but, at least initially, the new-look Eagles concert presented as if it were two shows—the Eagles and then a guest spot from Walsh. Walsh soon learned the structured format that Henley and Frey preferred to play live, and so kept his wild improvisational performing for his occasional solo gigs and recordings. The focus for the Eagles on stage was the same as it was for the recording studio: cohesion. It was important that they present themselves as a united and controlled unit, especially as rumors abounded among the rock fraternity in LA that the band was close to breaking up.

After recording the live album with Walsh, and with him settled into the Eagles, the band devoted itself to the pursuit of studio excellence in March 1976. Henley indulged his perfectionism and they spent around eight months in the studio, recording songs over and over to get the sound right. This time they worked at LA's Record Plant as well as in Miami at the famed Criteria Studios, where Eric Clapton had recorded his 1974 mainstream breakthrough album *461 Ocean Boulevard*. Henley was determined that *Hotel California*, with Felder integrated and Walsh now in the armory, would be the band's ultimate statement.

The album's artwork was designed to reinforce the dichotomy between good and evil, darkness and light. The front cover shot sees Hollywood's most prestigious meeting place for tinsel town's high-rolling movers and shakers, the Beverly Hills Hotel, shot from across the street in soft grainy pastel tones.

Inside, a collage of characters in a hotel lobby tell their own story. According to Henley, "Once upon a time it used to be very elegant, now it's a home for old people, some pimps, and young starting actors. It used to be very grand, and it's still a little that way except they've put up Formica, phony plastic wood on the walls, a coke machine in the lobby . . . even plastic chandeliers. That represented to us what happened to California and to the country in general, so we got a lot of our friends and we hired a bunch of people to come in and stand

The limos are waiting.
Most of the time.
This is normal.
An illusion
most of the time.
Right?
Am I normal?
I am waiting.
& we drive through the city
& the city stares back.
I observe &
make metaphors.
I'm polite with my words
while I study with my
eyes.
That's finally how you get to know.
Though a good word's
a good indication.
A Chinese restaurant goes by.

At the airport
the Enterprise is waiting.
I dig it.
I love it.
No waiting for tickets.
No baggage to check.
Just beamed aboard
beaming.
Four tons of equipment are
already on their way
in two semi-trailers.
The hare in the air &
the tortoise is rolling.
The fairy tale never changes.

On the plane
I'm a passenger
with a rock 'n roll
headache.
Food's in a pirate's box
& I nibble fruit
& look out the window
& recognize clouds
more familiar than any city.
We're flying.
It's turbulent.
Outside &
inside.
My stomach hurts.

We begin ou
Beaming dov
but it's hard
when you've

There's seat belt playtime
in the air.
Sometimes we're children
with expensive toys
that aren't so much fun.
I remember the last minute
through a dark cloud
with a child in its lap.

there. Then the back of the cover is the same lobby, except it's empty. The poor Mexican janitor is all alone packing it up at five o'clock in the morning . . . the Spanish people are left to clean up. It's a symbolic sleeve and it's not very pretty."

Opposite: Felder and Frey in full flight on the *Hotel California* tour, Wembley Empire, UK, January 1977.

The reggae-tinged title track started life in the hands of Don Felder. He was in the habit of recording musical ideas for songs, and sometimes, just guitar licks by himself before bringing them to Henley and Frey for consideration and comment. As Felder recalls:

> "I had just leased this house on the beach at Malibu—I guess around '74 or '75. I remember sitting in the living room, with the doors wide open, on a spectacular July day. I had a bathing suit on and I was on this couch, soaking wet, thinking the world is a wonderful place to be. I had this acoustic 12-string and started tinkling around with it, and those 'Hotel California' chords just kind of oozed out. I had a TEAC four-track set up in one of the back bedrooms and I ran back there to put this idea down before I forgot it. I also had one of those old Rhythm Ace things, and I remember it was set to play this cha-cha beat. I played the 12-string on top of that. A few days later, I came up with a bass line and mixed the whole thing to mono, ping-ponging back and forth on this little four-track."

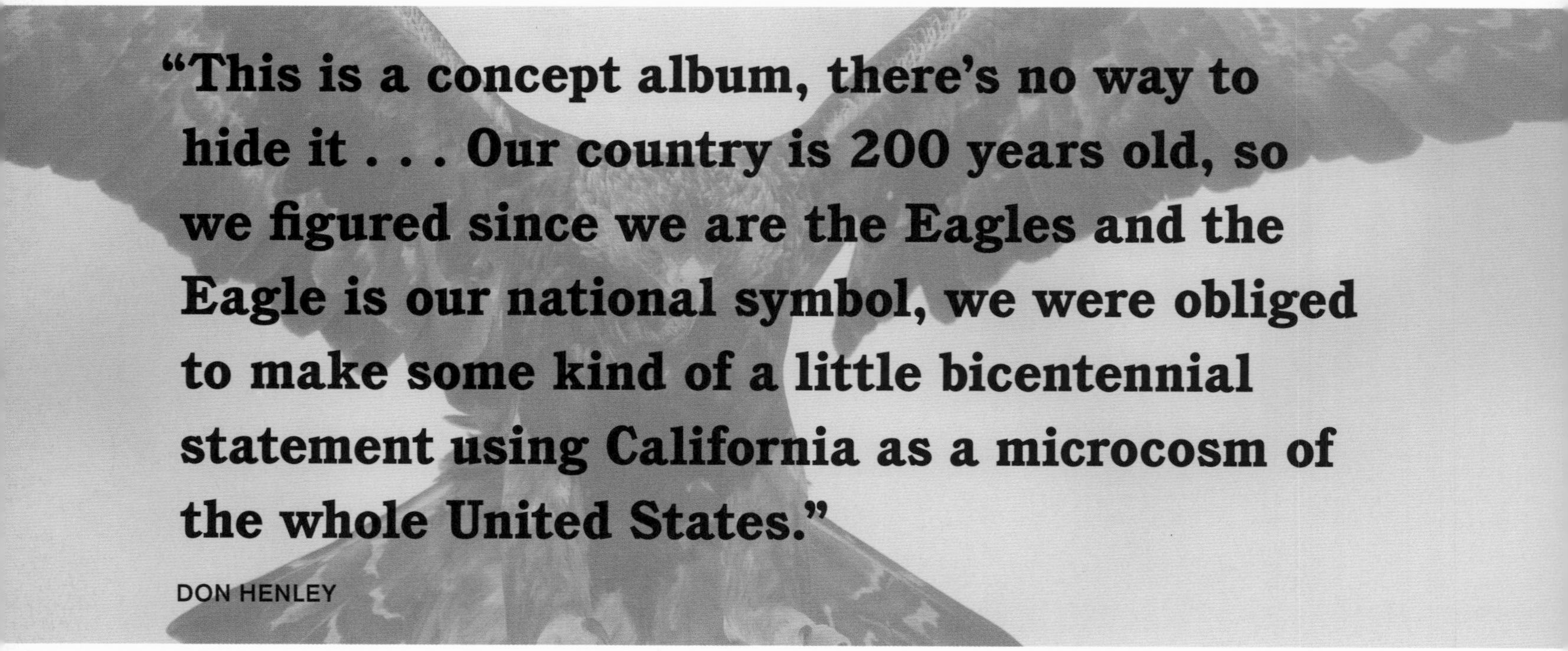

"This is a concept album, there's no way to hide it . . . Our country is 200 years old, so we figured since we are the Eagles and the Eagle is our national symbol, we were obliged to make some kind of a little bicentennial statement using California as a microcosm of the whole United States."

DON HENLEY

Hotel California

Producer: Bill Szymczyk

Recorded: Criteria Studios, Miami, and Record
Plant, Los Angeles, March to October 1976

Label: Asylum Records

Released: December 1976

Chart position: U.S.A. Billboard *pop albums #1*

T R A C K S

Side One

1. Hotel California
2. New Kid in Town
3. Life in the Fast Lane
4. Wasted Time

Side Two

1. Wasted Time (reprise)
2. Victim of Love
3. Pretty Maids All in a Row
4. Try and Love Again
5. The Last Resort

The Eagles

Henley took Felder's haunting chords and wistful melody and created one of the most memorable songs of the 1970s. It was a song that would be played in cars, by swimming pools, and on beaches all around the world, from Barcelona to Bombay throughout 1977 (and beyond). The sound of California was the sound of America, and the sound of America in 1977 was the Eagles.

Above: The inside gatefold of the *Hotel California* album. As Don Henley put it: "We hired a bunch of people to come in and stand there."

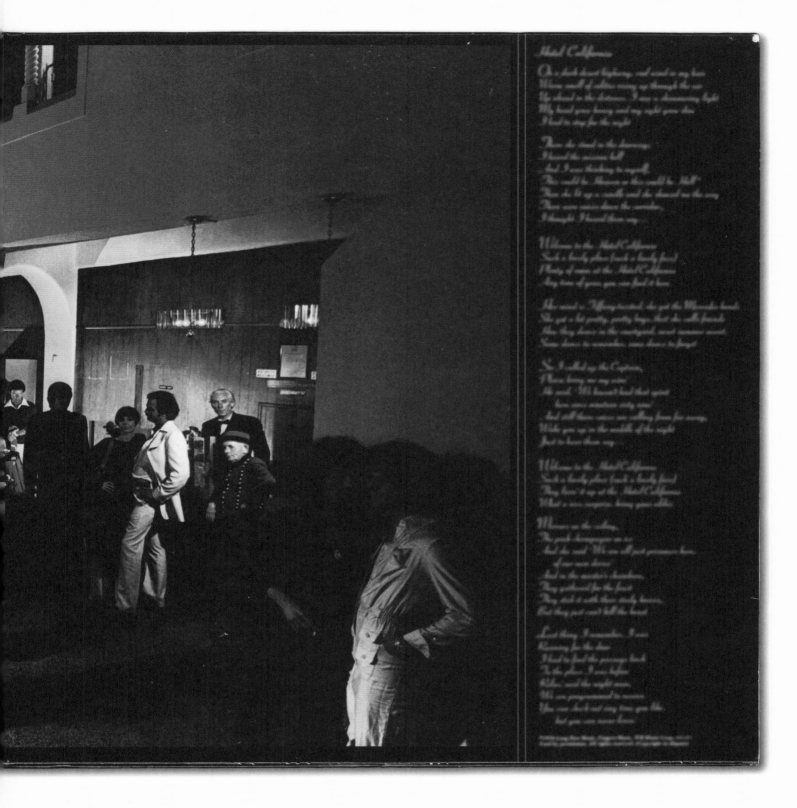

"New Kid in Town," co-written by Henley and Frey with J. D. Souther, is almost as good as the title track, and features some tremendous vocal harmony work from the group. "The Last Resort" continues the theme of decadent despair in America, and is a precursor for Henley's involvement in numerous environmental issues throughout the forthcoming years. Given the addition of Walsh, much was expected of the upbeat rockier tunes and "Life in the Fast Lane," co-written with the Cleveland cowboy, is rock and roll with a dark sense of humor. Walsh had immediately brought some Midwestern panache to the otherwise quite serious Eagles and it sounded pretty good. This is also in evidence on Felder's "Victim of Love," where Walsh and Felder, two master craftsmen, weave seamlessly into each other's lines on one of the band's best rock songs.

The album was tougher, more substantial sonically than anything they had achieved before and, while they had left the banjo and steel behind, the Eagles remained consummate songwriters and studio perfectionists. In the days before computers and pro-tool applications, perfection meant a tedious and painstaking recording process. But the overall sound was so full, so lush, and so musically well crafted that the band in fact set a new standard in production quality. Producer Bill Szymczyk had made some adaptations to the soundboard and was utilizing the punch-in system of editing that would become industry practice after *Hotel California*'s release. The painstaking attempts to get things just right led to countless retakes and overdubs, and rock albums taking not just months, but years to complete.

Henley had by now taken his place as the face and sound of the Eagles. He was also the band's chief lyricist. Henley had come a long way from the quiet drummer sitting at the back and hardly noticed on their debut album. Frey was still an essential part of the Eagles, but he was not particularly happy about the change; his moods and general attitude became more sullen and volatile as Henley emerged as the Eagle that everyone knew.

Above: The back cover of the *Hotel California* **album, with only the solitary Mexican janitor left to clear everything up.**

Opposite: On the road again in 1976.

"**They never got the respect they deserved, probably because when you get to be really successful and huge, people look to knock you down. But we all knew how good they were.**"

BYRON BERLINE

They order
six glasses of juice &
four glasses of milk.
The talk goes over & above my head
& settles in my ears.
I digest everything.

I see a mirage:
they discover a lost, dusty menu
on parchment
& share it with me.
Together they sit.
They don't look like explorers.
The talk is small
& then louder
& I'm a part with a quiet
smart remark.

Hotel California

⋯R PANDORA PRODUCTIONS, LTD. Engineered by Bill Szymczyk, Allan Blazek, Ed Mashal & Bruce Hensal. ⋯Plant, Los Angeles, March–October 1976 • Mixed by Bill Szymczyk in Miami. Mastered at Sterling ⋯ucted by Jim Ed Norman. Concert Master: Sid Sharp. Cover photography by David Alexander • direction: Don Henley & Kosh.

⋯son of 'Home at Last', Richard Irwin & Bruce Plummer of Northwest Sound & Lights, Harper Dance, ⋯Lou Stewart, Michael Rosenfeld, Bob Hurwitz, Walter Wanger, Ron Stander, Roger Montgomery, ⋯Shellist, Linda McGalliard, Pete Wagner, Jimmy Wachtel, Terry Bassett, David Rensin, Larry Solters, & our friends at Elektra / Asylum Records. Past due thanks to Alex Sadkin. Direction: Front Line ⋯Tom Nixon & Richard Fernandez. Everything and more: Irv Azoff. Special thanks to: John David Souther ⋯d, most of all, thanks to our respective families and friends for their patience and support.

Where Is Hotel California?

Hotel California, the best-known song from the Eagles' most popular album, has proved itself a timeless classic, but not just for its immediately identifiable guitar intro or its hypnotic tropical beat. Don Henley's lyrics have for many years caused rigorous debate as to the true meaning of the song. Some have called it a Satanist's hidden call to action; others have spent years trying to pinpoint the exact location of the "real" Hotel California.

Just why the Satanism rumor started is not clear, but the various theories focus on two main issues. First is that the Church of Satan used to be located in a converted hotel on California Street, San Francisco. It was the address of Anton LaVey, church founder and author of the *Satanic Bible* and something of a hero figure to Charles Manson, among others. So the story goes, Henley wrote the song about the hotel on California Street. It might seem tenuous except that the second set of rumors contend that LaVey is also pictured on the *Hotel California* album sleeve. There is indeed a shadowy figure shown, but it could be almost anyone. However, those so inclined feel that the "clues" are persuasive. And of course the band did record a song called "Good Day in Hell."

Alternately, many people have spent hours researching the exact location of the actual Hotel California in Henley's song. For some it's in Baja California, for others it's the Pacific highway between Cabo San Lucas and La Paz—or further north, near Santa Barbara. Some have claimed it to be a mental institution in California. Henley himself, the man responsible for the lyrics, has denied all the rumors—but of course, argue the theorists, he would!

See the list opposite for the many international artists who have covered "Hotel California."

HOTEL CALIFORNIA COVERS

Sam Hui ★ *(Cantonese, pop, 1977)*

Gypsy Kings ★ *(Spanish, flamenco, 1990)*

Al B. Sure ★ *(U.S., soul, 1990)*

Jam on the Mutha ★ *(The Orb, In Cali Mix) (England, chill-out, 1990)*

Nashville Superpickers ★ *(U.S., country, 1994)*

Roo'ra ★ *(Korean, hip-hop, 1995)*

The Moog Cookbook ★ *(U.S., electronica, 1997)*

Majek Fashek ★ *(Nigerian, reggae, 1998)*

Moonraisers ★ *(Swiss, reggae, 1998)*

Ska Daddyz ★ *(U.S., ska, 1998)*

Wilson Phillips ★ *(U.S., pop, 2000)*

Alabama 3 ★ *(English, swamp goth, 2000)*

William Hung ★ *(U.S., American Idol contestant, 2004)*

The Cat Empire ★ *(French, reggae, 2005)*

2pac vs. Biggie ★ *[Runnin' to . . .] (U.S., rap, 2006)*

Rascal Flats ★ *(U.S., country, 2007)*

Marc Anthony ★ *(U.S., latin, 2007)*

Sylvain Cossette ★ *(French-Canadian, 2008)*

The Killers ★ *(U.S., alt-rock, 2009)*

Life in the Fast Lane

As the album sold in huge numbers early in 1977 (having been released in December 1976), the title track was released as a single in February '77 and became the Eagles' fourth number 1 hit—and something of a signature tune. However, it was "Life in the Fast Lane," released in May 1977 and reaching number 11 in the pop charts, that best described the life of the Eagles after the release of their seminal album.

Azoff had impressively negotiated a mighty royalty rate for the Eagles at $1.50 an album, a figure unheard of at the time. They set out on their biggest world tour yet with Jimmy Buffett as support act in January 1977.

The band's return to London was a triumph. Two years earlier they had appeared less confident when supporting Elton John and the Beach Boys at London's Wembley venue. This time around, with the added confidence and sonic beef of Felder and Walsh, they were in their element. The 1977 world tour was executed with military precision, with no expense spared. The Eagles themselves, sure that they were promoting their masterpiece album, played at their peak. As the audience took in the beautifully lit backdrop of the *Hotel California* album cover, the Eagles were backstage, bonding musically with a group vocal warm-up of Steve Young's "Seven Bridges Road." As they took their place on stage, Felder slid into his by then famous "Hotel California" guitar run. Most bands would keep their ace song up their sleeves for a finale, or maybe encore, but not the Eagles vintage '77.

The Meisner and Henley rhythm section performed to perfection while Felder's laid-back approach disguised a technically gifted player, easily the best musician in the band. Joined by the dynamic and explosive Joe Walsh, the Eagles of 1977 were as powerful a live band as any to come out of America. They may have lacked the on-stage visuals of Kiss or Alice Cooper, the sheer raw energy of Springsteen, or the charisma of Lou Reed, but for millions of new stereo owners in the late 1970s this was a magical moment, when a live rock band sounded exactly like the record. Musically, it was as good as it got—at least to Eagles fans.

But not everyone felt warmly about the laid-back, West Coast–rock sound typified by the Eagles. A musical revolution had sprung up in New York and London in 1976 and was taking hold of the UK by

Opposite and following double page: A humorous take on the Eagles' hedonistic lifestyle appeared in *Crawdaddy* magazine in April 1977, when the band were at the very height of their fame. In the article the Eagles talked about the intense pressures of fame and life on the road. Was it all about to come crashing down?

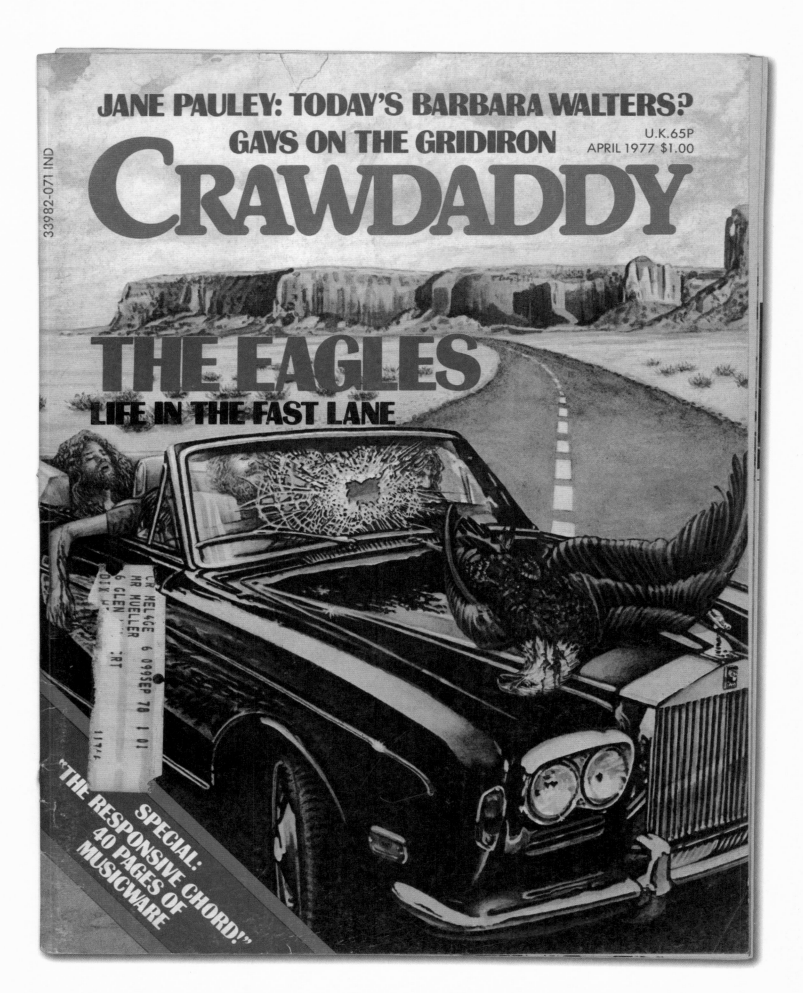

ONE OF THESE

Say a Prayer for the Pretenders....

BY BARBARA CHARONE

NIGHTMARES

illustration by Arthur Thompson

1977. Three-chord crunching punks were spitting and snarling at old-school rock music in England, where the Sex Pistols and the Clash poured scorn on "old" bands like the Eagles who spent years learning to play their instruments and then months in recording studios. New York punks, among them the Ramones and Blondie, Patti Smith, and Television, were similarly battling the establishment. The Eagles were already looked down upon by some sectors of the music press for supposedly lacking passion or social awareness, and now were once again under assault from journalists who simply didn't "get" the band.

Thankfully radio and huge swathes of the public thought differently, and in the first few weeks of its release *Hotel California* was selling in excess of half a million copies a week. The "Hotel California" single went to number 1 in America (number 8 in the UK) and stayed there for fifteen weeks. All that summer, "Life in the Fast Lane" was a radio constant as the band sold out venues across the country. In August 1977, the Eagles arrived in Memphis for a concert and to make a prearranged meeting with Elvis Presley. Sadly, Presley pulled out of the meeting because of ill-health. Barely a week later, he was dead.

The tour continued, although it was not without its difficulties. Randy Meisner was dealing with a particularly nasty stomach condition and suffered ulcers, which flared up on the road. The bickering and power trips continued within the band, too. Aside from the ulcers, Meisner was missing his family. They had remained in Nebraska throughout the Eagles rock and roll madness, and the touring lifestyle was taking its toll on him and his relationship with them. There was an air of inevitability about it, and finally, at the end of the *Hotel California* tour, Randy Meisner became a bit of Eagles history. The official announcement made was that he had left because of exhaustion.

Randy Meisner was the second original Eagle to say goodbye. The band's links with 1960s country rock—Leadon and Meisner—were now gone. While the Eagles had made a classic album, proved themselves the most popular band in the world, and enjoyed the trapping of excess like few others, there were new doubts over their continued existence. With Henley and Frey's friendship strained, and a new style of music emerging from the streets, the Eagles faced the toughest question for any successful band: how to maintain that incredible level of success.

Yes, the Eagles can rock

WE all know why the Eagles are one of the most popular bands of the Seventies. They write nice, tuneful songs which they sing with immaculate harmonies: an ideal package for, in America, FM and AM radio. And in Britain their records can be found on everything from the middlest-of-the-road afternoon Radio 2 show to the heaviest evening rock programme. The word is tasteful.

But is that enough to give them credibility as a ROCK band? As the decade rolls on, it's becoming more and more apparent that yesterday's rockers are today's MOR artists. There's a massive audience for tuneful ditties — music you hear, rather than listen to — and too many bands are copping out of progression and experimentation with the excuse that they're "giving people what they want."

Depending on what you believe, the Eagles are either the prime example of this, or a cunning bunch who adroitly walk the line between Muzak and music.

I've been sitting on the fence on this burning problem of the day for a long time, and it was with the hope of being dislodged from this uncomfortable position that I went along to the first of four nights of Eagles concerts at Wembley's Empire Pool on Monday.

The portents were bad: a programme filled with pretentious blank verse, and when the lights went down, blue neon signs bearing the legend Hotel California lit up and a backcloth unfurled to reveal the Hotel in all its glory, fringed by palm trees, silhouetted against an orange sky. Very tasteful.

The band start up, appropriately, with "Hotel California," note-perfect, just like the record. Halfway through there's an ominous "thunk" from stage right. It sounds like a restless guitarist — and lo and behold, Joe Walsh breaks out of the studio straitjacket with a blistering solo. Tastefulness be damned — this is rock 'n' roll!

And there's more. A quick pause for adulation, and Walsh shoots into "It Seems To Me," blasting out the chords with an energy and enthusiasm that would put a heavy metal band to shame. What a pleasure it is to hear TUNEFUL heavy rock again.

Then the pace gradually slows down, the momentum crumbles as the band churns through a couple of dirges until finally the backdrop rises again to reveal a 30-plus string orchestra, neatly decked out in white dinner jackets and black bow ties. They wend their way through "Wasted Time," "Take It To The Limit," "New Girl In Town" and "Desperado."

Beautiful harmonies; lovely songs; wonderful playing — all very tasteful. But I'm always suspicious when the orchestra earns more applause than the band.

That dispensed with, it's back into rock with a vengeance via a storming version of "One Of These Nights."

Now they're really sizzling, Walsh, Don Felder and Glenn Frey taking electrifying solo after electrifying solo, building the pressure relentlessly, as they rock up to a thundering version of Walsh's "Rocky Mountain Way."

Don't be fooled by the wimpish delicacy of their records: the Eagles haven't hung up their rock 'n' roll shoes yet. — MICHAEL OLDFIELD.

WEMBLEY

Robin Denselow

The Eagles

IF THE Beach Boys provided the sound track for California in the Sixties, the Eagles are doing the same for the Seventies. But while the Beach Boys summed up their time and place, first with catching surfing fans, then with far more progressive harmony material, the Eagles represent the new all-pervasive commercial rock culture with the ultimate in high quality, hip easy listening.

The first of their sold-out shows at Wembley, was on a par with their best-selling albums—lavishly produced, meticulously performed, and altogether quite superb if they hadn't left me with a nagging feeling that something, somewhere was sadly lacking. It was a confection perfect for a quick taste but ultimately insubstantial.

No question, it was clever though. Since the band started six years ago, its members (who had formerly been with the likes of Poco and Linda Ronstadt) have blended country, soft and heavy rock, and Mexican styles with five piece harmony and a lot of strong melodies, to create their string of hit songs, from One of these Nights to Hotel California.

Looking as emotionless and anonymous as the Pink Floyd in their jeans and long hair they stood statically behind their guitars and keyboards to successfully reproduce a thunderous version of their studio sound. A huge curtain behind the band occasionally lifted to reveal 28 violinists and seven cellists, perched incongruously and waiting somewhat ironically to battle with the hall's acoustics on Wasted Time.

There were some fine and varied passages—from the slow, pianobacked version of Desperado to Joe Walsh's noisy guitar breaks. The lead singing swopped all round the band. So why the slight disappointment? Ultimately, because the best of rock music takes chances and is an emotional experience. The Eagles were just very pleasant and very clever. That's California in the Seventies.

Don

Glenn Frey

Don Felder

Randy Meisner

EMPIRE POOL, WEMBLEY

HARVEY GOLDSMITH ENTERTAINMENTS
in association with TRINIFOLD LTD.
present

THE EAGLES
WITH SPECIAL GUEST
DAN FOGELBERG
TUESDAY, 26 APRIL, 1977
at 7.30 p.m.

SOUTH UPPER TIER
£4.25

APRIL
26
ENTER AT
SOUTH DOOR
ENTRANCE

57
ROW
F
SEAT
72

J. D. Souther

A key figure in California's country rock and singer-songwriter movement of the early '70s, Souther co-wrote some of the Eagles' finest songs of that era including "Heartache Tonight," "Victim of Love," "New Kid in Town," and "Best of My Love." He also penned a few classics for one-time girlfriend Linda Ronstadt, including "Faithless Love," "Simple Man, Simple Dream," and "Prisoner in Disguise."

Like the Eagles, J. D. Souther gravitated towards the flowering music scene in California back in the late 1960s. Raised in Texas, Souther had a natural affinity for country music but, unlike some of his peers, was educated in all kinds of music as a kid.

Moving to Hollywood as a musician and songwriter, he naturally gravitated toward the Troubadour. "The Troubadour in LA was an incredible place. Well you know, everybody at 22 wanted fame and attention. But my groups of friends were all serious about doing it well. The year that we were all there was 1969." Souther teamed up with another Troubadour regular Glenn Frey, formed Longbranch Pennywhistle, and they made one largely ignored album together before Frey started the Eagles with Don Henley (see Chapter 1). Souther saw it all begin. "They were good right from the start. I played with them at one rehearsal but there was no need for me in the band. They had everything."

Tipped for the top by everyone in the LA music scene, Souther never found the same level of commercial success as his Troubadour friends, but the critics adored him. He released three respected solo albums, *John David Souther, Black Rose,* and *You're Only Lonely* as well as two albums while a member of the commercially unsuccessful but critically acclaimed Souther Hillman Furay Band, the "supergroup" which united Souther with Poco's Richie Furay and the Byrds' Chris Hillman. His greatest commercial moment came in 1979 with the Top 20 hit "You're Only Lonely" from the album of the same name.

In 1985, Souther decided to walk away from his solo career. "I just wanted to be a good songwriter. I wanted to stay home and write." Which he did, when not acting in the television series *Thirtysomething*. He also scored a small part in the movie *Postcards from the Edge*. But he continued to devote himself to songwriting, for and with artists as diverse as Jimmy Buffett, Glen Campbell, Joe Cocker, Crosby, Stills and Nash, the Dixie Chicks, Don Henley, One Flew South, Roy Orbison, Bernadette Peters, Bonnie Raitt, George Strait, Brian Wilson, Trisha Yearwood, and Warren Zevon. In October 2008, he returned to the recording studio to make his first solo album in twenty-five years, *If the World Was You*. He followed that with his first live recording, *Rain*, which was recorded at Nashville's Belcourt Theatre. The albums appeared on his own indie label Slow Curve.

"The business model for the record industry has changed. Now the artist has more control. You need to devote a lot of time to the internet, to making contact; lots of touring, and you have to be creative and hard-working to replace the huge mechanism we used to be part of. In the late 1970s, there were just a few hundred albums released each year. In 2008, there were 115,000 albums and out of that only 15,000 sold 10,000 or more copies!"

Always part of the Eagles' inner circle throughout the years, Souther popped up again with a classic song for their 2007 *Long Road out of Eden* album. "How Long" was a song the Eagles performed in the early days but never recorded, since Souther wanted it for his own solo album, *John David Souther* (1972). But the track was classic Eagles country rock, perfect for the new recording, and with it the Eagles won the 2008 Grammy Award for Best Country Performance by a Duo or Group with Vocals. After the award J. D. Souther said, "I'm going to keep on playing and touring; I have a new album in mind, probably more cohesive than the last one. I'm enjoying it and when you get to play with young people like I did in New York recently, you get inspiration from their enthusiasm and creativity. It's a cool time, and I'm looking forward to this next year."

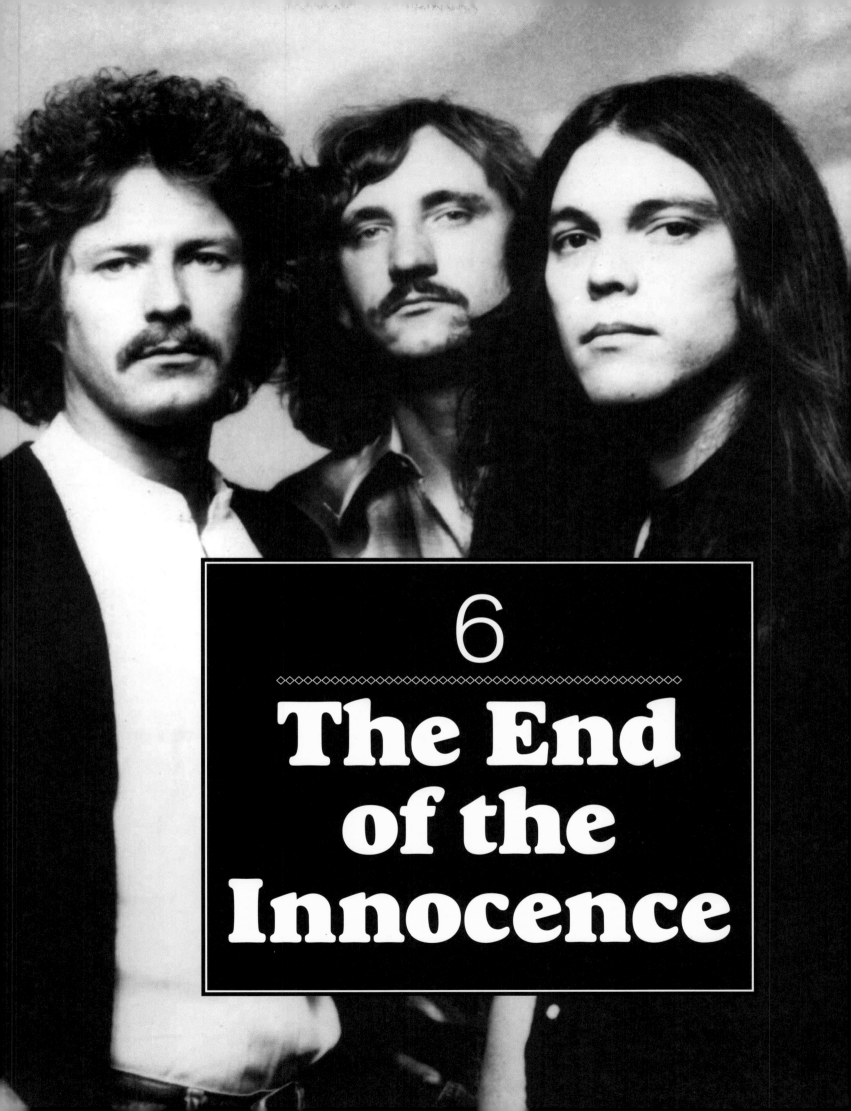

6

The End
of the
Innocence

WHEN RANDY MEISNER left LA and headed back to Nebraska to spend more time with his family, the Eagles looked around for a replacement. Five years of experience told them that personality would be as significant in their choice as musical ability. One name came to mind immediately, Timothy B. Schmit, nicknamed "Woodstock" for his laid-back hippie persona. He certainly had the right profile and had previously replaced Meisner when the latter left Poco.

Unlike the rest of the California-based Eagles circa 1976, Schmit was a native Californian, having grown up in Sacramento. His father had been a small-time musician and was happy with Schmit junior playing in bars at the tender age of fifteen. He joined a group in Sacramento, The New Breed, and played on the LA club and bar circuit in the mid-'60s. They released a single in 1965, "Green Eyed Woman," which was a minor local success, and recorded an album's worth of unreleased material (which would finally see the light of day in 2007 as *The New Breed Wants You*). Thinking that a name change would change their fortunes, they were rechristened Glad and attempted an album with another independent label—but nothing substantial transpired.

In the meantime Schmit had made a name for himself on the LA scene as a dependable bass player and auditioned for Poco, though he missed out to Randy Meisner. Meisner, of course, only stayed with Poco a year before jumping ship to work with Rick Nelson in his Stone Canyon Band. This time, Schmit. got the gig with Poco. However, when Glenn Frey called and asked him about joining the Eagles, he did not hesitate. "It was a twist of fate," says Schmit. "Think about it—I take Randy's place in Poco, then I get asked to replace him in the Eagles". His father's advice would come in handy over the next twenty years. "He told me 'I gotta tell you two things. The first is, don't get upset by press criticism. The second is never trust anyone in the business.'" Maybe Schmit would be able to survive the Eagles after all.

Schmit toured with the Eagles from July 1978. They had been gigging around the world for almost a year, enjoying sold-out shows in four different continents, and *Hotel California* had been number 1 almost everywhere they went.

Poco

Poco were one of country rock's most consistent and enduring outfits. They arose from the ashes of Buffalo Springfield in 1968. When Neil Young and Stephen Stills left the band in April '68, remaining members Jim Messina and Richie Furay oversaw the release of the third Buffalo Springfield album in as many years. This was the aptly titled *Last Time Around* (the first two were the rather unimaginatively titled *Buffalo Springfield* and *Buffalo Springfield Again*), which was released in July. Then they decided to form a new band. Steel guitar player Rusty Young had played on that

Springfield final album and he, George Grantham on drums, and Randy Meisner were recruited for a new group which was initially called Pogo. They debuted at the Los Angeles Troubadour club in November 1968.

Unfortunately Pogo was also the name of a well-known comic strip at the time, and the band was therefore prevented from using the name by the strip creator Walt Kelly, who filed a lawsuit against them. Changing just one letter to make themselves Poco, they signed a record deal with Epic in early

1969. Randy Meisner, however, left the band in order to play for Ricky Nelson's backing band at the invitation of producer John Boylan—before, of course, joining the Eagles.

Working as a four-piece, Poco released their debut album, *Pickin' Up the Pieces*, in summer 1969. The album was critically well received and it put the band on the rock and roll map. The original band was in fact one of the most exciting and pioneering live acts in late-1960s Los Angeles. Richie Furay and Jim Messina had, after all, been vital elements in the now legendary Buffalo Springfield. When they performed live, it was Rusty Young's idiosyncratic steel playing that gave the band an immediate edge and by 1970 they had perfected the soft rock, harmony vocals that would soon be taken to another level by the Eagles.

Meisner was replaced by Timothy B. Schmit (another future Eagle), who was on board for the recording and release of the band's second album, *Poco*.

Following the release of a live album, *Deliverin'*, which became the band's first to break into the Top 30 album chart, it was clear that Poco would be first and foremost a touring band. Jim Messina was not as keen on the idea as everyone else, and so left to become a studio producer for CBS (and to subsequently find success as a duo with Kenny Loggins). Paul Cotton from the Illinois Speed Press replaced Messina on the next album release, which was produced by Steve Cropper (*From the Inside*), but the hits were few and far between and—after both the 1972 release *A Good Feelin' to Know* and 1973's *Crazy Eyes* failed to sell in any large number—Richie Furay quit the band.

The Eagles, meanwhile, had just taken the charts by storm with the Jackson Browne-penned "Take It Easy," which was exactly the kind of song Furay was writing, but for some reason failing with. He joined J. D. Souther and ex-Byrd Chris Hillman to form a so-called supergroup, the imaginatively titled Souther Hillman Furay Band.

Poco continued through the 1970s with modest success, releasing eleven albums before bass player Timothy Schmit left to join the by then massively successful Eagles in 1977. Poco's next album, *Legend*, with Steve Chapman joining Young, Cotton, and bassist Charlie Harrison, was released at the end of 1978 and became their biggest selling album ever. A single, "Crazy Love," got as high as number 17 on the *Billboard* pop chart, making it far and away their biggest seller to date. However, their next few albums did not perform as well. Richie Furay rejoined his old pals briefly in 1984, with Schmit as a guest musician, and made the *Inamorata* album—which did even worse.

Poco decided to lay low for the next five years before trying their luck again in 1989 with a reasonably good album, *Legacy*, which made the Top 40. Moderate success followed in the 2000s when the band started to concentrate on website distribution and focused on keeping their large fan base happy. In 2002, they issued *Running Horse* through their website at www.poconut.com. They continue to be active.

Look What You've Done

By the end of the *Hotel California* tour the Eagles had ridden through the 1970s blazed in ever-increasing glory, with each album surpassing the last, and had become world superstars. They were rubbing shoulders with movie stars, politicians, and royalty—in public and private. But living in the bubble of the Eagles on the road through 1977, they became removed from the changes that were occurring rapidly in pop music. It wasn't just punk that was shaking things up; there was disco and a new concept in music marketing, the video. When Queen made a promotional film on videotape, rather than the more expensive cinefilm, for "Bohemian Rhapsody" in 1975, they unintentionally began a new age of music exploitation via television that would result in the creation of MTV, VH1, and CMT. After the success of "Bohemian Rhapsody," slowly at first, but increasingly as the decade drew to a close, bands felt that they had to be visual as well as audio performers.

Los Angeles was changing too. It had been ten years since the Beatles sang "All You Need Is Love" and Californians had tuned in, turned on, and dropped out. While the streets may have looked the same, the culture and attitude of California was far removed from that of 1967's summer of love.

The energy crisis of 1973 had slowed the U.S. economy, offering a warning that America could no longer live in splendid isolation. Watergate, the messy end of the Vietnam War, and the failure of the 1960s' ideals of peace, love, and harmony to alter American society for the better had left the younger generation feeling isolated and alienated. There was a definable sense of nihilism rising, in stark contrast to the naïve idealism of just a few years before. The pot-smoking camaraderie of the kaftan- and sandal-wearing hippies in Hollywood was quickly replaced by Day-Glo hair, torn leather, chains, and a new kind of music. Bands emerged out of nowhere inspired by the Ramones, Johnny Thunders, the Sex Pistols, and the Clash. None would be seen dead on stage in tee shirt, jeans, and sneakers, with long hair and playing guitar solos. Bands like the Bangs, the Dils, the Screamers, and the Weasels in Los Angeles and the Dead Kennedys and Negative Trend in San Francisco preferred something much harsher, more aggressive and artistic.

Above: Ticket stub from an Eagles concert at Miami Baseball Stadium, July 2, 1977.

Opposite: Poster from the Eagles' appearance in Oahu, Hawaii, alongside longtime supporter and friend, Jimmy Buffett.

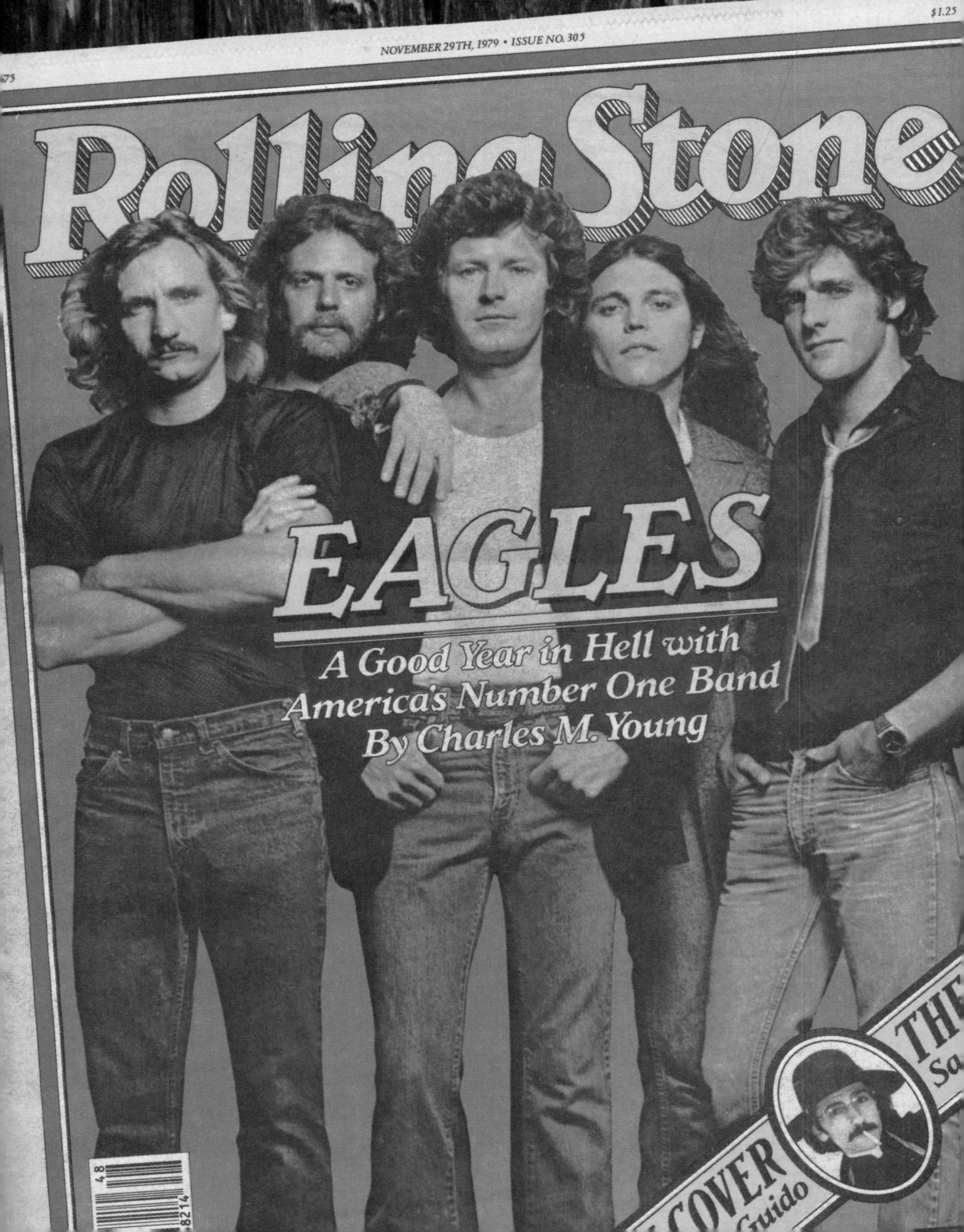
$1.25
NOVEMBER 29TH, 1979 • ISSUE NO. 305
Rolling Stone
EAGLES
A Good Year in Hell with
America's Number One Band
By Charles M. Young
THE
COVER

Just as the music revolution in the 1960s led to the flower-power migration to California, so the punk movement, ten years later, reverberated all around America. New York's CBGB was the epicenter, but LA and San Francisco were close behind. The media watched and responded; magazines switched editorial stances and embraced the new music. The punks threw scorn upon the naivety of the hippies and the word "hippie" became a favored insult.

At the same time that punk was taking a hold another youth explosion, disco, came out of the black and gay club scene of New York. Born from the early 1970s funk scene, the trend began with artists like Sylvester and Donna Summer mixing repetitive heavy beats with bass-laden dance music that was perfect for the glitzy, new-look clubs. When the Bee Gees offered their mainstream take on the genre with the soundtrack to *Saturday Night Fever* in 1977, disco became the rage around the world. More mainstream than punk, disco—or so it seemed for a while—threatened the very essence of rock and roll. Who needed guitar bands and years in a studio when a synthesizer could be played with two fingers and DJs could scratch their way to another 12" remix?

"The Eagles were incredible musicians, great harmonies and, you know, the songs we all loved in the 1970s."

TOM PETTY

How would the Eagles respond to disco, to new wave, and to the new challenge of making videos? When interviewed by *Rolling Stone* in the fall of 1979 in the bar of the Troubadour, Frey and Henley were in combative moods as a punk band from Ohio, Rubber City Rebels, blasted punk hits from the stage. "In '72, the punks had long hair and wore cowboy boots," said Henley. When the band on stage launched into the Sex Pistols' furiously antiestablishment "God Save the Queen," Henley scornfully looked across the bar at the band and mocked, "They don't look so tough, they look like dorks."

Side One OVER AND OVER SECOND HAND STORE INDIAN SUMMER AT THE STATION
Side Two TOMORROW INNER TUBE THEME FROM BOAT WEIRDOS LIFE'S BEEN GOOD
Produced by Bill Szymczyk, for Pandora Productions, Ltd. © 1978 AN ELEKTRA/ASYLUM Recording Distributed by WEA Records Ltd Ⓦ A Warner Communications Company
Printed and made by Garrod & Lofthouse Ltd.

But Seriously, Folks

Even after a year on the road, the restless guitarist Joe Walsh seemed
fresher than the jaded and exhausted Eagles. Not content to wait
around to record with the Eagles, he opted to capitalize on his new
found superstardom and record a solo album. *"But Seriously Folks . . ."*
was recorded early in 1978 and released in May that year. The album

**Above: The front and back cover
of *"But Seriously, Folks . . ."*. All the
other Eagles joined in the fun, which
provided a welcome relief from
their more serious band projects.**

did reasonably well, but the first single taken from it, "Life's Been Good," reached number 12 on the *Billboard* chart and made Walsh a pop star, not just an acclaimed guitarist. His sense of humor and zest for life were helping the Eagles remain intact, and all four contributed to his solo project, Felder with guitar and vocals and the rest on backing vocals.

Despite the pressures the band were under to match a mega successful album like *Hotel California*, and seemingly unaware of the deepening rift between Henley and Frey, Irving Azoff pushed ahead with plans for a follow-up album. The Eagles had become something of a cash cow for Asylum Records.

"The Eagles talked about breaking up from the day I met them. There'd be one mini-explosion followed by a replacement in the band, then another mini-explosion followed by another replacement. You just had to step back and give things time to calm down."

IRVING AZOFF

To give themselves time to regroup, the band went into the studio in late 1978 and recorded two Christmas tracks, "Please Come Home for Christmas" and "Funky New Year." It seemed an odd decision from a group who supposedly took themselves far too seriously. Humorously, the record company issued the single in a picture sleeve showing the five Eagles lounging around a palm tree–shaded swimming pool entertaining "ladies" while sitting next to a white artificial Christmas tree complete with wrapped holiday gifts. Walsh, always the joker, wears a snorkel and mask in a reference to the cover of his *"But Seriously, Folks . . ."* album, for which he had been photographed underwater (see previous page). The Eagles being the Eagles in 1978, the single charted in the Top 20, becoming the first Christmas song to chart that high for over twenty years.

Yet they couldn't put off the inevitable for too long, however much they prevaricated, and their sixth album, wittily entitled *The Long Run*, proved a painful album to make. They spent the best part of two years in the studio, either waiting for inspiration or working a song over and

EAGLES

VINYL BLANC

PLEASE COME HOME FOR CHRISTMAS
B/W FUNKY NEW YEAR

PRODUCED AND ENGINEERED BY BILL SZYMCZYK FOR PANDORA PRODUCTIONS LTD.

13145

WE 1 7 1

DISTRIBUTION : WEA FILIPACCHI MUSIC A WARNER COMMUNICATIONS COMPANY

DIRECTION: IRV AZOFF Art Direction and Design: Don Henley, Johnny Lee...

asylum

℗ & © 1978 Elektra/Asylum Records, 962 North La Cienega Boulevard, Los Angeles, Californ...

CHRISTMAS

over until it passed their test of by-now almost obsessive perfectionism. Whole songs would be taken apart and edited line by line, with words and notes patched in to make a finished song. As Joe Walsh would recall, "The *Hotel California* success made us very paranoid. People started asking us, 'What are you going to do now?' and we didn't know. We ended up on the next album in Miami with the tapes running, but nobody knowing what was going on. We lost perspective. We just kinda sat around in a daze for months."

The Long Run had more creative peaks and valleys than any previous Eagles album. The songs that worked, such as "Heartache Tonight," the title track, and "Sad Café," were as good as anything they had recorded. Unfortunately, despite Frey and Henley's avowed intent to avoid fillers, there were several below-standard songs on the finished release.

The band knew it, too, even if they weren't willing to admit that in 1979. Looking back on the process of making *The Long Run*, Don Henley said, "The romance had gone out of it for Glenn and me. I mean, *The Long Run* was not as good as *Hotel California*, and it was an excruciatingly painful album to make. We were having fights all the time about the songs—enormous fights about one word—for days on end. That record took three years and cost $800,000, and we burned out. I think we knew early on that fame was a fleeting thing. That's really what *Desperado* was all about: that you get up just to get torn down eventually, and that this is a fickle business. We knew we would all be hung sooner or later. Or we would hang ourselves. Also, we were growing in different directions, and there was a tremendous pressure on us after *Hotel California* to keep that commercial and creative momentum going. But you can't really do that again."

The Albums

The Long Run

Producer: Bill Szymczyk

Recorded: One Step Up Recording Studio, Los Angeles, CA; Love 'n' Comfort Recording Studio, Los Angeles, CA; Britannia Recording Studio, Los Angeles, CA; Record Plant Studios, Los Angeles, CA; and Bayshore Recording Studio, Coconut Grove, FL, March 1978 to September 1979

Label: Asylum Records

Released: September 1979

Chart position: U.S.A. Billboard pop albums #1

TRACKS

Side One
1. The Long Run
2. I Can't Tell You Why
3. In the City
4. The Disco Strangler
5. King of Hollywood

Side Two
1. Heartache Tonight
2. Those Shoes
3. Teenage Jail
4. The Greeks Don't Want No Freaks
5. The Sad Café

EAGLES
THE LONG RUN

Above: Don Felder and Joe Walsh
enjoying *The Long Run* tour.

"The Long Run" is a typical Henley song. The melody and harmonies
are pure Eagles, the lyrics romantic, and the production lush but
subtle, allowing Henley's vocals to dominate. Schmit proves himself
a more than adequate replacement for Meisner as both writer and
performer on "I Can't Tell You Why," and Joe Walsh shines on a
reworking of "In the City," which he had previously cut for the
Warriors movie soundtrack. "Heartache Tonight" was an obvious
single and a hit as soon as it was released. It's exactly the R&B sound
that Frey and Henley had been working towards and with Szymczyk's
Miami production stamped all over it, it proved that the Eagles could

move with the times and respond to new pop demands. With Henley dominating the previous album, Frey fights back with an impressive vocal, although it's his only chance to shine on the album with a solo performance. Frey called on old buddies J. D. Souther and Detroit hero Bob Seger for help writing the tune, and it's definitely one of Frey's finest moments.

Attempts to vary the Eagle menu stall and splutter, however, on "The Disco Strangler" and "King of Hollywood," both of which try too hard to be different and in doing so lose that Eagles essence that flowed so vibrantly through "Heartache Tonight."

Henley saves his best for last with the truly magnificent "Sad Café," on which he displays a sentimental yearning for the old days at the Troubadour. It's a song about the innocence of hopes and dreams and the sadness of those who miss out—as well as the sadness of those whose success doesn't match their dreams.

Can't Tell You Why

The cover artwork for *The Long Run* was suitably somber. There was no image, just a black background with lettering that made it look almost as if it were a tombstone. It was certainly a pointer to the end of the road. Reviews of the album on its release in September 1979 were mixed. Henley, acutely aware that the band was attempting to follow on from a truly classic album in the shape of *Hotel California*, was nervous about its critical reception. When the album was knocked in the *Village Voice* and *Rolling Stone*, Henley fired off letters attacking the critics, which did little to win the band friends in the press. But times had changed since *Hotel California*, and the press were now championing bands that they thought had more social relevance to the world than the California superstars. To them, *The Long Run* simply showed that the Eagles were running short on themes and ideas and had attempted to disguise some of the weaker songs with over-elaborate production work.

The public, of course, still loved the Eagles and rushed out in their millions around the globe to buy what would be the last Eagles album of the decade. On its release *The Long Run* entered the *Billboard* album chart at number 2, moving up a place the following week and remaining there until the end of November. In what had become the norm for the Eagles with the release of a new album, they embarked for another international tour, this time starting in Japan before heading back to America for their first Los Angeles show since 1976.

LA would be a special event, with three shows at the Los Angeles Forum in three days marketed as "The Eagles Come Home." Hollywood turned out in force and the band brought a series of special guests onto the stage with them, including Roy Orbison, Jackson Browne, and Elton John. They even had flavor-of-the-moment The Blues Brothers, John Belushi and Dan Aykroyd, who danced as the band played "The Greeks Don't Want No Freaks."

It was the perfect end to the year and to the decade for the Eagles. They had "owned" the 1970s and defined an era that would forever be associated with their easy-going, laid-back, country-flavored soft rock sound. *The Long Run* was a different kind of album to the rest, but it still topped the charts, was number 1 for thirteen weeks, went platinum in record time, and was the biggest selling album of the year.

But all was not well in the Eagles camp, as usual. Tensions that had existed to differing degrees over the past few years were exacerbated by another long stint on the road, and the band argued about everything from hotels and restaurant menus to which candidate to endorse in the 1980 presidential election. Henley was relieving his stress with more bouts of hedonism and, shortly after the band split, found himself in deep water when he was arrested after paramedics had to be called to attend to a sixteen-year-old female who had overdosed on drugs at a party at his LA home. Cocaine, marijuana, and Quaaludes were taken by the police. Henley was placed on probation. Recalling 1980 to the *LA Times* a couple of years later he commented, "It was a terrible year. The band broke up. I broke up with my girlfriend. I did a stupid thing and got into trouble with the law [cocaine arrest]. Then I met the girl I'm with now and we almost got killed in a [private] plane crash in Colorado. John Lennon got killed and that devastated me for a while."

The Eagles had tolerated and lived with pressure for five years, but as the decade passed, a new intensity to their disputes was threatening to break up the band. According to Frey, "Everything changed for me

Above: The Eagles are joined by Jackson Browne (second from left) in concert in March 1980. Four months later, the band would break up.

during *The Long Run*. There was so much pressure that Don and I didn't have time to enjoy our friendship. We always had to worry about doing this or living up to that. We could talk about girls or football for a while, but it wouldn't be long before we'd remember that we had to make a decision about this or that we had to get another song written for the next album."

Live On?

Not wanting to risk another two-year gap between recordings, Asylum Records decided to follow *The Long Run* with an Eagles live album release, culled mainly from live recordings from the 1979/1980 tour. If the record company thought that it was going to be any easier to put together a live release than another studio one, however, they were mistaken. The tour itself was fraught with difficulty, and looked as though it might not even be completed.

As well as playing straightforward album promotional gigs, the band had begun to make political appearances. The Eagles had long supported California Governor Jerry Brown with various benefit performances, partly because his liberal politics suited the majority of the band but also, and maybe more importantly, due to his ongoing

Above: The Eagles with Linda Ronstadt and California governor Jerry Brown. This was one of a number of benefit concerts for Brown that eventually caused friction within the band and played a part in their decision to break up.

romance with their old Troubadour friend Linda Ronstadt. However, Glenn Frey, having taken a liking to political candidate Alan Cranston, a liberal Democrat from California, committed the band to play a benefit concert on July 31, 1980 in Long Beach. It turned out not to be a good night. Frey felt that Felder had been disrespectful to Alan Cranston's wife before the show and Felder was tired of Frey's controlling attitude. They spent the gig trading insults and threats to such an extent that the sound desk turned down their microphones between songs. In Felder's version of events, when the concert ended the two Eagles went for each other but were calmed down. Showered and changed, Felder, enraged, walked out of the stadium towards their waiting cars and smashed an acoustic guitar against a column in frustration and anger. Standing right behind him were Glenn Frey and special guests Alan Cranston and wife.

Everyone involved knew that that night in Long Beach marked the end of the Eagles. They could no longer put the infighting down to creative tension. The band could barely tolerate each other. They traveled separately, stayed in different hotels, and only really communicated on stage and in the studio. The game was up and the on-stage fighting was the final straw. Of course the live album still had to be completed, so Henley and Frey finished the final mixes separately while living as far apart as they could—with Henley in Miami and Frey and the rest of the band back home in California. The tapes were couriered to Henley's house by producer Bill Szymczyk.

"We were exhausted, and we were sick and tired of each other. We needed a vacation, and we didn't get one. So we just flamed out."

DON HENLEY

At the end of the mixing process Glenn Frey called Henley and chatted about football and sports . . . before telling his writing partner that he was done with the Eagles. Henley was hardly surprised, though he was unsettled by the abruptness of the decision.

Frey was simply tired of the band. "I think my decision may have boiled down in the end to the fact that I just couldn't see myself spending all of the '80s making just three more Eagles albums . . . three albums that wouldn't be any fun. I needed to be more involved with music than that. I wanted to do solo albums and friends had been urging me to produce records. The idea of working on 50 pieces of music a year instead of struggling through three or four while dealing with all the other tensions and intrigues of being in the Eagles was just too appealing to ignore."

The management and record company behaved like a dumped spouse, regularly issuing statements of denial, claiming that the band were taking a sabbatical, that members were working on solo projects. Nobody could bear to announce that the Eagles were over. Joe Smith, then head of Asylum, offered the band a staggering two million dollars for some new songs for the live album. Frey said no.

Eagles Live was released in November 1980, just a month before the shocking death of John Lennon—an event that traumatized Henley into inertia and depression. The album, featuring songs recorded at the various Santa Monica concerts the year before, went to number 1 and yielded a modestly successful single, the band's previously unrecorded old warm-up song, "Seven Bridges Road."

The world had still not heard that the Eagles were no more. It wasn't until two years later in the spring of 1982 Glenn Frey put everyone out of their misery in interviews for his new solo album, *No Fun Aloud.* "I have no regrets," he said. The Eagles were no more.

In a parting shot at the press' bestowal of posterity on music and musicians of the past he continued, "A lot of people in the media attach more importance to bands that came out of the '60s than bands that came out of the '70s, so I don't know how the Eagles will be remembered. The '70s sort of got passed off as the decade that wasn't very important in music. Someday, though, I think people may look back and say, 'Some of that stuff was pretty good after all.'"

In the aftermath of the split Glenn Frey relaxed in California, healed his wounds as best he could, and made tentative plans for a solo album.

Below: One of the inner sleeves of the *Eagles Live* double album. Standing room only.

Joe Walsh headed back to the studio and the road while Schmit and Felder also began work on solo projects. Asylum Records offered each member of the band a solo deal. Felder surfaced first with his contributions to the soundtrack *Heavy Metal* in 1981. In interviews for the record, he stated that the Eagles were on hold waiting for Glenn Frey to come back to the fold. There was still hope, it seemed. Henley, however, was still traumatized, seemingly more than the others, and feeling the loss of the band like a bereavement.

The Albums

Eagles Live

Producer: Bill Szymczyk

Recorded: The Forum Los Angeles October 20–22, 1976; Santa Monica Civic Auditorium, July 27–29, 1980; and Long Beach Arena, July 31, 1980

Label: Asylum Records

Released: November 1980

Chart position: U.S.A. Billboard pop albums #6

TRACKS

Side One
1. Hotel California
2. Heartache Tonight
3. I Can't Tell You Why

Side Two
1. The Long Run
2. New Kid in Town
3. Life's Been Good

Side Three
1. Seven Bridges Road
2. Wasted Time
3. Take It to the Limit
4. Doolin-Dalton
5. Desperado

Side Four
1. Saturday Night
2. All Night Long
3. Life in the Fast Lane
4. Take It Easy

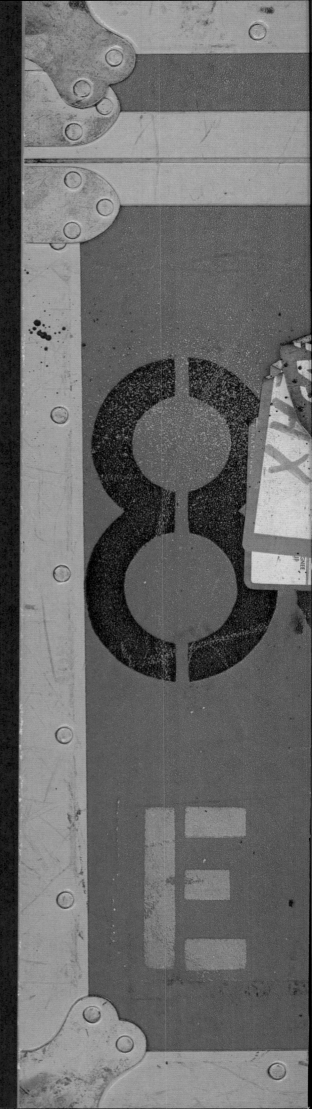

EAGLES LIVE

EAGLES

Side One:
HOTEL CALIFORNIA
HEARTACHE TONIGHT
I CAN'T TELL YOU WHY
Side Two
THE LONG RUN
NEW KID IN TOWN
LIFE'S BEEN GOOD
Side Three
SEVEN BRIDGES ROAD
WASTED TIME
TAKE IT TO THE LIMIT
DOOLIN-DALTON (REPRISE II)
DESPERADO
Side Four
SATURDAY NIGHT
ALL NIGHT LONG
LIFE IN THE FAST LANE
TAKE IT EASY

EAGLES LIVE

PRODUCED BY BILL SZYMCZYK
FOR PANDORA PRODUCTIONS LTD.

Live albums typically fall into one of two camps: either a "warts and all" capturing of an artist on one night or a series of live shows culled from several concert dates and cleaned up before release. Given the Eagles' predilection for perfection, it's hardly surprising that *Eagles Live* falls into the latter category. Taken from an assortment of live recordings from 1976 and 1980, the album is indistinguishable from a studio record, thanks to both the excellence of their on-stage work as well as some deft amendments completed in the studio before release. "Life's Been Good" checks in at a rollicking nine-plus minutes and, along with a majestic "Hotel California," is the outstanding performance. The surprises for Eagles fans on the live set are perhaps the dynamic vocal performance of Timothy B. Schmit on "I Can't Tell You Why" and certainly the previously un-recorded group harmony showcase on Steve Young's "Seven Bridges Road."

Above: The front and back cover artwork for *Eagles Live*.

Opposite and below: Pages from a 1980 tour program, with appropriate sign-off.

HOTEL CALIFORNIA July 29, I
Santa Monica Civic Auditor
HEARTACHE TONIGHT July 27
Santa Monica Civic Auditor
I CAN'T TELL YOU WHY July 2
Santa Monica Civic Auditor
THE LONG RUN July 27, 1980,
Santa Monica Civic Auditor
NEW KID IN TOWN October 2
The Forum, L.A.
LIFE'S BEEN GOOD July 29, 19
Santa Monica Civic Audito
SEVEN BRIDGES ROAD July 2
Santa Monica Civic Audito
WASTED TIME October 22, I
The Forum, L.A.
TAKE IT TO THE LIMIT
October 20, 1976, The Foru

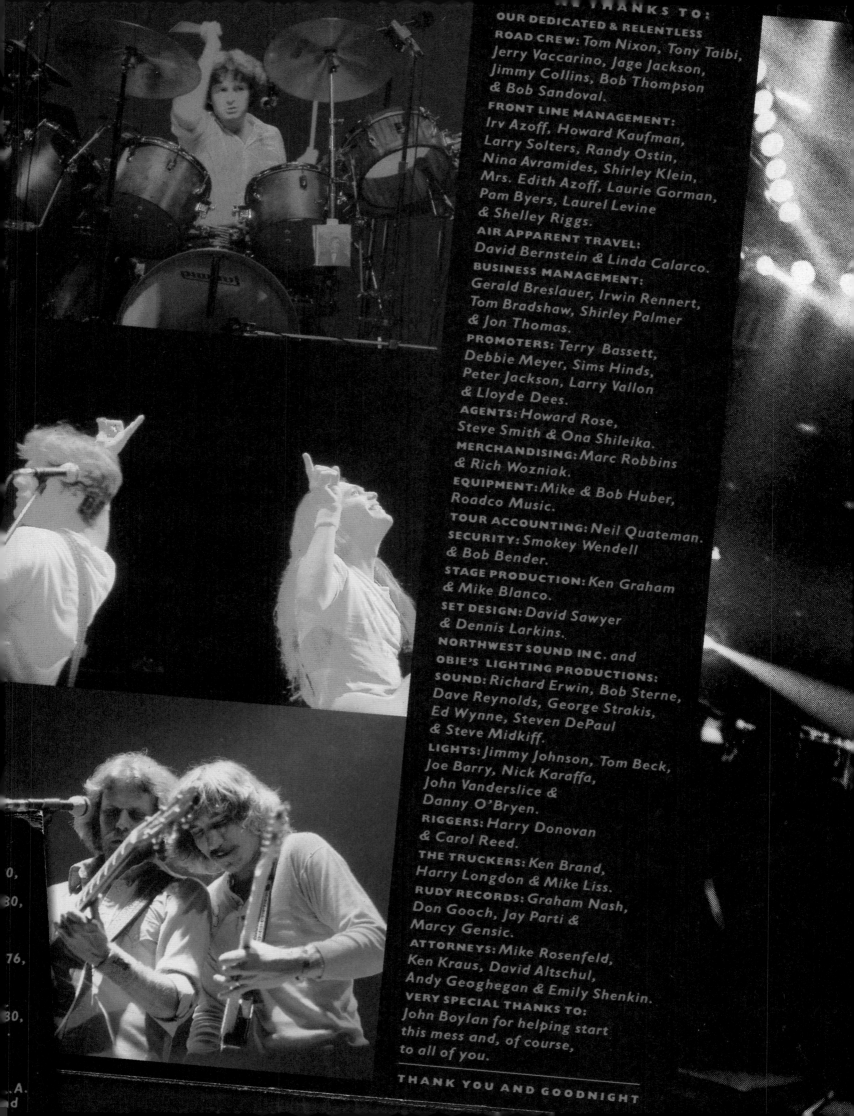

THANKS TO:

OUR DEDICATED & RELENTLESS
ROAD CREW: Tom Nixon, Tony Taibi,
Jerry Vaccarino, Jage Jackson,
Jimmy Collins, Bob Thompson
& Bob Sandoval.
FRONT LINE MANAGEMENT:
Irv Azoff, Howard Kaufman,
Larry Solters, Randy Ostin,
Nina Avramides, Shirley Klein,
Mrs. Edith Azoff, Laurie Gorman,
Pam Byers, Laurel Levine
& Shelley Riggs.
AIR APPARENT TRAVEL:
David Bernstein & Linda Calarco.
BUSINESS MANAGEMENT:
Gerald Breslauer, Irwin Rennert,
Tom Bradshaw, Shirley Palmer
& Jon Thomas.
PROMOTERS: Terry Bassett,
Debbie Meyer, Sims Hinds,
Peter Jackson, Larry Vallon
& Lloyde Dees.
AGENTS: Howard Rose,
Steve Smith & Ona Shileika.
MERCHANDISING: Marc Robbins
& Rich Wozniak.
EQUIPMENT: Mike & Bob Huber,
Roadco Music.
TOUR ACCOUNTING: Neil Quateman.
SECURITY: Smokey Wendell
& Bob Bender.
STAGE PRODUCTION: Ken Graham
& Mike Blanco.
SET DESIGN: David Sawyer
& Dennis Larkins.
NORTHWEST SOUND INC. and
OBIE'S LIGHTING PRODUCTIONS:
SOUND: Richard Erwin, Bob Sterne,
Dave Reynolds, George Strakis,
Ed Wynne, Steven DePaul
& Steve Midkiff.
LIGHTS: Jimmy Johnson, Tom Beck,
Joe Barry, Nick Karaffa,
John Vanderslice &
Danny O'Bryen.
RIGGERS: Harry Donovan
& Carol Reed.
THE TRUCKERS: Ken Brand,
Harry Longdon & Mike Liss.
RUDY RECORDS: Graham Nash,
Don Gooch, Jay Parti &
Marcy Gensic.
ATTORNEYS: Mike Rosenfeld,
Ken Kraus, David Altschul,
Andy Geoghegan & Emily Shenkin.
VERY SPECIAL THANKS TO:
John Boylan for helping start
this mess and, of course,
to all of you.

THANK YOU AND GOODNIGHT

7
Solo Years

B Y THE TIME that they had finally called it a day as a band, solo careers must have seemed positively relaxing to all the Eagles. The offer of a solo album deal from Asylum arrived as each member of the band was attempting recovery from the conflict, animosity, and fighting the Eagles had suffered for the best part of a year. It wasn't going to be easy for any of them, beginning a new decade not only as a former member of the previous decade's bestselling act but having to carry a new project entirely by himself. The Eagles had been cocooned in a super-band environment for ten years and if something

Below: Glenn Frey's first solo album release, *No Fun Aloud*. The white suit would become a staple of the Frey solo years.

Opposite: The back cover and inner sleeve artwork for *No Fun Aloud*.

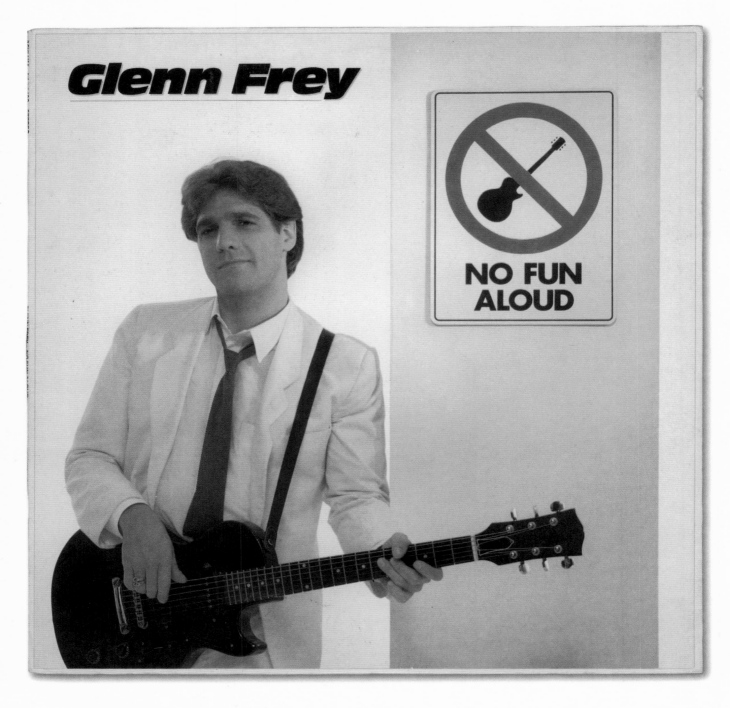

went wrong, or they failed to impress the critics—or, God forbid, the public—there was always somebody else in the group to blame. The release of albums made on their own into what had become a very unpredictable and fickle pop music market was a daunting prospect. Their fame could work for and against them. As the unofficial sixth Eagle, J. D. Souther put it, "Probably it helps if you do have name recognition. But it also makes it more difficult because this is such a youth oriented culture. Everyone wants something that's new. It's a double-edged sword."

Glenn Frey was the first of the big two to release a solo album in May 1982, beating Henley by almost three months. *No Fun Aloud* had Glenn Frey smiling on the cover (which was a radical departure from Eagles albums). He is wearing a white sports coat and tie, looking like the star of the soon-to-be-hugely-successful series *Miami Vice*. There was no doubt about his intention to shake off the California cowboy image. Here he was, clean shaven, looking almost suave in a South Beach way, ready to hop onto a boat to Cuba for a night at the casino. Musically, Frey chose to make a complete break with his country rock past. It must have been tempting to ride the Eagles' sound a little longer, play it safe, and slide gently into the 1980s as a solo act sounding like the hugely successful band he'd just left. But having fought all those years for the freedom to add some soul and Detroit-style R&B to the Eagles mix, Frey stuck by his convictions

Above and opposite: Don Henley's first solo offering, *I Can't Stand Still*. The matches reappear on Glenn Frey's later release, *The Allnighter*.

and delivered a soulful record that was at times reminiscent of the Bee Gees' Miami sound in its electronic production style.

The album was looser and less perfect in its production values than anything the Eagles had recorded. "After spending a year and a half on *The Long Run*, recording was not fun for me," explained Frey when *No Fun Aloud* was released. "I got to the point where I was like a kid who doesn't want to go to school. You can sure sleep in the morning when you don't want to get up. When I had that attitude about the studio, there was something wrong and I had to correct that. So the

way I corrected it was just by starting to do other records and recording more the way I think Rock 'n' Roll records should be made: faster, but still real good. I don't think I'm compromising quality. I just don't think every single note has to be perfect."

For assistance with the creative process Frey teamed up with old writing partner and creator of "Peaceful Easy Feeling" Jack Tempchin, who collaborated with him on five songs. The new material could hardly compete with Frey's greatest moments over an almost ten-year run with the Eagles, but the first single, "The One You Love," rose to number 15 on the singles chart and helped establish Frey as, if not exactly a solo star, then at least an act with a chance of building a new career.

No Standing Still

Don Henley meanwhile recharged his batteries by moving back to Texas for a while, where he teamed up with session guitarist and songwriter Danny Kortchmar. If Frey wanted to be a solo act, then Henley would too. He was "inspired" to make a solo album by his former partner's offhand way of informing him that they'd be working apart. As he explained it, "Glenn called up one day and told me that he wanted to go and do some recording on his own. It was a casual conversation that started out being about football and then he interjected that he wanted to go do something on his own. He didn't necessarily mean by that that he wanted to break the group up but it pissed me off so bad, because I always thought in my mind that when the group broke up, we'd all get in the room together and get good and drunk and sort of cry on each other's shoulders and say, 'Well it was great and I love you and we're gonna just quit now.' He didn't mean to do it that abrupt a way but it was too painful for him to do it any other way. He just sorta had to whip it out like that. I understand it now, but at the time it pissed me off. I just said to myself, 'Well, if he's going to make an album, I'm going to make an album, too!'"

Henley had enjoyed some non-Eagles single success in 1981 when his duet with ex-girlfriend Stevie Nicks of Fleetwood Mac, "Leather and Lace," made the pop singles Top 10. A year after that Henley released his debut solo album, *I Can't Stand Still*. Like Frey, Henley attempted to remove himself from the old Eagles sound, although he didn't go quite as far as Frey, opting instead to bring the sound up to date with state-of-the-art synthesizers and drum machines. The album's success was driven by an Eagles-style song, the hit single "Dirty Laundry," in which he addresses concerns with celebrity culture.

"I watch the news a lot. National news, local news; I got tired of these talking heads up there stripping people of their dignity," he explained to MTV in 1990. "I got tired of the sensationalism of the death of certain celebrities—John Belushi, Natalie Wood, Marilyn Monroe, Elvis. I just got sick of reporters running up to some grieving Mexican

Opposite: Joe Walsh having fun again with his album cover artwork. Behind the scenes, however, Walsh was increasingly battling with drink problems.

woman down in the barrio whose child had just got shot in a gang fight and saying how do you feel about that—that is the most absurd question you could ask."

The Other Side

Joe Walsh was a reasonably successful solo artist before joining the Eagles so he knew about the pressures of going solo. While the Eagles disintegrated, Walsh's excessive drinking, which had begun when his

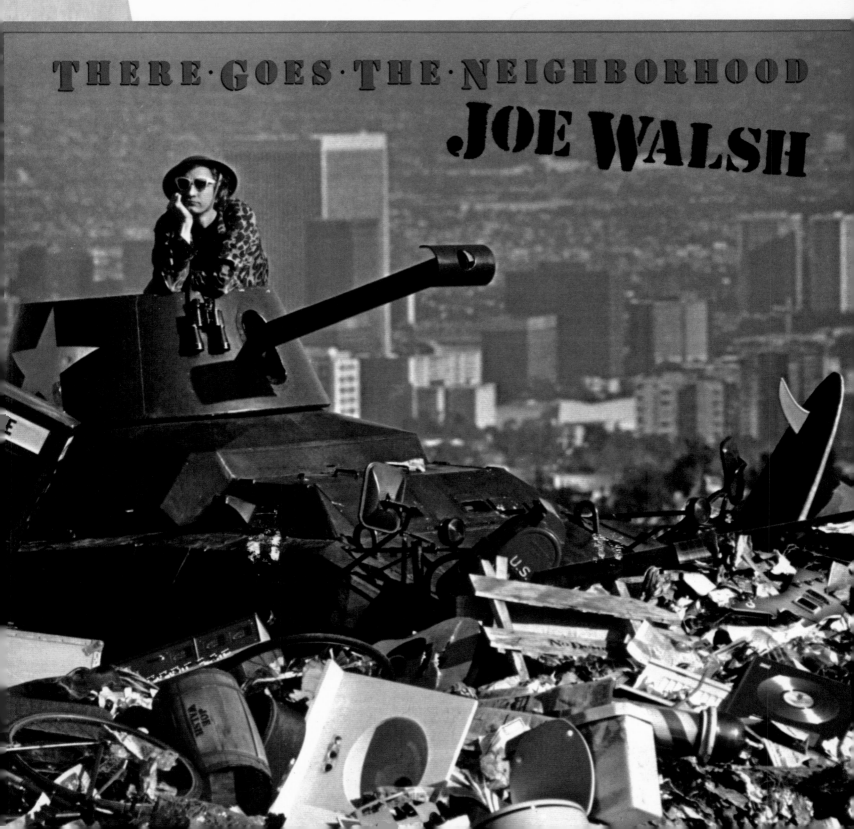

young daughter was tragically killed by a drunk-driver in 1974, became more extreme. He tried a couple of solo albums with *There Goes the Neighborhood* in 1981 and *You Bought It, You Name It* in 1983. But he was clearly in bad shape and seemed to be going through the motions.

> # "I mean, there was a whole long period of being an alcoholic, when I didn't pursue any hobby other than vodka. I like to say I only got drunk once—for thirty years."
>
> **JOE WALSH**

In 1989, Walsh joined up with Ringo Starr's All-Starr Band and recorded an *MTV Unplugged* that same year. Concerts with The Doobie Brothers in 1991 were largely a shambles as he slurred and forgot his words. His 1992 album *Songs for a Dying Planet* quickly vanished into obscurity.

Don Felder, although the target of much of the latter-day animosity from the head Eagles, was devastated by the breakup of the band. A working musician most of his life, he got back in the studio quickly and contributed a song to the soundtrack of the movie *Heavy Metal* and then accepted the solo record deal offered by Warner. He built a studio in his house to record what would become his only solo album. *Airborne*, unfortunately, was a typical sideman's project. It exhibited an incredibly high standard of musicianship but lacked the star quality that Frey and Henley were able to conjure up, even under trying circumstances.

Instead of coming out of the solo gates with an album, Timothy B. Schmit, the quietest, newest, and least well-known Eagle, chose to go back to session and touring work as a musician. He recorded with Crosby, Stills and Nash, Boz Scaggs, Bob Seger, and even Don Henley,

Timothy B. Schmit

Randy Meisner

as well as touring with rock star friends like Jimmy Buffett and Warren Zevon. He did contribute "So Much in Love" to the *Fast Times at Ridgemont High* soundtrack, a project that several ex-Eagles worked on thanks to their friendship with writer Cameron Crowe, the former *Rolling Stone* roving reporter.

In 1983 Schmit felt ready to embark on a solo career and produced the jazzy and mellow *Playin' It Cool*, which was released in 1984. Nothing much surfaced by way of singles or radio play and Schmit went back to

Above: Randy Meisner's eponymous debut album, one of two self-titled albums released by the Eagles bassist.

Below: Bernie Leadon teamed up with Michael Georgiades and released *Natural Progressions* in 1977.

sideman work, licked his wounds, and tried again in 1987 with *Timothy B.*, a better record than his debut, and one that delivered a number 26 single, "Boys Night Out."

Randy Meisner faced problems similar to those of other former Eagles, although he left of his own choice rather than seeing the group collapse around him. Once he had the Eagles out of his system he recorded solo album *Randy Meisner* in 1978, which did very little. As the Eagles were beginning to seriously fall apart, Meisner reached out to Don Henley to help him on his next solo attempt, *One More Song*, released in 1980. Henley decided he would contribute to his former colleague's project. Soon Meisner was back on the charts, first with a duet with Kim Carnes, "Deep Inside My Heart," which reached number 22 on the *Billboard* singles chart, and then with the impressive and catchy "Hearts on Fire," which made number 14 early in 1981. Unfortunately, Meisner was unable to use that promising start to establish himself as a *bona fide* solo act. His next album, also called *Randy Meisner*, failed to live up to expectations and he went back to session and touring work as a musician. Meisner did return to the limelight but only briefly in 1989, when he rejoined Poco for the *Legacy* album from which "Call It Love" was a minor hit single.

Always ready to team up with others from the old days, Meisner tried the Meisner-Roberts Band in 1987, with ex-Firefall member Rick Roberts. Then there was Black Tie, formed in 1992 with Sun rocker-turned-country-crooner Charlie Rich, Billy "I Can Help" Swan, and Jimmy Griffin, once of soft-rockers Bread. Again, Meisner found only modest success.

The always independent-minded Bernie Leadon had been the first to leave the Eagles and, after a lengthy recuperation in Hawaii, he went back to country music. His first post-Eagles album was a dual recording with Michael Georgiades, *Natural Progressions*, in 1977. Leadon preferred life behind the scenes, producing records for alternative folk acts like Michelle Shocked and teaming up with old music buddies when the mood took him. He played for a while with the Nitty Gritty Dirt Band, plucked banjo for Eagles sound-alike country band Restless Heart, and in the 1990s formed the tongue-in-cheek country outfit called Run C&W that gave a bluegrass spin to modern country. With

GLENN FREY

SEXY GIRL

From the MCA LP, MCF 3232, "THE ALLNIGHTER"

Produced by: BARRY BECKETT, GLENN FREY, and ALLAN BLAZEK for N.F.

Opposite: Glenn Frey's single, "Sexy Girl," showing typically eighties artwork.

Bernie, Jim Photoglo, Vince Melamed, and ex-Amazing Rhythm Aces Russell Smith taking on characters for the project—Crashen Burns, Wash Burns, Side Burns, and Rug Burns—they spoofed mainstream country for a couple of years before disbanding in 1995.

Smuggler's Blues

With both Frey and Henley receiving positive reactions to their first solo attempts, the next task for each was to consolidate and build. They were starting over, and two names from the Eagles' early days would once again surface and play significant roles in the next stage of a solo career for both men: David Geffen and Irving Azoff.

Frey was not happy with the Warner Brothers organization in 1983. The label had changed since the glory days of the Eagles and he was no longer considered a priority act. Fortuitously, old Eagles manager Irving Azoff was about to change all that.

On April 27, 1982, MCA announced that Irving Azoff had been made President of the MCA Record Group and Vice President of MCA Inc. Competitive to the core, he was well aware that David Geffen had caused quite a stir with Geffen Records and was determined to make his mark on a similar scale. Azoff being Azoff of course, he made more than a mark and in just a few years turned MCA from a struggling dinosaur into one of the most powerful labels in the music business, diversifying into concert promotion, venue management, and merchandising in the process.

When Asylum decided that they weren't sure about the tracks they heard from Frey's second solo album, *The Allnighter*, Frey immediately made an appointment to see Azoff at MCA. The new big boss man loved the idea of doing what Asylum could not and breaking Frey big time as a solo artist. The deal was done and the album came out promptly in June 1984. Remarkably, the first single "Sexy Girl" went to number 20 on the pop charts. But that was nothing—Frey was about to hit the big time.

A new cop show, *Miami Vice*, had become the latest TV phenomenon in America and around the world. Filmed in exotic locales around South Beach, Miami, the show's fast-paced action scenes and particularly the two dashing leads, Don Johnson and Philip Michael Thomas, dressed in trademark Armani jackets and t-shirts, revolutionized television and changed men's fashion in the mid-1980s. Nobody ever thought to explain how a vice cop could afford to drive a Ferrari or why he would wear numerous Armani, Boss, and Versace outfits while tracking criminals on the back streets of Miami, but it didn't really matter; this was a triumph of style over substance writ large and *Miami Vice* was all about style, fashion, and music.

As much a part of the new music TV scene along with video-only station MTV, *Miami Vice* allied itself with the record business by featuring new acts and releases to such a degree that the *USA Today* newspaper went to the lengths of listing which music acts were to be featured on the following episode every week. The program proved to be a global showcase for the top acts of the day, from Phil Collins to Tina Turner, Peter Gabriel, The Police, Depeche Mode, Iron Maiden—the list goes on and on. The show's soundtrack by Jan Hammer was everywhere at the time and even went to number 1 and won a couple of Grammy awards (in 1986).

Michael Mann, producer and creator of *Miami Vice*, liked Frey's "Smuggler's Blues," the follow-up single to "Sexy Girl," and set up a meeting with the ex-Eagle.

Opposite: The stars of *Miami Vice*, Don Johnson and Philip Michael Thomas, sporting their signature Armani suits.

Below: "Smuggler's Blues," the song that first attracted the attention of *Miami Vice* producer Michael Mann.

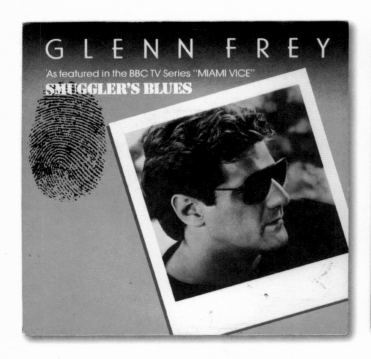

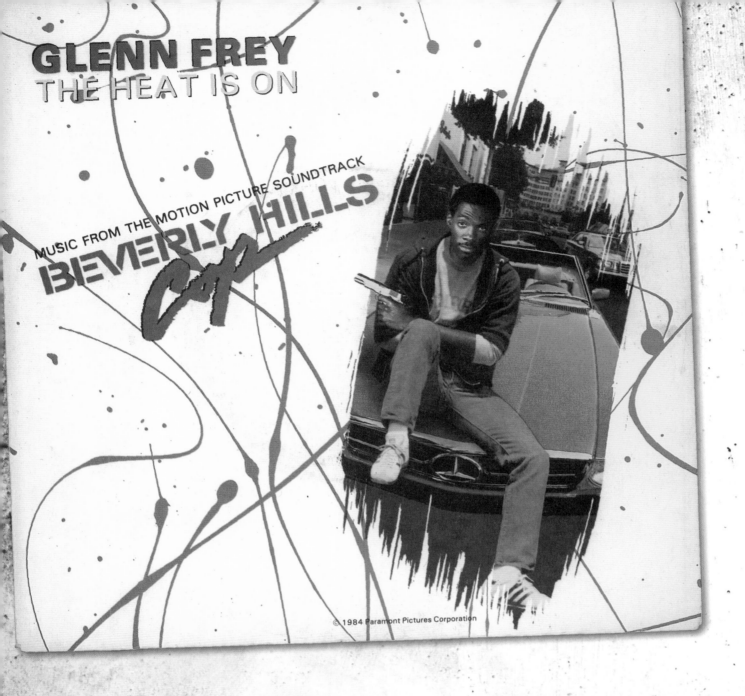

GLENN FREY
THE HEAT IS ON

MUSIC FROM THE MOTION PICTURE SOUNDTRACK
BEVERLY HILLS COP

© 1984 Paramont Pictures Corporation

"I was contacted when I was filming the video for 'Smuggler's Blues,'
recalled Frey. "*Miami Vice* was filming its first episode and they wanted
to get the show somehow involved in the video. Something like a
badge that said *Miami Vice* being flashed around or starting the video
with the camera locked on a black file cabinet labeled *Miami Vice*.
Then they offered footage from the show, but, in the end, we were too
rushed to work out the details and passed on involving them in the
video in any way. After we finished the shoot, Michael Mann called
and wanted to have lunch. I'd never met Michael Mann in person, so I
went the blue-suit routine—full Wall Street. I'm sitting at the bar
in Le Dome, awaiting the arrival of the executive producer of *Miami
Vice*, and in walks this guy in white Levi's, sandals, and a Hawaiian
shirt. I wore a suit so he wouldn't think I was a rock 'n' roll weirdo.

Above and opposite: The front and
back covers of Glenn Frey's "The Heat
is On" single, showing the young star
of *Beverly Hills Cop*, Eddie Murphy.

Boy, did I figure this guy wrong. Michael sat down with me, never asked me if I could act, and explained to me his concept of an episode based on 'Smuggler's Blues.' 'You're going to play this guy Jimmy, and you'll be great.'"

Frey solved the visual anonymity dilemma facing all the Eagles by acting in an international television program. After it aired, he was a household name in his own right. And then he recorded Harold Faltermeyer's "The Heat Is On" for the soundtrack of the Eddie Murphy movie *Beverly Hills Cop*.

The song was a massive hit all around the world and went to number 2 on the U.S. *Billboard* chart in March 1985. Frey had somehow transformed himself from mustachioed country rock singer in denim, torn jeans, and cowboy boots into a slick, 1980s Armani-loving man about town.

The Albums

The Allnighter

Producers: Glenn Frey and Allen Blazek

Recorded: Wilder Bros., Santa Monica, CA; Caribou Studios, Colorado; and Muscle Shoals Sound, Sheffield, Alabama, August 1983–March 1984

Label: Asylum Records

Released: June 1984

Chart position: Billboard album chart #22

TRACKS

Side One

1. The Allnighter
2. Sexy Girl
3. I Got Love
4. Somebody Else
5. Lover's Moon

Side Two

1. Smuggler's Blues
2. Let's Go Home
3. Better in the U.S.A.
4. Living in Darkness
5. New Love

DON
henley

BUILDING

THE

PERFECT

BEAST

Perfect Beast

When David Geffen had left the Eagles in the lurch (at least that's how it seemed to Henley, Frey, Leadon, and Meisner) and taken control of the Warner Elektra Atlantic empire, he was still in an ambitious frame of mind. Geffen, flushed with success, went after the biggest scalp of early 1970s pop music, Bob Dylan.

After much wining and dining Geffen signed Bob Dylan to Elektra/ Asylum in 1973 and, pulling out all his promotional stops, gave Dylan his first ever number 1 album, *Planet Waves*. The maverick Dylan however returned to his longtime record company Columbia for his next project, *Blood on the Tracks*. Perhaps jaded by the decision, Geffen accepted an offer to head Warner's film division. It was a short-lived career move since Geffen quit the entertainment business in 1976 when he was diagnosed with bladder cancer (a misdiagnosis, as it transpired) and returned to New York. Living in semi-retirement, he taught business classes at Yale.

However, Geffen bounced back when he discovered that he was in fact completely healthy and wanted to make a comeback in the record business. After accepting an advance of $25 million from Steve Ross at Warner Brothers, Geffen formed Geffen Records in 1980. Realizing he was no longer the man on the street who could spot new talent, he took a backseat, hired some good young A&R (artist and repertoire) personnel, and planned overall strategies from his lavish office. While the label scoured the clubs for new talent, Geffen won the company valuable press attention and media profile by drawing up a wish list of some heavyweight names, including John Lennon, Elton John, Joni Mitchell and, surprisingly, Don Henley. He would sign all of them.

Don Henley, like Glenn Frey, was not happy at Asylum. The label's old guard had gone and he did not feel important to them, despite performing well with his first album. Azoff had understood back in the early days of the Eagles that artists needed to feel valued and significant in their organization. Henley did not feel any of those things and when Geffen, back to his dynamic and sweet-talking best, pumped up the former superstar and wooed him, Henley jumped ship and released his next album *Building the Perfect Beast* in November 1984 on Geffen. The album was a success on every level with four hits: "All She Wants to

Do Is Dance," "Not Enough Love in the World," "Sunset Grill," and the powerful "The Boys Of Summer." The last put Henley back on the map as a serious artist and won him recognition at the 1986 Grammy Awards where he received nominations for Record of the Year, Song of the Year, and Producer of the Year. He walked away with a Grammy for Best Rock Vocal for "The Boys of Summer."

The track, co-written with Mike Campbell from Tom Petty's band, took the best of the Eagles free-flowing sound and lashed it to a contemporary beat. Henley's best vocal performance in years combined with tasteful guitars and the then in-vogue synthesizers beautifully evoke a sense of nostalgia and disappointment with the past.

If Frey could master the video age then so could Henley, who produced one of the most progressive and charismatic music videos of the early MTV era for "The Boys of Summer" and won the Video of the Year Award at the 1985 MTV Video Music Awards.

"That's what the last verse of 'The Boys of Summer' was about. I think our intentions were good, but the way we went about it was ridiculous. We thought we could change things by protesting and making firebombs and growing our hair long and wearing funny clothes. But we didn't follow through. After all our marching and shouting and screaming didn't work, we withdrew and became yuppies and got into the Me Decade."

DON HENLEY

Above: Glenn Frey and Don Henley
making a decent show of unity at the
MTV Awards in 1985. Thoughts of a
reunion were still far from their minds,
however, if not their manager's.

End Of Innocence

Frey may have stolen Henley's thunder in the short term, but his
Miami Vice–inspired fame proved brief. The TV show burned brightly
but dimmed quickly. Once the show lost its place on the cool register,
anything connected with *Miami Vice* looked dated. Frey was offered a
lead role in a movie in 1986, an adventure romp called *Let's Get Harry*,
but it was hardly a memorable or successful film. He was later offered
a lead in his own TV action series, *South of Sunset*, but that only had
a one-episode run. He did better in a smaller role in Cameron Crowe's
Jerry McGuire, a full ten years later, playing the manager of a football

team. Commercials worked better for Frey, as a performer and music composer. He starred in a Pepsi commercial with Don Johnson from *Miami Vice* in 1986 before turning to commercials for gyms, and, soon, the newly buff Frey was seen modeling ski wear in *Rolling Stone*.

There were no such trivial pursuits for Henley of course; he was saving the end of the 1980s for his best solo album yet. It put his past well behind him, and saw him accepted as a legitimate and significant solo artist. The album was 1989's *The End of the Innocence*, a record that contained several hits like "The Heart of the Matter," "The Last Worthless Evening," and "New York Minute." But it was the haunting title track that changed perceptions around the world and won Henley the Best Rock Vocal Grammy. Taking five years to produce after *Building the Perfect Beast*, this was Henley in serious and reflective mood. The social commentator who developed his observer's pen through the Eagles years was now capable of thoughtful, challenging, and exceptionally literate rock music. Musically it's a treat, more guitars and fewer synthesizers and some complex vocal arrangements, including background work from gospel vocal outfit Take 6 and rock and roll wild man Axl Rose.

In 1989 Henley, relaxing at home after a tiring tour in support of *The End of the Innocence* album, caught a TV news report that Walden Woods in Concord and Lexington, Massachusetts, the idyllic space inhabited by Thoreau for two years while writing *Walden*, was threatened by developers.

"I was appalled when I first heard that the place was in danger. You assume that these places are protected," Henley told Paul Verna of *Billboard* at the end of 1996. Henley began a campaign to save the site. "I've done this for two reasons," he told Verna. "One, because Ralph Waldo Emerson and Thoreau had an impact on me as a young man, when my father was dying and I was trying to figure out what life and death meant, and struggling to make sense of my life and become a songwriter. And two, because I've been very successful and fortunate in my career, and I do not want my life and career to be defined only in terms of taking. I want it to be said that I gave as good as I got, which I think is a duty of every individual."

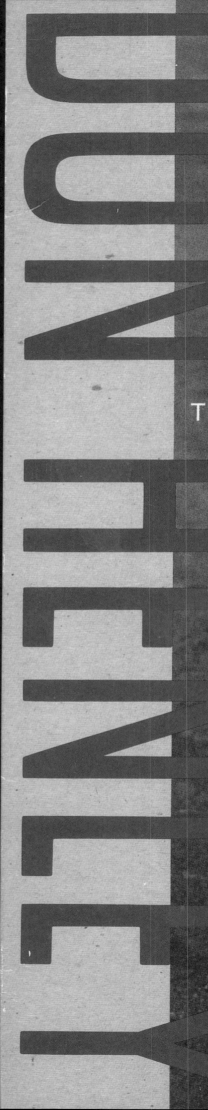

The End of the Innocence

Producers: Don Henley, Danny Kortchmar, Greg Ladanyi, Mike Campbell, John Corey, Bruce Hornsby, and Stan Lynch

Recorded: Los Angeles, CA 1987–1989

Label: Geffen Records

Released: June 1989

Chart position: U.S. Billboard album chart #8

TRACKS

1. The End of the Innocence
2. How Bad Do You Want It
3. I Will Not Go Quietly
4. The Last Worthless Evening
5. New York Minute

6. Shangri-La
7. Little Tin God
8. Gimme What You Got
9. If Dirt Were Dollars
10. The Heart of the Matter

GEFFEN RECORDS

STEREO GEMA/BIEM SIDE ONE

DON HENLEY
THE END OF THE INNOCENCE

924 217-1
WX 253

The Eagles

OF THE INNOCENCE

DON HENLEY

The Voice

of Hotel California,

One of these nights, Dirty

Laundry and the Boys of

Summer returns with a

brand new album of

ten songs.

THE END OF THE INNOCENCE

on CD Cassette and LP

Henley's project worked by buying up land before developers could get hold of it, relying on donations and fundraising in order to do so. Henley co-edited a collection of environmental essays entitled *Heaven Is Under Our Feet* with rock writer Dave Marsh. Proceeds from the book along with money donated by celebrity colleagues helped fund the project's initiatives. The rest of the Eagles later gave money in the form of part of the *Hell Freezes Over* reunion tour profits. At Henley's behest, Elton John, Sting, The Police, and Jimmy Buffett raised money through benefit gigs and the country music community chipped in with a sizeable chunk from the triple platinum *Common Thread* album.

As for the music business, that would take a backseat as Henley attempted to get out of his deal with Geffen and make a clean start after Geffen sold the company to MCA. His creative energies lay with the Walden Woods Project for which he opened an office in Boston, devoting himself to fundraising. Manager Irving Azoff recognized Henley's passion and thought that if he could just get Glenn Frey along to a Walden Woods benefit concert in Worcester Centrum, he could at least get the two men to think about working together again. That Frey would take part and help his ex-colleague was an exciting development for Azoff, who was still offered crazy money deals for an Eagles reunion tour. But money wasn't everything, even for the business savvy Eagles; music needed to play a part in any talks of a reunion. It was an unexpected rebirth in Eagles music that would finally bring about what they simply referred to as a resumption of the Eagles' career.

8
Back in the Saddle

B Y THE MIDDLE of the 1990s American music had reached a new and interesting place. Country music had slumped into a sickly swamp of rhinestone-encrusted mawkishness and kitsch in the 1970s, with countless records being made that sounded just like all the others, selling plentifully—but only to pure country music fans. At the end of the 1980s, however, a new influx of singer-songwriters including Lyle Lovett, Nanci Griffith, Steve Earle, Dwight Yoakam, and a lesbian vegetarian from Canada named k.d. lang brought tremendous change and effectively revolutionized the genre. This wave of New Country (as it was predictably named by marketing men and repeated by lazy journalists) took the sound of fiddles, pedal steel, twanging vocals, and soaring harmonies to a new audience of rock and pop fans—an audience which had perhaps once been into the Eagles.

Then, at the beginning of the 1990s a new sensation in country music took the sound of Nashville all around the world, and did so by playing incendiary live gigs and making cinematic promo videos: Garth Brooks dragged country music with a kick, a yelp, and a guitar solo towards the new millennium. He did it using a rock and roll approach, a theatrical stage show, and a music style not a million miles away from that of the California country rock bands of the 1970s.

Opposite: Trisha Yearwood with partner Garth Brooks, who was at the forefront of the rejuvenation of country music in the 1990s and whose records owed much to the Eagles' country rock sound of two decades earlier.

"I grew up on Dan Fogelberg, the Eagles and Billy Joel. That's what we listened to in high school and college. That was American music to us. Those Eagles songs were where country music is right now."

GARTH BROOKS

By 1993, country music was riding high on the hog. In September 1991, Brooks, a media graduate from Oklahoma, released *Ropin' the Wind*

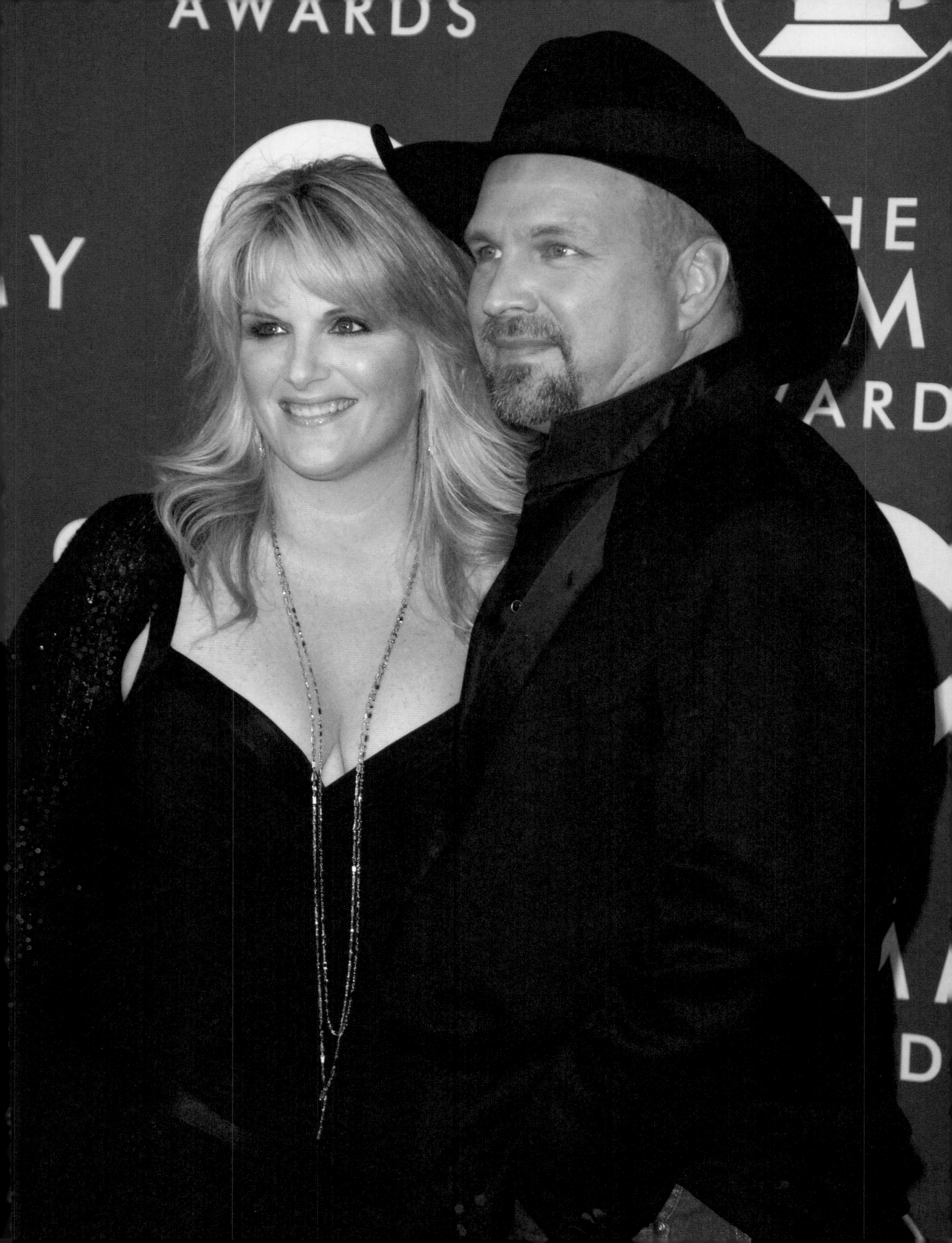
AWARDS

and it immediately went to the number 1 spot across all music genres.
The music industry had never seen anything like it. In September 1992
his follow-up release, *The Chase*, sold almost half a million copies in its
first week of sale. This was more than a one-off anomaly. It was hugely
surprising to the music business—after all, Nashville was supposed to
be a cottage industry, the sometimes embarrassing hillbilly cousin of

Los Angeles or New York which plodded along making music for the country folks but never challenging the sales supremacy of the real rock and roll business.

Clearly though, baby boomers raised on the Eagles found 1990s-style country music far more to their liking than much of the rock and dance music surrounding them at the time. This country music was close to 1970s rock in style, lyrical content, and increasingly in musical production. Music City dropped the steel and banjo on record after record. Other country artists emerging in the wake of Garth Brooks' success and making similarly rock-sounding music began to enjoy comparable crossover appeal. One of them, Travis Tritt, had no illusions about what was going on, and he had it from the Eagles themselves for proof: "People were looking for an alternative to same-sounding pop," Tritt said at the end of the '90s, adding that he knew it because "Don Henley told me at the time that 'country is doing so well now because country is where melody and lyric have come to live.' I couldn't agree with that more. It seems that when people get tired of one thing because it loses its originality or ability to reach out and touch somebody, they will leave."

If Tomorrow Never Comes

Aiding the spread of country music was a southern-fried version of MTV that had emerged in Nashville—Country Music Television (or CMT). Naturally, it programmed as many crossover hits as it could. CMT even had a program called "Jamming Country" that mixed country with rock and roll. Hal Willis, CMT general manager in 1993, believed that the growing country music audience of the early 1990s was partly made of disillusioned rock fans who yearned for the gentle mellow sounds of '70s California.

> "People who grew up listening to the Eagles are now finding that kind of music in country music. If you watch CMT, you will see that country music has changed; it really is much closer to 1970s country rock than anything else right now."

It is perhaps no wonder, then, that when Don Henley was approached by new country starlet Trisha Yearwood to sing with her on a single release entitled "Walkaway Joe," he happily volunteered to test the

country waters. Yearwood was an exceptional vocal talent and had
already been likened to one of Henley's previous musical partners,
Linda Ronstadt. The song was a huge hit, and Yearwood asked Henley
to perform the duet live with her on the Country Music Association
Awards show in Nashville in 1992. He agreed.

"I remember getting the call from Don Henley and I said 'No way!'
because it was one of those things, you know, I grew up on the Eagles
and meeting artists and someone that's a legend like that, it's like 'No
way!'" Yearwood was stunned. "We knew that the coup would be to
get him to come to Nashville and sing it with me at the CMAs and he
didn't do award shows that much—he'd done a few and then decided
he wasn't going to do any more but he said 'yes.' It was the coolest
night because everybody thought I was the coolest girl on the planet."

By 1993, Irving Azoff had left MCA and was running his own record
company, Giant Records. When Geffen Records was sold to MCA,
Warner looked to fill the gap with a new label and Azoff once again
found himself following in the footsteps of David Geffen. Giant did
well from the beginning of the Warner's tie-up. *Voices That Care* was
an all-star single released in 1991 with all proceeds going to the Red
Cross and intended as a morale booster for U.S. troops then involved
in the Gulf War. Among the lead singers on the Linda Thompson-,
Peter Cetera-, and David Foster-written number were Garth Brooks,
Stevie Wonder, Little Richard, Celine Dion, Bobby Brown, and
Randy Travis. It was truly all-inclusive musically and a reflection of
how musical genres were blurring and interacting. Later the same year
Giant released the massive-selling soundtrack to the movie *New Jack
City*, featuring the talents of, among others, Ice-T and 2 Live Crew. As
if to prove how all-encompassing Azoff's company was they also signed
some big names from the 1970s, among them Steely Dan, Warren
Zevon, Deep Purple, and Brian Wilson.

Missing You

Azoff was well aware of the industry shift toward country music and,
seeing the numbers being sold by Nashville acts in 1993, he developed
an idea for an Eagles tribute album, with Eagle songs performed by
some of the biggest names in country music. Aside from Garth Brooks,
the line-up on *Common Thread* featured all the heavyweights of early

Below: Lorrie Morgan, whose version
of "The Sad Cafe" is the final track on
the *Common Thread* tribute album.

Above: Travis Tritt, whose version of "Take It Easy" was the most successful single from the *Common Thread* album.

1990s country music: Vince Gill, Travis Tritt, Little Texas, Clint Black, John Anderson, Alan Jackson, Suzy Bogguss, Diamond Rio, Trisha Yearwood, Lorrie Morgan, Billy Dean, and Tanya Tucker.

Brady Seals, the keyboard player and vocalist for Little Texas, was such a fan of the Eagles that he pulled out of performing his band's contribution on the record. He did, however, rehearse with the band, and while they were practicing their version of "Peaceful Easy Feeling," Don Henley popped his head around the door, listened intently, and then remarked, "I miss this."

The first single from the album was to be Travis Tritt's version of "Take It Easy." At the time Tritt was riding high in country music circles and wanted his video to make a mark, as he explained when promoting it.

"When we first came up with the idea of doing a video I said 'Well, look guys, if you're wanting to do a video on this it needs to be something special cause this is a real special project.' They said, 'Well, what do you have in mind?' and I said, 'Well let's get the Eagles back together.'

The Albums

Common Thread: The Songs of the Eagles

WALDEN POND

COMMON THREAD:

THE SONGS OF THE EAGLES

74321 16677 2

TRACKS

1. Take It Easy, Travis Tritt

2. Peaceful Easy Feeling, Little Texas

3. Desperado, Clint Black

4. Heartache Tonight, John Anderson

5. Tequila Sunrise, Alan Jackson

6. Take It to the Limit, Suzy Bogguss

7. I Can't Tell You Why, Vince Gill

8. Lyin' Eyes, Diamond Rio

9. New Kid in Town, Trisha Yearwood

10. Saturday Night, Billy Dean

11. Already Gone, Tanya Tucker

12. Best of My Love, Brooks & Dunn

13. The Sad Café, Lorrie Morgan

After everybody stopped laughing it was like, 'Well, how exactly are we gonna do this?' We called up Don Henley first, I think, and he said, 'Hey, this is not about us, the Eagles, this is about you and we enjoy your music and we'd love to be a part of it.' Then we called up the other guys in the band and they said 'Yeah.' The morning we started everybody showed up—now this is the first time these guys had been back together in 14 years—and everybody showed up except for Don Henley. Now Henley was the key player, he was the guy, and if he doesn't show, nobody shows. He was late, about 45 minutes late, and boy there was a lot of nail-biting and itchy foreheads and that sort of thing going on. And then he came in, everybody hugged, they all had a great time and I got to be an Eagle for a day. The original idea was to have me singing the song and have Don Henley and Glenn Frey behind me basically beating the hell out of each other. That didn't happen but would have been great television. It was a real cool thing to do."

Before the shoot the Eagles actually jumped on stage and played "Rocky Mountain Way," the first time they had played together since 1980. Henley's now famous quote that the Eagles would get together again when Hell froze over was looking a little premature. The thaw was on. *Common Thread: The Songs of the Eagles* was one of the finest tribute albums ever recorded, and every artist included was a genuine fan who was delighted, like Travis Tritt, to be an Eagle for a day.

Travis Tritt fires up the album with a southern rock take on "Take It Easy." His is a gruffer version than the original but a respectful cover nonetheless. Trisha Yearwood conjures memories of Linda Ronstadt at her peak on "New Kid in Town," while Alan Jackson gives a "good ol' boy" reality to "Tequila Sunrise." Clint Black, who paid his dues singing Eagles covers in bars, sings *Desperado* as if it is a hallowed song, and Lorrie Morgan and Tanya Tucker bring powerful female voices to what is in essence very male-oriented material. With much of the album's profits going to charity to help out the Walden Woods Project, few could begrudge the good-natured bonhomie of the album.

Together Again

As well as allowing Nashville's finest to indulge in some wholesome hero worship, *Common Thread* signaled a shift in how the Eagles were now perceived. Post-1970s, the critics had painted the band as self-satisfied fat cats who got rich criticizing the very culture that they initially embraced and which had made them stars. But that was the critics. For musicians and artists and the four million record buyers who added *Common Thread* to their collections, it was an opportunity to wallow in some nostalgia. It also showed that the Eagles played a part in the life of every American of a certain age.

As Gregg Hubbard of 1990s country group Sawyer Brown said, "It's the Eagles thing, isn't it. There's this whole generation of Americans who grew up on the Eagles and I'm one of them."

Moreover, the Travis Tritt music video shoot proved to the Eagles that time had healed some internal wounds. They'd even enjoyed goofing off and just being the Eagles again, however briefly. The success of the album told shrewd operators like Henley and Frey that there was a sizeable audience ready to listen again.

"We just started jamming together during the making of the video," said Henley. "That was how it all began. We always maintained that if we were ever going to tour again we wouldn't want it to just be two or three of us. Had to have all five of us together."

Azoff worked diligently behind the scenes to capitalize on the Eagles' camaraderie and invited band members to be wined and dined in Aspen, and listen to him reinforce the benefits of a reunion. It didn't take that much, in truth, and once they'd all agreed to his plan, he orchestrated an MTV special, recorded at a Warner soundstage in Hollywood. "There was a bond, a great familiarity with the old stuff, so it came back to us fairly quickly," explained Glenn Frey. The first few days we were a little rusty, but it's all about repetition—doing it over and over."

After filming the MTV special the band went straight into rehearsals for a new tour, which began in May 1994 at the Irvine Meadow amphitheater near Los Angeles, a venue part owned by . . . Eagles manager Irving Azoff. Tickets for the show were over $100 each. It was a staggering figure but, as Azoff expected, the show was a sell-out. The *Hell Freezes Over* tour that followed would play to sold-out houses around the world until Frey fell ill with a stomach condition in September 1994. The tour continued when he was well enough,

Opposite: The thaw. Frey and Henley back together again in 1995 on the *Hell Freezes Over* tour. The marathon tour lasted for over two years and played to sell-out venues throughout the U.S., Canada, Europe, Australia, and Japan.

EAGLES

1996 WORLD TOUR

POP MUSIC REVIEW

The Eagles Soar

Eagles World Tour 1996

Glenn Frey
Don Henley
Don Felder
Joe Walsh
Timothy B. Schmit

Guitars/Keyboards/Vocals
Drums/Guitar/Vocals
Guitars/Vocals
Guitars/Keyboards/Vocals
Bass/Vocals

orey
y Drury
ago
n

Keyboards/Vocals
Keyboards/Vocals
Percussion/Drums
Sax/Violin/Vocals

zoff
ez

Personal Manager

Brian Ruggles
Chris Lantz
Scott Appleton
David Brantle

Sound Crew Chief
Monitor Mixer
Sound T

Opposite: Pages from a *Hell Freezes Over* tour program.

through 1995 and 1996. The live shows were in support of an album, *Hell Freezes Over*, which sold over seven million copies and was locked in the *Billboard* top 200 for almost two years. The new-look, mature, PG-rated tour was very much a model for all Eagles tours to come. The band brought family members, worked out, kept healthy, and Joe Walsh in particular stayed sober for the duration. Rather than risk fights and disagreement, they kept themselves separate while traveling.

After two years on the road, remarkably things were looking good for the Eagles. Walsh was out of his darkest alcohol-filled pits, and Henley and Frey had found a way to work together again. Felder was amiable and the whole band was able to exist in some kind of harmony. Henley surprised everyone by getting married and then solving his record company dispute with Geffen. Surely, it couldn't get much better?

Hall of Fame

Better was just around the corner, though, and on January 12, 1998, the Eagles—along with Lloyd Price, Carlos Santana, Fleetwood Mac, Jelly Roll Morton, and the Mamas and the Papas—were inducted into the Rock and Roll Hall of Fame at the Waldorf Astoria's Grand Ballroom in New York.

"For the record, we never broke up, we just took a fourteen-year vacation."

GLENN FREY

Jimmy Buffett, so often the band's favorite opening act, was entrusted with the task of introducing the Eagles. He said, "It's nice to see everybody I can recognize in their tuxedos, and we truly do look like the people our parents warned us about tonight. I've known the Eagles for nearly as long as they've been a band . . . .

"First, with about a jillion other war babies in America in 1972, I was converted instantly to the Eagles when I heard 'Take It Easy' on the radio. . . . They put their thumb on the pulse of popular music, where it remained for nearly twenty-seven years. As performers they came with a straightforward style, no smoke bombs or sacrificial guitars. The Eagles created their own style, blending banjos and electric guitars, harmonies from the heartland, and cutting-edge lyrics from the fault line, and God knows what they did for the chamber of commerce of Winslow, Arizona. ". . . The Eagles are going into the Rock and Roll Hall of Fame as one of the signature bands that began in the seventies and are still alive and kicking ass as we head for the millennium. They've laughed, frolicked, cried, fought, but most of all they have beaten the odds and are as popular today as they were in that incredible summer back in 1972. And here I am, still opening for this goddamn band! Now it's the Eagles' turn."

That night all seven Eagles (including Leadon and Meisner) shuffled on stage beaming and joking, hugging and gathering around the microphone for their acceptance comments.

Above: Jimmy Buffett, who led the tributes to the Eagles at the celebrations for their induction into the Rock and Roll Hall of Fame.

Don Henley went first. "We are all grateful and honored for the opportunity and good fortune that have brought us all here this evening on this suspicious occasion! I've had a lot of mixed emotions about the name 'Hall of Fame.' It's the fame part that bothers me a little, here in the waning hours of the twentieth century. In what we call Western culture, in this age of media, friends, fame is just not what it used to be. It's become an ugly, ugly thing! Andy Warhol was right; anybody can become famous for fifteen minutes—if you're sufficiently starved for attention and willing to be really obnoxious in public and make a complete fool of yourself, you too can be famous. . . . You know, the line between fame and accomplishment is becoming very blurred. I guess they couldn't call it the Hall of Accomplishment. Accomplishment enriches life, and fame always comes with a price. Fame is a by-product of accomplishment.

"I appreciate all the work these guys behind me have done. I want to thank Irving Azoff, without whom we wouldn't be here today."

At this point Glenn Frey chipped in with, "Well, we might still have been here, but we wouldn't have made as much money." Henley laughed and uttered, "Right. As I've said before, he may be Satan, but he's our Satan!" before continuing, "I want to thank Bill Szymczyk, who's here

this evening, our producer. . . I want to thank Glyn Johns . . . Hell, I'll even thank David Geffen! And I want to thank our good friends and compadres Jackson Browne and J. D. Souther, our crew, the many, many good men in our road crew . . . It's been a good trip, and we appreciate it. Last but not least, I want to thank my family, my mother and my father for believing in me early on, for getting me that drum set and letting me play it in the house. And I want to thank my wonderful wife for being patient and kind and loving and understanding. Thank you all."

Timothy B. Schmit, the newest Eagle, went next. "I'd like to thank whoever's responsible for my induction into this Hall of Fame. On a brief personal note, I'd like to say that I was not in the trenches with this particular band, and so I'd like to thank my predecessor for being there and paving the way for my being here tonight. With him beside me and the rest of these guys, I'm very honored. Thank you very much."

Giving Thanks

Next up was original Eagle Bernie Leadon, the first to leave the band. Leadon was typically witty and classy, remembering a few people who might have been forgotten on the Eagles rocket ride to glory. "Hi, my name is Bernie Leadon. I'm really honored to be here tonight. Thank you. Really proud to have lived long enough to be indicted. I'd like to thank everybody on the grand jury who voted for me. To the people already thanked, I want to add the names of a few less well known. One is John Boylan. He was Linda Ronstadt's manager and producer at the time that we got together and had a lot to do with my being included in the first group of four, and I'd really like to thank him personally tonight. I'd also really like to thank Ahmet Ertegun and Atlantic Records for having funded David Geffen and Elliot Roberts and the starting of Asylum Records. I know that Atlantic did a lot of work behind the scenes of the Eagles' success, and . . . also, thanks to my family."

Quiet and shy Randy Meisner was . . . well, quiet and shy with his speech. "I'd just like to say I'm very honored to be here tonight. Thank you, Timmy. It's just great playing with the guys again. I'd like to thank my mother and my father for supporting me during those years."

Next Joe Walsh ambled over to the microphone, grinned and said "Hey, how ya doin'? I would like to thank the people from Canton,

Ohio; Akron, Ohio; and Cleveland, Ohio for believing in me. I'd like
to thank Bill Szymczyk for finding me in the middle of nowhere. I'd
like to thank Don and Glenn for writing those songs; it makes my job
real easy. I'd also like to thank all the guys that drive this equipment
around—that drive the trucks, set it up, fix it, put it back in the truck,
so we can do what we do. God bless the road crew. Thank you!"

Next it was the other Don, Felder, to speak. "I'd like to again thank
Don Henley and Glenn Frey for writing an incredible body of work
that propelled this band through twenty-some-odd years of life . . .
Thank you guys . . . And I'd like to thank my wife, Susan, who put up
with me for twenty-six years while we did this."

And then, last but certainly not least, the man who started the band
and gave them their name, Detroit's Glenn Frey.

"Well, I'm doing mop up . . . There's much I'd like to say tonight . . . Anybody who's been in a band knows what it's like to go through changes . . . A lot has been made tonight about disharmony. The Eagles were a very laid-back band in a high-stress situation. A lot has been said and a lot has been speculated about the last twenty-seven years in terms of whether or not we got along. We got along fine! We just disagreed a lot! Tell me one worthwhile relationship that has not had peaks and valleys? That's really what we're talking about here. You cannot play music with people for very long if you don't genuinely like them. I guarantee you that over the nine years the Eagles were together during the seventies, over the three years we were together in our reunion, the best of times rank in the ninety-five percentile, the worst of times rank in the smallest percentile—that obviously everybody but the seven of us has dwelled on for the longest time. Get over it! On a personal note, you get a lot of free advice when you're coming up in the business. When I was still a kid, Bob Seger told me that if I didn't write my own songs I'd never get out of Detroit. I listened to him and said, 'Well, what if they're bad?' 'The first few will be really bad, but if you're good they'll get better,' he said. The next bit of free advice I got was from David Geffen, who told me I should get in a band and find a songwriting partner. I did both, and we're all here to celebrate the fruits of David's advice."

When the speeches were over the band made their way toward the stage. Henley took off his tuxedo and sat in a starched white shirt behind the drums while Leadon, Walsh, Frey, Felder, Schmit, and Meisner stood in a row at the front of the stage. It was the first and last time all seven Eagles would be on the same stage together. Frey started strumming his guitar, Leadon played that distinctive, twangy, string-bending intro, and they were into "Take It Easy," followed by a note-perfect "Hotel California."

The Eagles played a special New Year's show at the Staples Center in Los Angeles on December 31, 1999. The concert would be the last for Don Felder; yet another new-look Eagles would emerge in the new millennium.

9

On the Road Again

I N F E B R U A R Y 2 0 0 1 , Don Felder was officially sacked from the Eagles. Shocked and dismayed, he took legal advice and sued the band for wrongful dismissal and $200 million in damages. Felder argued that since he was a full partner in Eagles Ltd., his part in the band could not be terminated. He was promptly countersued by Don Henley, Glenn Frey, and manager Irving Azoff. The counterargument stated that the partnership stipulated that the agreement with any member could be terminated for a number of reasons, and the one they selected as the reason for Felder's termination was "disruption of band activities." That argument had arisen from Felder's claim that he had been left in the dark about band finances and believed he was not getting his fair share of money raised by the Eagles' activities. Felder alleged that from the 1994 tour onward, Henley and Frey had received a higher percentage of the band's profits and had coerced him into signing an agreement under which they would receive three times as much of the proceeds from the *Selected Works: 1972–1999* as he would. In return it seemed that Henley and Frey were unhappy with Felder's general attitude.

Despite the lawsuits, Felder's firing became official when a statement was issued on April 10, 2001 announcing that he was to be replaced by Nashville session guitarist Steuart Smith. Felder's claims would remain in litigation until 2007 when he wrote a biography of his years with the Eagles entitled *Heaven and Hell: My Life in the Eagles 1974–2001*. Initial publication of the book by Wiley & Sons was delayed because of more litigation from the Eagles' camp, but a settlement was reached between both camps, and the book was published in October that year.

There was a lot of Eagles-related activity at the start of the new millennium, though most of it was solo stuff. Henley released his fourth album, *Inside Job*, in the spring of 2000 after extricating himself from his deal with Geffen. The album showed that he still had relevance in the contemporary music market-place and, while not breaking any sales records, it did win a Grammy nomination for Best Pop Vocal album. *Inside Job* showed a softer side of Henley, featuring songs about marriage and family life as well as his favored environmental issues.

In 2001 Henley found time to form a record industry pressure group, the Recording Artists' Coalition, along with Sheryl Crow, Alanis

Above: Henley and Frey perform at the 16th Annual Conference to Erase MS, May 8th, 2009, in Century City, California.

Morissette, and a host of other big names, to campaign for and protect musicians' rights against the power of the major recording companies.

After the terrorist attack on the World Trade Center in New York on September 11, 2001, Henley and Frey responded with the song, "Hole in the World," which was recorded by the Eagles for inclusion on a new greatest hits compilation, *The Very Best of the Eagles*. This was the first collection to span their entire recording career from the debut album to 1994's *Hell Freezes Over*. The record debuted at number 3 on the *Billboard* album charts.

In early summer 2001 the Eagles jetted off for a mammoth world tour, which would take them through to July 2002. Inter-band relationships had improved to the extent that the band again contemplated new recordings. Don Henley remarked in a 2001 interview to a British magazine, "We're gonna attempt to write a new album, the general mood of the band is so good and so positive right now that I think we might just pull it off. A couple of years ago we tried to get together with the same purpose and after a few weeks it really just fizzled out. But, at the same time, nobody said, 'That's it. It's not gonna work. We quit.' That sentiment was never there. So I think that these breaks that we take from each other are a positive thing. Somehow it's one of the ingredients."

Glenn Frey was equally enthusiastic about another future resumption of band proceedings. "The Eagles don't have a record deal. We're going to make a new record with our own money, our way, and we're going to put it out ourselves. Call me kooky, but that's what I want to do. We feel we're a better band now, with a better feel for the way each other plays. And we're not high, so we know what's going on."

Less than a year after completing the 2001–2 tour, the Eagles were back on the road to support the new greatest hits collection on the Farewell 1 tour. In the break between tours, three of the Eagles—Henley, Walsh and Schmit—worked on old friend Warren Zevon's final album, *The Wind*, along with Bruce Springsteen, Tom Petty, Dwight Yoakam, and Emmylou Harris. Zevon, part of the Los Angeles Troubadour crowd, had been diagnosed with terminal cancer and recorded the album knowing it would be his final project. The Farewell 1 tour brought another new release, this time a DVD, *Farewell 1 Tour—Live from Melbourne*. It featured two new songs, Glenn Frey's "No More Cloudy Days" and Walsh's "One Day at a Time."

In the first week of November 2007 the Eagles defied all odds and beat pop star Britney Spears in the race for the number 1 album in America. They topped the *Billboard 200 Top Albums* chart with their album

**Moscow
Helsinki
Stockholm
Hannover
Cologne
London
Sheffield
Manchester
Belfast
Dublin
Paris
Ghent
Rotterdam
Berlin
Frankfurt
Zu**

Above: Frey, Henley, Walsh, and Schmit announce the Farewell 1 tour.

Below: Pages from the Millennium tour program, 2001–2002.

Long Road Out of Eden. It debuted at number 1, and sold 711,000 copies during its first week of release. The album not only debuted at number 1 in their homeland but also in the United Kingdom, Australia, New Zealand, the Netherlands, and Norway. Within a few weeks it would reach number 1 in eleven countries around the world and be Top 10 in another thirteen.

The album, their first studio project since 1979, had taken almost seven years to produce. It started life on a 2001 tour of Europe, about which Frey commented, "We didn't just play; we started hanging out again. It was a pleasure to go to sound check. There was a lot of fun and a lot of laughs on the charter flights from country to country."

Long Road was recorded over an extended period when mood and schedules permitted, and released on their own record label, Eagles Recording Company II. Blessed with their own studios, Henley and Frey were able to pick and choose their session times and slowly build an album strong enough for the record-buying public of 2007.

As ever with the Eagles, the creative process was not straightforward. "We were done with the album a few times," Joe Walsh said, "but it wasn't done with us." But it was worth the wait. *Long Road* received great acclaim from critics around the world. Just as Johnny Cash, Neil Diamond, and Glen Campbell had all found critical acclaim with the music press in their later years, so the Eagles were now regarded with affection and respect by many in the media. UK magazine *Uncut* remarked "that the band's ambition is intact, is remarkable—that they've made an album that captures the zeitgeist is maybe even more

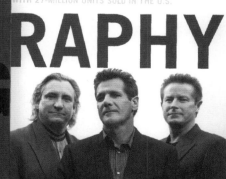

so." The website AllMusicGuide.com said, "The album is savvier
still, crafted to evoke the spirit and feel of the Eagles' biggest hits."
Billboard decided that the album was a "testament to the durable Eagles
footprint on the pop landscape." *Entertainment Weekly* gushed that
"the Eagles sidestep self-parody, serving up the rarest of musical blends:
freshly brewed nostalgia you'll actually want to savor." Irish music
magazine *Hot Press* admired the album for its relevance. "There is more
than nostalgia at work here. Lyrically at least, the cocaine cowboys of
yore strive to engage with the modern world's ills and idiosyncrasies."

How Long

The release of *Long Road* had been preceded by the single release of
"How Long," written by long-time friend and collaborator J. D. Souther.
It was a song from the 1970s that they had performed live on several
occasions but had never recorded, since Souther wanted it for his own
album. On the same day that *Long Road Out of Eden* went to number
1 on the album chart, the Eagles went to Nashville to perform "How
Long" for the Country Music Association Awards show—the first
music awards show they had ever attended as a band. Henley had
performed with Trisha Yearwood in 1992 for the nominated duet
"Walkaway Joe" and the band had been welcomed by country music

Above: Schmit, Henley, Frey, and
Walsh in harmony at the 2008
Stagecoach Country Music
Festival in Indio, California.

since the remarkable success of the *Common Thread: The Songs of the Eagles* tribute compilation in 1993. Vince Gill, host of the awards show, introduced the band to a predominantly industry audience.

"For thirty-five years or more these guys have been writing songs like this entire room wished they could write. They've been making records like we wished we could make and playing music like we wished we could play. These guys for thirty-five years have been the blueprint of what country rock is all about. We are honored to have them on the CMA stage, ladies and gentlemen, the Eagles . . ."

Dressed all in black and looking healthy, trim, and younger than they had a right to, Henley and Frey stood next to each other, guitars in hands between Schmit, Walsh, and Steuart Smith. They launched into a classic country rock sound that could have come straight out of the Troubadour in 1972. The crowd of new country superstars like Keith Urban and legends like Kris Kristofferson rose as one for an extended standing ovation. The Eagles have often been accused over the years of orchestrating the fun out of their live shows, but here was a group of men clearly enjoying every second of their time on stage. Nobody could fake the smiles and enjoyment of the band that night in Nashville.

Long Road Out of Eden

Producers: The Eagles, Steuart Smith, Richard F. W. Davis, Scott Crago, and Bill Szymczyk

---

Recorded: The Doghouse, Los Angeles, CA; Samhain Sound, Malibu, CA; O'Henry Studios, Burbank, CA; Henson Recording Studios, Hollywood, CA; Mooselodge, Calabasas, CA; The Panhandle House, Denton, Texas; Luminous Sound, Dallas, TX (2001–2007)

Label: Eagles Recording Company II/Lost Highway

Released: October 2007

Chart position: U.S.A. Billboard pop albums #1

TRACKS

Disc One	Disc Two
1. No More Walks in the Wood	1. Long Road Out of Eden
2. How Long	2. I Dreamed There Was No War
3. Busy Being Fabulous	3. Somebody
4. What Do I Do with My Heart	4. Frail Grasp on the Big Picture
5. Guilty of the Crime	5. Last Good Time in Town
6. I Don't Want to Hear Any More	6. I Love to Watch a Woman Dance
7. Waiting in the Weeds	7. Business as Usual
8. No More Cloudy Days	8. Center of the Universe
9. Fast Company	9. It's Your World Now
10. Do Something	
11. You Are Not Alone	

VINYL ONE

SIDE A
1 NO MORE WALKS IN THE WOOD 2:00
2 HOW LONG 3:15
3 BUSY BEING FABULOUS 4:21
4 WHAT DO I DO WITH MY HEART 3:55
5 GUILTY OF THE CRIME 3:44
6 I DON'T WANT TO HEAR ANY MORE 4:21

SIDE B
1 WAITING IN THE WEEDS 7:47
2 NO MORE CLOUDY DAYS 4:04
3 FAST COMPANY 4:01
4 DO SOMETHING 5:13
5 YOU ARE NOT ALONE 2:22

VINYL TWO

SIDE A
1 LONG ROAD OUT OF EDEN 10:17
2 I DREAMED THERE WAS NO WAR 1:38
3 SOMEBODY 4:10
4 FRAIL GRASP ON THE BIG PICTURE 5:47

SIDE B
1 LAST GOOD TIME IN TOWN 7:08
2 I LOVE TO WATCH A WOMAN DANCE 3:16
3 BUSINESS AS USUAL 5:32
4 CENTER OF THE UNIVERSE 3:42
5 IT'S YOUR WORLD NOW 4:20

ALBUM PRODUCED BY THE EAGLES

Above: The back cover artwork for *Long Road Out of Eden*.

Never short on confidence, Henley and Frey offered fans twenty tracks on two CDs with almost ninety minutes of music, all of it immaculately considered and recorded. "We worried for a while about how to fit in with what's happening on radio," said Don Henley about the album. "Finally we decided we just needed to be who we are."

The high quality of the music on the album was a remarkable achievement for a group of road warriors, all aged around 60, who had spent most of their adult lives in the fast lane. Very few veteran rock and roll lineups have come anywhere near to reproducing the quality of music they made while at their youthful peaks, but by once again recognizing the changes in America and the music scene around them, the Eagles were able to write songs of relevance and dignity: *Long Road* is packed with them. Perhaps as a result of the infighting and unpleasantness of the late Felder-era Eagles, the band offers an immediate show of democracy among the ranks with a group vocal on "No More Walks in the Wood," Henley's vocally impressive musical adaptation of a poem by John Hollander. Then it's back to the classic early Eagles sound with "How Long," before each Eagle gets a chance to do his own thing on the rest of the opening few tracks. Joe Walsh is zesty and fiery as usual on "Guilty of the Crime," and on "I Don't Want to Hear Anymore," and on "Do Something" Timothy B. Schmit's vocal sounds more pure and angelic than it did when he was in his thirties.

Frey and Henley take the lion's share of the album's collection of more-than-competent songs. Frey focuses on love and emotion on songs like "No More Cloudy Days" and "What Do I Do with My Heart", whereas Henley shows himself the master of social commentary on the ten-minute title track and the terse "Business as Usual." Of course, for a band with such a long and illustrious history, their past glories do echo throughout the material, but it would be unreasonable to expect an improvised jazz album or some screaming heavy metal from a band of veteran brothers who'd always admired consistency over inspiration.

"I'd much rather make what I consider to be a really good album every twenty-eight years than to make a mediocre album every year. I'm proud of the album. And I'm glad we did it. And if we never make another one, that'll be fine too."

GLENN FREY

Both Frey and Henley were more than happy with the final results. "I think a great many of the songs on it will stand up with the best work we've ever done. So it took twenty-eight years. So what? You know? That's my answer to that. So what? There's something greater than money about this and that's the sense of satisfaction. There's no greater, more satisfying thing for me than hearing a song that I've written or co-written come to fruition in a recording studio," said Henley. "It's addictive. And you wanna keep doing it."

Opposite: Schmit, Walsh, and Frey on the U.S. leg of the Farewell 1 tour in 2003.

Busy Being Fabulous

There was one notable difference in the nature of the success of *Long Road Out of Eden* from previous Eagles releases; it debuted at number 1 on the *Billboard* Country album chart, signaling a shift in marketing for the pioneers of country rock. As Glenn Frey noted, "We have a very strong following in the country music audience, and it's not because we're a country band, but I think it's because we have respect for country music, American music, the popular song. Sometimes we rock a little more than country. What I like to say is we're kind of country-tinged. The first country band that I thought we influenced was Alabama. In the '80s, when Alabama broke through, they had a lot of songs where the choruses were always three-part harmony and there was a whole lot of singing going on. Then, as the '90s came around, country music became to me a little bit more like pop music. There are still the traditionalists, and still guys that stick to the sawdust, ashtrays, empty beers, broken hearts, trucks, Cadillacs—that sort of country music has always been there. There was also this other evolution where it sounded like pop songs with country lead vocalists. You'd say, 'Gosh, that sounds like a Fleetwood Mac track to me except Wynonna is singing.' That's a part of what country music has been, too. Actually, that's probably why we fit a little better now . . . because the songs they play are a little broader. There are horns and Hammond B-3 organs beside steel guitars, mandolins, violins, and other traditional country instruments."

Aside from the publicity that its unexpected chart success gave the band, the album grabbed headlines for other reasons. Instead of releasing the record through the usual channels, the Eagles set up their own recording company and sold it exclusively through Wal-Mart. The giant discount retailer had already had an exclusive deal with Garth Brooks and was delighted to follow up on it with mega-sellers the

Eagles. "Our partnership with the Eagles demonstrates how serious we are about giving our customers a choice of new, unique, world-class entertainment products! We are very pleased to be able to bring our customers an alliance with America's greatest rock icons," explained David Porter, Wal-Mart's vice president of home entertainment, triumphantly.

Hardly the favorite store of environmental activists, Wal-Mart seemed an odd choice for the band, but the thoughtful Henley had some answers for those who questioned the decision. He accepted that there would be criticism but felt that "there's not a big corporation in this country that has clean hands, and certainly the major labels don't. This is a one-album deal. We got flak for it, but everyone's screaming for a new paradigm, so we found one." Moreover, he shared

"We needed to do this album for our own personal fulfillment. People tell us, 'You've got enough money and fame. Why do this album?' Being musicians is not a hobby. It's a calling. There's a life-affirming aspect to creating music. There's more to it than getting songs on the radio and touring. It keeps us young and vital and off the shrink's couch."

DON HENLEY

D F. W. DAVIS, SCOTT CRAGO AND BILL SZYMCZYK
GLENN FREY ~ GUITAR, KEYBOARDS, BASS AND VOCALS
KEYBOARDS AND VOCALS · TIMOTHY B. SCHMIT ~ BASS
DRUMS AND PERCUSSION · RICHARD F. W. DAVIS ~
D TROMBONE WILL HOLLIS ~ KEYBOARDS · AL GARTH ~
ALTO SAX • GREG SMITH ~ BARITONE SAX • GREG LEISZ
TRATIONS BY RICHARD F. W. DAVIS AND GLENN FREY ·
TAR TECHNICIANS: BOBBY CARLOS, VICTOR RODRIGUEZ,
HANK LINDERMAN, STEVE CHURCHYARD, CHRIS BELL,
R, JASON LADER, THAN VAN NISPEN, JEREMY JANEZCKO
I, TOM NIXON, SMOKEY WENDELL, HARRY SANDLER,
, MALIBU · ADDITIONAL STUDIOS: O'HENRY STUDIOS,
HE PANHANDLE HOUSE, DENTON; LUMINOUS SOUND,
MANAGEMENT: IRVING AZOFF · ART DIRECTION AND
HY: OLAF HEINE.

aking of this album.

Above: Walking the long road on the gatefold of *Long Road Out of Eden*.

his concerns with the issue of Wal-Mart forcing small companies out of business. "I've never been a fan of big-box retailers. My daddy was a small businessman."

And to keep Henley's liberal activist friends happy, the Eagles organization was also quick to point out via their website that the CDs were produced using environmentally friendly materials such as Domtar Earth Choice paper, which is endorsed by the Forest Stewardship Council and supported by the World Wildlife Fund and

Forest Ethics. The CD package, they said, contained thirty percent post-consumer recycled fiber, and virgin fiber from FSC Certified forests or other controlled sources. Henley was further impressed that the mega–retail chain had announced future plans to be supplied 100% by renewable energy, to create zero waste and to sell products that sustained the earth's resources and environment.

In the final analysis, the Wal-Mart deal was simply a smart business move. As Don Henley admitted to *Billboard* magazine, "There aren't many places where 60-year-old men, no matter how good their record is, can get this kind of promotion and widespread retail coverage. We're artists but we're also businessmen, and we try to live in the real world."

Assisted Living

As ever, the Eagles had a long and sophisticated schedule set up to promote the new release. In 2007, the music industry was living in a brave new world, and in a move that exhibited a well-informed appreciation of the new digital elements of the business, the Eagles refused to allow Eagles songs to be downloaded via iTunes, instead striking a deal with Amazon.com. "Amazon's new MP3 store has better quality, and the songs are 10 cents cheaper," Henley explained.

In preparing for the tour to support the album release, the Eagles performed a dress rehearsal at the Forum in Los Angeles on March 9, 2008. The audience included a corporate client (NetJet) and numerous celebrities, all there to "remember when music sounded this good," as the publicity material for the worldwide trek put it. A few months later, the Eagles, dressed impeccably in sober suits, took the stage at Nashville's Sommet Center in the middle of the *Long Road Out of Eden* tour, looking somewhat serious. And then Glenn Frey opened his Detroit mouth and announced, "This is the Eagles 'Assisted Living' tour, and we're the Eagles—the band that wouldn't die." Showing no signs of road weariness, they played as impeccably as they ever had, albeit with extra musicians adding to the sound. Joe Walsh, clean and sober, seemed to enjoy his mugging for the crowd even more than in the drink-fueled days and amusingly strapped a camera to his head to film the audience during his evergreen crowd pleaser "Life's Been Good." Glenn Frey appeared genuinely enthused to be still on stage, appreciative that after all these years there was not an empty seat in the house.

Above: Frey and Walsh at the 2008 Stagecoach Country Music Festival. Life's been good.

The Eagles were still that famously well-oiled machine. The note-perfect guitar solos, choreography, and much-practiced harmonies continued to surpass those of any other live act. If at times, over the years, the Eagles had relied too much on musicianship and songwriting over personality, this was no longer the case. They appeared warm, engaged, and thrilled to be playing live. When they returned to encore with "Take It Easy" and "Desperado," it was as if the 1980s and 1990s had never happened.

And if that wasn't enough for the workaholic Eagles, in 2009 Tim Schmit released a new album, while Don Henley put out a compilation, *The Very Best of Don Henley*. The Henley CD/DVD featured fourteen remastered classics including "Dirty Laundry," "The Boys of Summer," "The End of the Innocence," and "Taking You Home."

Opposite: The dramatic setting of
the Olympiahalle in Munich, Germany,
where the Eagles played on the
European leg of their *Long Road
Out of Eden* tour, June 15th, 2009.

Timothy B. Schmit's *Expando* album was recorded at his home studio near LA with an amazing cast of collaborators including Keb' Mo', Graham Nash, Kid Rock, The Blind Boys of Alabama, the Band's Garth Hudson, Dwight Yoakam, the Heartbreakers' Benmont Tench, and Timothy's son, Ben. It was more diverse than his work with the Eagles but retained that mellow presence and pure vocal sound that had been heard around the world for the past thirty years.

Eden Regained

In the final reckoning, the Eagles proved all the doubters wrong, again. *Long Road* was one of the biggest selling albums of 2007, and won two Grammys for songs from the album—Best Country Performance by a Duo or Group with Vocals for "How Long" in 2008, and Best Pop Instrumental Performance for "I Dreamed There Was No War" in 2009.

The Eagles have sold more than 120 million albums worldwide, earning five U.S. number 1 singles and six Grammy Awards in the process. For many years *Their Greatest Hits 1971–1975* was the best-selling U.S. album of all time, and currently exceeds sales of twenty-nine million units. (It is now tied at the top with Michael Jackson's *Thriller*.) The *Hotel California* album and *Eagles Greatest Hits Volume 2* have sold more than sixteen and eleven million albums respectively. In 2010 the Eagles played the Hollywood Bowl on April 16, 17, and 20 on their *Long Road Out of Eden* tour—and almost all the shows sold out.

More than forty years after Glenn Frey arrived in Los Angeles and met a fellow songwriter with similar dreams, the band they formed together was continuing to defy critics around the world with their accomplished and masterfully performed music. If the Beatles wrote the soundtrack for the swinging 1960s, then the Eagles scored the movie of the laid-back 1970s. Despite personnel changes, drugs, alcohol, and too much time spent living life in the fast lane, the band survived, pretty much intact, to become vibrant and relevant today. As they enter the fifth decade of their existence, Eagles' concerts are much more than golden oldie nostalgia shows. Henley and Frey were astute social commentators when they surfaced as songwriters in the early 1970s; that skill has not left them. To misquote one of their old Los Angeles Troubadour pals, Neil Young, "long may they run."

SOLO DISCOGRAPHY

Don Felder

AIRBORNE

Producer: *Don Felder*
Recorded: *1983*
Label: *Asylum*
Released: *1983*
Chart position: *Did not chart*
Tracks:
Side One: 1. Bad Girls
2. Winners 3. Haywire
4. Who Tonight
Side Two: 1. Never Surrender
2. Asphalt Jungle 3. Night
Owl 4. Still Alive

Glenn Frey

NO FUN ALOUD

Producers: *Glenn Frey, Allen
Blazek, and Jim Ed Norman*
Recorded: *Wilder Bros. Studios;
Rudy Records, Los Angeles;
Muscle Shoals Sound, Sheffield,
Alabama; and Bayshore
Recording Studio, Miami*
Label: *Asylum Records*
Released: *November 1982*
Chart position: *Billboard
album chart #32*
Tracks:
Side One: 1. I Found Somebody
2. The One You Love
3. Partytown 4. I Volunteer
5. I've Been Born Again
Side Two: 1. Sea Cruise 2. That
Girl 3. All Those Lies 4. She
Can't Let Go 5. Don't Give Up

THE ALLNIGHTER

Producers: *Glenn Frey
and Allen Blazek*
Recorded: *Wilder Bros.,
Santa Monica, CA; Caribou
Studios, CO; and Muscle
Shoals Sound, Sheffield, AL
(August 1983–March 1984)*
Label: *Asylum Records*
Released: *June 1984*

Chart position: *Billboard
album chart #22*
Tracks:
Side One: 1. The Allnighter
2. Sexy Girl 3. I Got Love
4. Somebody Else
5. Lover's Moon
Side Two: 1. Smuggler's Blues
2. Let's Go Home 3. Better
in the U.S.A. 4. Living in
Darkness 5. New Love

SOUL SEARCHIN'

Producers: *Elliot Scheiner
and Glenn Frey*
Recorded: *1986–1988 at Fool on
the Hill, Studio 55, Bill Schnee
Studio, Ocean Way Recording,
Cherokee Studios, and Capitol
Studios, Los Angeles; The Hit
Factory and Automated Sound,
New York; Muscle Shoals Sound,
Muscle Shoals, Alabama; and
The Sandbox, Connecticut*
Label: *MCA Records*
Released: *August 1988*
Chart position: *Billboard
album chart #36*
Tracks:
Side One: 1. Livin' Right
2. Some Kind of Blue 3. True
Love 4. Can't Put Out This
Fire 5. I Did It for Your Love
Side Two: 1. Let's Pretend We're
Still in Love 2. Working Man
3. Soul Searchin' 4. Two Hearts
5. It's Your Life 6. It's Cold in
Here (released on Japanese
version and as B-side)

STRANGE WEATHER

Producers: *Elliot Scheiner
and Glenn Frey; "Part of Me,
Part of You" produced by Dan
Was, co-produced by Elliot
Scheiner and Glenn Frey*
Recorded: *Mad Dog Ranch,
Snowmass, CO; Cherokee Studios,
Los Angeles, CA; Bill Schnee
Studios, North Hollywood, CA; and*

SoundCastle, Los Angeles, CA
Label: *MCA Records*
Released: *June 1992*
Chart position: *Did not chart*
Tracks:
1. Silent Spring (instrumental
prelude) 2. Long Hot Summer
3. Strange Weather 4. Agua
Tranquilla (instrumental) 5. Love
in the 21st Century 6. He Took
Advantage (Blues for Ronald
Reagan) 7. River of Dreams
8. I've Got Mine 9. Rising Sun
(instrumental) 10. Brave New
World 11. Delicious 12. A Walk
in the Dark 13. Before the Ship
Goes Down 14. Big Life 15. Part
of Me, Part of You 16. Ain't It
Love (Japanese release only)

GLENN FREY LIVE IN
DUBLIN (1992)

Producers: *Elliot Scheiner
and Glenn Frey*
Recorded: *The Stadium,
Dublin, Ireland, July 8, 1992*
Label: MCA Records
Released: *July 1993*
Chart position: *Did not chart*
Tracks:
1. Peaceful Easy Feeling
2. New Kid in Town 3. The
One You Love 4. Wild Mountain
Thyme 5. Strange Weather
6. I've Got Mine 7. Lyin' Eyes/
Take It Easy (Medley) 8. River
of Dreams 9. True Love
10. Love in the 21st Century
11. Smuggler's Blues 12. The
Heat is On 13. Desperado

SOLO COLLECTION

*Producers: Elliot Scheiner and
Glenn Frey, Jim Ed Norman, Allen
Blazak, Barry Beckett, Keith Forsey,
Harold Faltermeyer, and Don Was*
Recorded: *1982–1994*
Label: *MCA Records*
Released: *March 1995*
Chart position: *Did not chart*

Tracks:
1. This Way to Happiness
2. Who's Been Sleeping in
My Bed? 3. Common Ground
4. Call on Me 5. The One You
Love 6. Sexy Girl 7. Smuggler's
Blues 8. The Heat Is On 9. You
Belong to the City 10. True Love
11. Soul Searchin' 12. Part of Me,
Part of You 13. I've Got Mine
14. River of Dreams 15. Rising
Sun 16. Brave New World

THE BEST OF GLENN
FREY: 20TH CENTURY
MASTERS—THE MILLENNIUM
COLLECTION

Producers: *Elliot Scheiner and
Glenn Frey, Jim Ed Norman, Allen
Blazak, Barry Beckett, Keith Forsey,
Harold Faltermeyer, and Don Was*
Recorded: *1982–1994*
Label: *MCA Records*
Released: *September 2000*
Chart position: *Did not chart*
Tracks:
1. The Heat Is On 2. Smuggler's
Blues 3. You Belong to the
City 4. Sexy Girl 5. Love in the
21st Century 6. True Love
7. The Allnighter 8. The One You
Love (live) 9. Strange Weather
10. I've Got Mine 11. Soul
Searchin' 12. Part of Me,
Part of You (from *Thelma
& Louise* soundtrack)

SINGLES

I Found Somebody (Asylum;
released 1982 U.S. #31)
The One You Love (Asylum;
released 1982 U.S. #15)
All Those Lies (Asylum;
released 1982 U.S. #41)
That Girl (Asylum; released
1982)
Sexy Girl (MCA; released
1984 U.S. #20)
The Allnighter (MCA;
released 1984 U.S. #54)

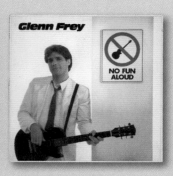

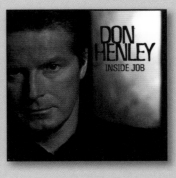

The Heat Is On (MCA;
released 1984 U.S. #2)
Smuggler's Blues (MCA;
released 1985 U.S. #12)
You Belong to the City (MCA;
released 1985 U.S. #2)
True Love (MCA; released
1988 U.S. #13)
Soul Searchin' (MCA;
released 1988 U.S. #5)
Some Kind of Blue (MCA;
released 1988)
Livin' Right (MCA; released
1988 U.S. #90)
Part of Me, Part of You (MCA;
released 1991 U.S. #55)
I've Got Mine (MCA; released
1992 U.S. #91)
River of Dreams (MCA;
released 1992)
Love in the 21st Century (MCA;
released 1993 U.S. #112)
Strange Weather (live)
(MCA; released 1993)
This Way to Happiness
(MCA; released 1995)

Don Henley

I CAN'T STAND STILL
Producers: *Don Henley, Danny
Kortchmar, and Greg Ladanyi*
Recorded: *Los Angeles, CA*
Label: *Asylum Records*
Released: *August 1982*
Chart position: *U.S. #24*
Tracks:
SIDE ONE: 1. I Can't Stand
Still 2. You Better Hang Up
3. Long Way Home 4. Nobody's
Business 5. Talking to the
Moon 6. Dirty Laundry
SIDE TWO: 1. Johnny Can't
Read 2. Them and Us 3. La Eile
4. Lilah 5. The Unclouded Day

BUILDING THE
PERFECT BEAST
Producers: *Don Henley, Danny
Kortchmar, and Greg Ladanyi*
Recorded: *Los Angeles, CA*
Label: *Geffen Records*
Released: *November 1984*

Chart position: *U.S. #13*
Tracks:
SIDE ONE: 1. The Boys of
Summer 2. You Can't Make
Love 3. Man with a Mission
4. You're Not Drinking Enough
5. Not Enough Love in the World
6. Building the Perfect Beast
SIDE TWO: 1. All She Wants
to Do is Dance 2. A Month
of Sundays 3. Sunset Grill
4. Driving with Your Eyes
Closed 5. Land of the Living

THE END OF THE INNOCENCE
Producers: *Don Henley, Danny
Kortchmar, Greg Ladanyi, Mike
Campbell, John Corey, Bruce
Hornsby, and Stan Lynch*
Recorded: *Los Angeles, CA*
Label: *Geffen Records*
Released: *June 1989*
Chart position: *U.S. #8*
Tracks:
1. The End of the Innocence
2. How Bad Do You Want It?
3. I Will Not Go Quietly 4. The
Last Worthless Evening 5. New
York Minute 6. Shangri-La
7. Little Tin God 8. Gimme What
You Got 9. If Dirt Were Dollars
10. The Heart of the Matter

ACTUAL MILES: HENLEY'S
GREATEST HITS
Producers: *Don Henley, Danny
Kortchmar, Greg Ladanyi, Mike
Campbell, John Corey, Bruce
Hornsby, and Stan Lynch*
Recorded: *1982–1995*
Label: *Geffen*
Released: *November 1995*
Chart position: *U.S. #16*
Tracks:
1. Dirty Laundry 2. The Boys of
Summer 3. All She Wants to do
is Dance 4. Not Enough Love
in the World 5. Sunset Grill
6. The End of the Innocence
7. The Last Worthless Evening
8. New York Minute 9. I Will
Not Go Quietly 10. The Heart
of the Matter 11. The Garden
of Allah 12. Everybody Knows

INSIDE JOB
Producers: *Don Henley
and Stan Lynch*
Recorded: *Los Angeles, CA*
Label: *Warner Bros. Records*
Released: *May 2000*
Chart position: *U.S. #7*
Tracks:
1. Nobody Else In the World
but You 2. Taking You Home
3. For My Wedding 4. Everything
Is Different Now 5. Workin' It
6. Goodbye to a River 7. Inside
Job 8. They're Not Here, They're
Not Coming 9. Damn It, Rose
10. Miss Ghost 11. The Genie
12. Annabel 13. My Thanksgiving

SINGLES
Johnny Can't Read (Asylum;
released 1982 U.S. #41)
Dirty Laundry (Asylum;
released 1982 U.S. #3)
You Better Hang Up (Asylum;
released 1982)
I Can't Stand Still (Asylum;
released 1983 U.S. #48)
The Boys of Summer (Geffen;
released 1984 U.S. #5)
All She Wants to Do Is Dance
(Geffen; released 1985
U.S. #9)
Not Enough Love in the
World (Geffen; released
1985 U.S. #34)
Sunset Grill (Geffen; released
1985 U.S. #22)
Driving with your Eyes Closed
(Geffen; released 1985)
Who Owns This Place?
(Soundtrack *The Color of
Money*; released 1986)
The End of the Innocence (Geffen;
released 1989 U.S. #8)
The Last Worthless Evening
(Geffen; released 1989 U.S. #21)
I Will Not Go Quietly (Geffen;
released 1989)
If Dirt Were Dollars (Geffen;
released 1989)
The Heart of the Matter (Geffen;
released 1989 U.S. #21)
How Bad Do You Want It?
(Geffen; released 1989)

New York Minute (Geffen;
released 1989 U.S. #48)
Sit Down You're Rockin' the
Boat (Soundtrack *Leap of
Faith*; released 1993)
The Garden of Allah (Geffen;
released 1995)
Everybody Knows (Geffen;
released 1995)
You Don't Know Me At All
(Geffen; released 1995)
Through Your Hands (Soundtrack
Michael; released 1996)
The Boys of Summer (UK
re-release 1998)
Workin' It (Warner Bros.;
released 2000)
Taking You Home (Warner
Bros.; released 2000)
Everything Is Different Now
(Warner Bros.; released 2000)
For My Wedding (Warner
Bros.; released 2000)

Bernie Leadon

NATURAL PROGRESSIONS
(with Michael Georgiades)
Producer: *Glyn Johns*
Recorded: *1977*
Label: *Asylum Records*
Released: *1977*
Chart position: *Did not chart*
Tracks:
SIDE ONE: 1. Callin' for Your
Love 2. How Can You Live
without Love? 3. Breath
4. Rotation 5. You're the Singer
SIDE TWO: 1. Tropical Winter 2. As
Time Goes On 3. The Sparrow
4. At Love Again 5. Glass Off

MIRROR
Producer: *Ethan Johns*
Recorded: *2005*
Label: *Really Small Entertainment*
Released: *2003*
Chart position: *Did not chart*
Tracks:
1. Vile and Profane Man
2. Volcano (I Identify) 3. Center
of the Universe 4. What
Do I Own 5. Backup Plan

6. Everybody Want 7. Sears and Roebuck Catalog 8. Rich Life 9. Hey, Now Now 10. God Ain't Done with Me Yet

Randy Meisner

RANDY MEISNER

Producers: *Mike Flicker and Randy Meisner*
Recorded: *1981*
Label: *Epic Records*
Released: *February 1982*
Chart position: *Did not chart*
Tracks:
SIDE ONE: 1. Never Been in Love 2. Darkness of the Heart 3. Jealousy 4. Tonight
SIDE TWO: 1. Playin' in the Deep End 2. Strangers 3. Still Runnin' 4. Nothing Is Said ('Til the Artist Is Dead) 5. Doin' It for Delilah

ONE MORE SONG

Producer: *Val Garay*
Recorded: *1980*
Label: *Epic Records*
Released: *November 1983*
Chart position: *U.S. #50*
Tracks:
SIDE ONE: 1. Hearts on Fire 2. Gotta Get Away 3. Come on Back to Me 4. Deep Inside My Heart
SIDE TWO: 1. I Need You Bad 2. One More Song 3. Trouble Ahead 4. White Shoes 5. Anyway Bye Bye

RANDY MEISNER

Producers: *Mike Flicker, Randy Meisner*
Recorded: *1981*
Label: *Epic Records*
Released: *February 1982*
Chart position: *Did not chart*
SIDE ONE: 1. Never Been in Love 2. Darkness of the Heart 3. Jealousy 4. Tonight
SIDE TWO: 1. Playin' in at the Deep End 2. Strangers 3. Still Runnin' 4. Nothin' Is Said 5. Doin' it for Delilah

LIVE IN DALLAS

Producers: *Randy Meisner and Buford Jones*
Recorded: *December 1982*
Label: *Rev-Ola Records*
Released: *February 2002*
Chart position: *Did not chart*
Tracks:
1. Lonesome Cowgirl 2. Jealousy 3. Strangers 4. Gotta Get Away 5. Try and Love Again 6. Tonight

7. I Need You Bad 8. Hearts on Fire 9. Darkness of the Heart 10. Take It to the Limit 11. Take It to the Limit (alternate)

LOVE ME OR LEAVE ME ALONE

Producers: *Randy Meisner and Joey Stec*
Recorded: *2004*
Label: *Sound City*
Released: *2004*
Chart position: *Did not chart*
Tracks:
1. Long Time Blue 2. In a Minute 3. Don't Keep It Inside 4. Love Me or Leave Me Alone 5. Midnight Rain 6. My How Things Have Changed 7. Walk of Life 8. Trust Your Heart 9. Leaving on Tuesday 10. Salt in My Tears 11. All Alone in Paradise 12. Ain't Gonna Take It 13. Lonely Alone 14. Take It Easy 15. One Less Fool 16. Take It to the Limit (live) 17. When the Dam Breaks

SINGLES

I Really Want You Here Tonight (Asylum; released 1978)
Deep Inside My Heart (Epic; released 1980 U.S. #22)
Hearts on Fire (Epic; released 1980 U.S. #19)
Never Been in Love (Epic; released 1982 U.S. #28)

Timothy B. Schmit

PLAYIN' IT COOL

Producers: *Timothy B. Schmit and Josh Leo*
Recorded: *1985*
Label: *Asylum*
Released: *October 1984*
Chart position: Did not chart
Tracks:
SIDE ONE: 1. Playin' It Cool 2. Lonely Girl 3. So Much in Love 4. Something's Wrong 5. Voices
SIDE TWO: 1. Wrong Number 2. Take a Good Look Around You 3. Tell Me What You Dream 4. Gimme the Money

TIMOTHY B.

Producer: *Dick Rudolph*
Recorded: *1987*
Label: *MCA*
Released: *October 1987*
Chart position: *Did not chart*
Tracks:
1. Boys Night Out 2. Don't Give Up 3. Hold Me in Your Heart

4. Everybody Needs a Lover 5. Into the Night 6. A Better Day is Coming 7. Jazz Street 8. I Guess We'll Go On Living 9. Down Here People Dance Forever

TELL ME THE TRUTH

Producers: *David Cole, Bruce Gaitsch, Don Henley, Danny Kortchmar, John Boylan, and Timothy B. Schmit*
Recorded: *1990*
Label: *MCA*
Released: *October 1990*
Chart position: *Did not chart*
Tracks:
1. Tell Me the Truth 2. Was It Just the Moonlight 3. Something Sad 4. Down by the River 5. In Roxy's Eyes 6. Let Me Go 7. Perfect Strangers 8. All I Want to Do 9. Tonight 10. For the Children

FEED THE FIRE

Producers: *Timothy B. Schmit and Mark Hudson*
Recorded: *2000*
Label: *Lucan*
Released: *May 2001*
Chart position: *Did not chart*
Tracks:
1. The Shadow 2. Every Song Is You 3. Make You Feel My Love 4. I'll Always Let You In 5. Running 6. I'm Not Angry Anymore 7. Give Me Back My Sight 8. You Are Everything 9. Top of the Stairs 10. Moment of Truth 11. Song for Owen 12. Just Say Goodbye (bonus track—Japanese printing only)

EXPANDO

Producers: *Timothy B. Schmit and Mark Hudson*
Recorded: *2009*
Label: *Lost Highway*
Released: *October 2009*
Chart position: *Did not chart*
Tracks:
1. One More Mile 2. Parachute 3. Friday Night 4. Ella Jean 5. White Boy from Sacramento 6. Compassion 7. Downtime 8. Melancholy 9. I Don't Mind 10. Secular Praise 11. A Good Day

SINGLES

So Much in Love (Asylum; released 1982)
Boys Night Out (MCA; released 1987)
Don't Give Up (MCA; released 1987)

Joe Walsh

THE SMOKER YOU DRINK, THE PLAYER YOU GET

Producers: *Joe Walsh and Bill Szymczyk*
Recorded: *Late 1972–Early 1973*
Label: *ABC-Dunhill*
Released: *1973*
Chart position: *U.S. #6*
Tracks:
1. Rocky Mountain Way 2. Book Ends 3. Wolf 4. Midnight Moodies 5. Happy Ways 6. Meadows 7. Dreams 8. Days Gone By 9. Daydream (Prayer)

SO WHAT

Producers: *Joe Walsh, John Stronach, and Bill Szymczyk*
Recorded: *December 1973–March, 1974*
Label: *Dunhill*
Released: *December 1975*
Chart position: *U.S. #11*
SIDE ONE: 1. Welcome to the Club 2. Turn to Stone 3. Falling Down 4. Time Out
SIDE TWO: 1. All Night Laundry Mat Blues 2. Help Me Through the Night 3. Song for Emma 4. Pavanne for the Sleeping Beauty 5. County Fair

YOU CAN'T ARGUE WITH A SICK MIND

Producer: *Joe Walsh*
Recorded: *25 March 1976*
Label: *ABC Records*
Released: *October 1976*
Chart position: *U.S. #20*
SIDE ONE: 1. Walk Away 2. Meadows 3. Rocky Mountain Way
SIDE TWO: 1. Time Out 2. Help Me Thru the Night 3. Turn to Stone

"BUT SERIOUSLY, FOLKS . . ."

Producers: *Joe Walsh and Bill Szymczyk*
Recorded: *March 1978*
Label: *Asylum*
Released: *May 1978*
Chart position: *Billboard #1*
SIDE ONE: 1. Over and Over 2. Second Hand Store 3. Indian Summer 4. At the Station
SIDE TWO: 1. Tomorrow 2. Inner Tube 3. Theme from Boat Weirdos 4. Life's Been Good

THERE GOES THE NEIGHBORHOOD

Producers: *Joe Walsh and George Perry*
Recorded: *October 1980*

Label: *Asylum Records*
Released: *March 1981*
Chart position: *U.S. #20*
SIDE ONE: 1. Things 2. Made Your Mind Up 3. Down on the Farm 4. Rivers (of the Hidden Funk)
SIDE TWO: 1. A Life of Illusion 2. Bones 3. Rockets 4. You Never Know

YOU BOUGHT IT—YOU NAME IT
Producers: *Joe Walsh, Bill Szymczyk, and George Perry*
Recorded: *September 1982*
Label: *Warner Bros. Records*
Released: *May 1983*
Chart position: *U.S. #48*
SIDE ONE: 1. I Can Play That Rock and Roll 2. Told You So 3. Here We Are Now 4. The Worry Song 5. "I.L.B.Ts"
SIDE TWO: 1. Space Age Whiz Kids 2. Love Letters 3. Class of '55 4. Shadows 5. Theme from Island Weirdos

THE CONFESSOR
Producers: *Joe Walsh and Keith Olsen*
Recorded: *1985*
Label: *Full Moon*
Released: *1985*
Chart position: *U.S. #65*
Tracks
1. Problems 2. I Broke My Leg 3. Bubbles 4. Slow Dancing 5. 15 Years 6. The Confessor 7. Rosewood Bitters 8. Good Man Down 9. Dear John

GOT ANY GUM?
Producer: *Terry Manning*
Recorded: *Spring 1987*
Label: *Full Moon*
Released: *October 1987*
Chart position: *U.S. #113*
Tracks
1. The Radio Song 2. Fun 3. In My Car 4. Malibu 5. Half of the Time 6. Got Any Gum? 7. Up to Me 8. No Peace in the Jungle 9. Memory Lane 10. Time

ORDINARY AVERAGE GUY
Producers: *Joe Walsh and Joe Vitale*
Recorded: *August 1990*
Label: *Epic*
Released: *April 1991*
Chart position: *U.S. #112*
Tracks:
1. Two Sides to Every Story 2. Ordinary Average Guy 3. The Gamma Goochee 4. All of a Sudden 5. Alphabetical Order 6. Look at Us Now 7. I'm Actin' Different 8. Up All Night 9. You Might Need Somebody 10. Where I Grew Up (Prelude to School Days) 11. School Days

SONGS FOR A DYING PLANET
Producers: *Bill Szymzyck and Joe Vitale*
Recorded: *February 1992*
Label: *Epic*
Released: *March 1992*
Chart position: *U.S. #112*
Tracks:
1. Shut Up 2. Fairbanks Alaska 3. Coyote Love 4. I Know 5. Certain Situations 6. Vote for Me 7. Theme from Baroque Weirdos 8. The Friend Song 9. It's All Right 10. Will You Still Love Me Tomorrow? 11. Decades 12. Song for a Dying Planet

LOOK WHAT I DID
Compiled: *Joe Walsh, David Spero and Andy McKaie*
Label: *MCA*
Released: *May 1995*
Chart position: *Did not chart*
Tracks:
DISC 1: 1. Tuning, Part 1 2. Take A Look Around 3. Funk #48 4. The Bomber 5. Tend My Garden 6. Funk #49 7. Ashes, the Rain & I 8. Walk Away 9. It's All the Same 10. Midnight Man 11. Here We Go 12. Midnight Visitor 13. Mother Says 14. Turn to Stone 15. Comin' Down 16. Meadows 17. Rocky Mountain Way
DISC 2: 1. Welcome to the Club 2. All Night Laundry Mat Blues 3. County Fair 4. Help Me Thru The Night 5. Life's Been Good 6. Over And Over 7. All Night Long 8. A Life of Illusion 9. Theme from Island Weirdos 10. I Can Play That Rock and Roll 11. "I.L.B.Ts" 12. Space Age Whiz Kids 13. Rosewood Bitter 14. Shut Up 15. Decades 16. Song for a Dying Planet 17. Ordinary Average Guy

JOE WALSH'S GREATEST HITS—LITTLE DID HE KNOW . . .
Producers: *Joe Walsh, Bill Szymczyk*
Label: *MCA*
Released: *November 1997*
Chart position: *Did not chart*
Tracks
1. Funk #49 2. Tend My Garden 3. The Bomber 4. Walk Away 5. Midnight Man 6. Mother Says 7. Turn to Stone 8. Meadows 9. Rocky Mountain Way 10. Help Me Thru the Night 11. Life's Been Good 12. All Night Long 13. The Confessor 14. A Life of Illusion 15. Ordinary Average Guy

SINGLES
Rocky Mountain Way (Dunhill; released 1973 U.S. #23)
Meadows (Dunhill; released 1974 U.S. #89)
Turn to Stone (ABC-Dunhill; released 1974 U.S. #93)
Life's Been Good (Asylum; released 1978 U.S. #12)
All Night Long (Asylum; released 1980 U.S. #19)
A Life of Illusion (Asylum; released 1981 U.S. #34)
The Waffle Stomp (Soundtrack *Fast Times at Ridgemont High*; released 1982)
Space Age Whiz Kids (Full Moon; released 1983 U.S. #52)
I Can Play That Rock and Roll (Warner Bros.; released 1983)
The Confessor (Full Moon; released 1985)
The Radio Song (Warner Bros.; released 1987)
In My Car (Warner Bros.; released 1987)
Ordinary Average Guy (Epic; released 1991)
All of a Sudden (Epic; released 1991)
Vote for Me (Epic; released 1992)

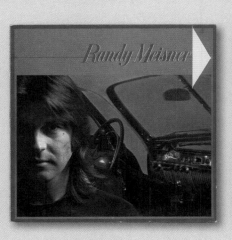

INDEX

SOURCES

Chapter 1

Page 17
"In a town that size . . ." Don Henley (Cameron Crowe, *Rolling Stone*, #196, Sept. 25, 1975)

Pages 17–18
"I was pretty well known in Texas . . ." (author interview with Al Perkins)

Page 18
"We met Kenny in a clothing boutique . . ." Don Henley (*Goldmine*, 1998)

Page 20
"Only a few were making it out of Detroit . . ." Glenn Frey (Blair Jackson, *Bam*, #133, Jul. 2, 1982)

Page 23
"Jackson Browne, J. D. Souther, and I all lived . . ." Glenn Frey (Cameron Crowe, "Conversations with Don Henley and Glenn Frey," *The Very Best of the Eagles Booklet*, Aug. 2003)

Page 28
"We just wanted to be the Beatles . . ." (author interview with David Crosby)

Page 29
"This was the center of the music universe . . ." David Crosby (*ibid.*)

Page 33
". . . hundreds of kids on the street . . ." Pamela Des Barres (Rodney Bingenheimer, *Mayor of the Sunset Strip*, DVD)

". . . humiliate curfew-violators with insults and obscene jokes . . ." Mike Davis ("Notes and Documents: Riot Nights on Sunset Strip," *Labour/Le Travail* 59, Spring 2007)

Page 35
"The year that we were all there, 1969 . . ." (author interview with J. D. Souther)

Page 36
"The troubadour was this incredibly influential place . . ." (author interview with John Boylan)

"There I was, this young kid, sitting next to folk legends . . ." Jackson Browne ("Jackson Browne in London, Part 2," from Barney Hoskyns, *Rock's Backpages Audio*, Oct. 18, 1993)

"It was the club you played in to hired . . ." Jackson Browne (*ibid.*)

Page 38
"Joni Mitchell lives in Laurel Canyon . . ." Susan Gordon Lydon (Susan Gordon Lydon, *New York Times*, Apr. 20, 1969)

Page 41
"We'd already known that a country influence would work . . ." Roger McGuinn of the Byrds (BBC/WGBH documentary series *Dancing in the Street*)

Page 45–6
"I realized that the most exciting music for me . . ." (author interview with John Boylan)

Page 46
"I heard that Randy Meisner had left . . ." John Boylan (*ibid.*)

Chapter 2

Page 52
"It was Glenn and Don; . . ." (author interview with John Boylan)

". . . the first night of our tour . . ." Glenn Frey (Cameron Crowe, *Rolling Stone*, #196, Sept. 25, 1975)

"Right from the start the Eagles were good . . ." (author interview with Al Perkins)

"I went to a rehearsal after they got together . . ." (author interview with J. D. Souther)

"We had it all planned . . ." Don Henley (Cameron Crowe, *Rolling Stone*, #196, Sept. 25, 1975)

"Money was a much saner goal than adoration . . ." Don Henley (*ibid.*)

Page 67
"At the beginning he was an executive . . ." (author interview with Jackson Browne)

"A lot of credit has to go to Jackson . . ." Don Henley (Cameron Crowe, *Rolling Stone*, #196, Sept. 25, 1975)

Page 68
"Bernie Leadon strode up to Geffen . . ." Don Henley (Cameron Crowe, *Rolling Stone*, #196, Sept. 25, 1975)

Page 69
"At the time everything was strawberry that . . ." Don Henley (interview with John Tobler, *Rock On*, BBC Radio One, 1977)

Page 71
"We all wanted to record in London . . ." Bernie Leadon (Ray Coleman, "Where Eagles Dare," *Melody Maker*, June 17, 1972)

"He pretty much insisted that we use . . ." Don Henley (interview with BBC Radio, 1977)

Page 72
"We were driven to the studio . . ." Don Henley (Blair Jackson, *Bam*, Nov. 19, 1982)

"We thought 'We'll get to see London . . .'" Don Henley (interview with BBC Radio, 1977)

"Glyn had a very particular style . . ." Don Henley (*Goldmine*, 1998)

Chapter 3

Page 83
". . . we had David Geffen behind us . . ." Glenn Frey (Blair Jackson, *Bam*, #133, Jul. 2, 1982)

"It's sad when you learn . . ." Glenn Frey (*Los Angeles Phonograph Record*, vol. 5, Jun. 1975)

Page 88
"The Eagles proved to everyone watching . . ." (author interview with Dwight Yoakam)

Page 90
"We didn't use any fake blood . . ." Henry Diltz (*Uncut*, May 2007)

Page 93
". . . it contained the story of Bill Dalton . . ." Glenn Frey (Penelope Ross, *Circus*, 1973)

Page 97
"The only two people . . ." Don Henley (Cameron Crowe, *Rolling Stone*, #196, Sept. 25, 1975)

"The Eagles took things to another level . . ." (author interview with Jackson Browne)

Page 101
(caption) "The gear they got . . ." Henry Diltz (*Uncut* magazine, May 2007)

"When a kid sees a guitar . . ." Glenn Frey (Penelope Ross, *Circus*, 1973)

Page 103
Jim Ed Norman feature (all quotes: author interview)

Chapter 4

Page 111
"The thing about Gram . . ." (author interview with Byron Berline)

"It was difficult for artists like Gram . . ." (author interview with Emmylou Harris)

Page 116
"I was a nervous wreck." Irving Azoff (Cameron Crowe, *Rolling Stone*, #267, Jun. 5, 1978)

"The first night we met Irving . . ." Glenn Frey (Cameron Crowe, *Rolling Stone*, #267, Jun. 5, 1978)

". . . always the young guys down there . . ." Don Henley (Cameron Crowe, *Rolling Stone*, #196, Sept. 25, 1975)

Page 118
"They had already had a couple of hits . . ." Bill Szymczyk (Dan Daley, *Sound on Sound*, Nov. 2004)

Page 119
"Don Henley asked me how many microphones I used on drums . . ." Bill Szymczyk (*ibid.*)

"Glenn and I assumed this bulldozer attitude . . ." Don Henley (Cameron Crowe, *Rolling Stone*, #196, Sept. 25, 1975)

"When I was living in New York..." Don Felder (Dennis Hunt, "The Ex-Eagle Has Landed ... on a Solo Career," *Los Angeles Times*, 1983)

Page 120
"The biggest problem that we had was..." Glenn Frey (John Tobler, *Rock On*, BBC Radio One, 1977)

Page 121
"Glenn called me up and said..." Don Henley (*ibid.*)

Page 125
"'My Man' was written by Bernie..." Don Henley (John Tobler, *Rock On*, BBC Radio One, 1977)

Page 126
Al Perkins feature (all quotes: author interview)

Page 132
"We fight with our manager, we fight..." Glenn Frey (Tom Nolan, *Phonograph Record*, June 1975)

Page 133
"We wrote that when we were just getting into our R&B period." Glenn Frey (Blair Jackson, *Bam*, #133, Jul. 2, 1982)

Page 137
"Mainly, I was burnt out." Bernie Leadon (John Bream, *Minneapolis Star Tribune*, Jun. 9, 2002)

Chapter 5

Page 141
"We were scared." Glenn Frey (Michael Barackman, *Phonograph*, vol. 76, 1977)

Page 145
"I was tremendously influenced by the Beatles..." Joe Walsh (David Gans, *Bam*, #108, Jul. 17, 1981)

"I majored in English, minored in music..." Joe Walsh (*ibid.*)

Page 146
"[They] were a good, five-piece band..." Joe Walsh (Alexis Korner, BBC Radio One, 1982)

Page 147
"Around that time, I was just fed up with a solo career..." Joe Walsh (*ibid.*)

"It was good training for me..."

Joe Walsh (*ibid.*)

Page 150
"So I went to Colorado..." Joe Walsh (*ibid.*)

Page 151
"We're not exactly going to win friends..." Don Henley (Joseph Rose, "The Eagles Make California Sounds," *Hit Parader*, winter 1977–78)

Page 152
"I personally thought that adding Joe Wash was a dangerous move." Glenn Frey (Michael Barackman, *Phonograph*, vol. 76, 1977)

Page 154
"Once upon a time it used to be very elegant..." Don Henley (*Zigzag*, Jun. 1976)

Page 156
"I had just leased this house out on the beach at Malibu..." Don Felder (Alan di Perna, *Guitar World Acoustic*, March 2007)

"This is a concept album, there's no way to hide it..." Don Henley (*Zigzag*, Jun. 1976)

Page 160
(caption) "We hired a bunch of people to come in and stand there." Don Henley (*ibid.*)

Page 162
"They never got the respect they deserved..." (author interview with Byron Berline)

Page 172
J. D. Souther feature (all quotes: author interview: "Conversation Corner with J.D. Souther," *American Music Channel*, November 2009)

Page 173
"I'm going to keep on playing and touring." J. D. Souther (*ibid.*)

Chapter 6

Page 176
"It was a twist of fate." Timothy B. Schmit (MCA Press Statement)

"He told me 'I gotta tell you two things.'" Timothy B. Schmit (*Rolling Stone*, #306, Nov. 29, 1979)

Page 185
"The Eagles were incredible musicians..." (author interview with Tom Petty)

"In '72, the punks had long hair and wore cowboy boots." Don Henley (Charles M. Young, *Rolling Stone*, #306, Nov. 29, 1979)

"They don't look so tough, they look like dorks." Don Henley (*ibid.*)

Page 188
"The Eagles talked about breaking up from the day I met them." Irving Azoff (Robert Hilburn, *LA Times*, May 23, 1982)

Page 191
"The *Hotel California* success made us very paranoid." Joe Walsh (Robert Hilburn, *LA Times*, May 23, 1982)

"The romance had gone out of it for Glenn and me." Don Henley (*Rolling Stone* 20th Anniversary Issue, #512, Nov. 5–Dec. 10, 1987)

Page 196
"It was a terrible year. The band broke up." Don Henley (Robert Hilburn, *LA Times*, May 23, 1982)

"Everything changed for me during *The Long Run*." Glenn Frey (Robert Hilburn, *LA Times*, May 23, 1982)

Page 199
"We were exhausted, and we were sick and tired of each other..." Don Henley (*Rolling Stone*, 20th Anniversary Issue, #512, Nov. 5–Dec. 10, 1987)

Page 200
"I think my decision..." Glenn Frey (Robert Hilburn, *LA Times*, May 23, 1982)

"A lot of people in the media attach more importance..." Glenn Frey (*ibid.*)

Chapter 7

Page 211
"Probably it helps if you do have name recognition." (author interview with J. D. Souther)

Page 212
"After spending a year and a half on *The Long Run*..." Glenn Frey

("An Eagle Alone," *International Musician and Recording World*, Sept. 1982)

Page 214
"Glenn called up one day and told me..." Don Henley (interview with Mitchell Glazer)

"I watch the news a lot. National news, local news..." Don Henley (MTV Rockumentary, 1990)

Page 216
"I mean, there was a whole long period of being an alcoholic..." Joe Walsh (Erik Hedegaard, *Rolling Stone*, #1101, Aug. 9, 2006)

Page 224
"I was contacted when I was filming the video for 'Smuggler's Blues,' ..." Glenn Frey (Glenn Frey from Jeff Yarbrough, *Interview Magazine*, Apr. 1986)

Page 230
"That's what the last verse of 'The Boys of Summer' was about." Don Henley (*Rolling Stone*, 20th Anniversary Issue, #512, Nov. 5–Dec. 10, 1987)

Page 232
"I was appalled when I first heard that the place was in danger." Don Henley (Paul Verna, *Billboard*, Dec. 28, 1996)

Chapter 8

Page 240
"I grew up on Dan Fogelberg..." (author interview with Garth Brooks)

Page 243
"People were looking for an alternative..." Travis Tritt (http://www.CMT.com, 1999)

"People who grew up listening to the Eagles..." (author interview with Garth Brooks)

Page 244
"I remember getting the call from Don..." Trisha Yearwood (*Intimate Portrait*, Lifetime TV, 2000)

Page 245
"When we first came up with the idea..." Travis Tritt (http://www.CMT.com, 1999)

Page 248

"It's the Eagles thing, isn't it." (author interview with Gregg Hubbard)

"We just started jamming together . . ." Don Henley (Sue Gold, *Cleveland Plain Dealer*, Jul. 8, 1994)

"There was a bond, a great familiarity . . ." Glenn Frey (*ibid.*)

Page 251

"For the record, we never broke up . . ." Glenn Frey (*Hell Freezes Over* reunion tour, April 1994)

"It's nice to see everybody I can recognize . . ." Jimmy Buffett (Speech at the Rock and Roll Hall of Fame, Jan. 12, 1998)

Chapter 9

Page 259

"We're gonna attempt to write a new album . . ." Don Henley (*What's On in London*, Jun. 6, 2001)

Page 260

"The Eagles don't have a record deal." Glenn Frey (Joseph Dunn, *The Herald Sun*, Melbourne, Oct. 28, 2001)

Page 261

"We didn't just play; we started hanging out again." Glenn Frey (Geoff Boucher, *Los Angeles Times*, Nov. 6, 2007)

"We were done with the album a few times . . ." Joe Walsh (*ibid.*)

". . . that the band's ambition is intact, is remarkable . . ." Bud Scoppa (*Uncut*, 2007**)**

Page 266

"We worried for a while about how to fit in . . ." Don Henley (Edna Gundersen, *USA Today*, Oct. 30, 2007)

Page 267

"I'd much rather make what I consider to be a really good album . . ." Glenn Frey (Steve Kroft Interviews Members of the Legendary Band, *60 Minutes*, CBS News, Nov. 25, 2007)

Page 268

"I think a great many of the songs on it will stand up . . ." Don Henley (*ibid.*)

"We have a very strong following in the country music audience . . ." Glenn Frey (Terry Bumgarner, *CMT Insider Interview: The Eagles*, CMT News, Dec. 4, 2007)

Page 270

"Our partnership with the Eagles demonstrates . . ." David Porter (Gabe Meline, "Music & Nightlife," *metroactive*, Nov. 29–Dec. 5, 2006)

"There's not a big corporation in this country . . ." Don Henley (Edna Gundersen, *USA Today*, Oct. 30, 2007)

"We needed to do this album for our own personal fulfillment . . ." Don Henley (*ibid.*)

Page 272

"There aren't many places where 60-year-old men . . ." Don Henley (Don Henley, *Billboard*, Oct. 12, 2007)

"Amazon's new MP3 store has better quality . . ." Don Henley (Edna Gundersen, *USA Today*, Oct. 30, 2007)

PICTURE CREDITS